CLASS AND THE COMMUNIST PARTY OF CHINA, 1978–2021

By examining the changing political economy in China through detailed studies of the peasantry, workers, middle classes, and the dominant class, this volume reveals the Communist Party of China's (CCP's) impact on social change in China between 1978 and 2021.

This book explores in depth the CCP's programme of reform and openness that had a dramatic impact on China's socio-economic trajectory following the death of Mao Zedong and the end of the Cultural Revolution. It also goes on to chart the acceptance of Market Socialism, highlighting the resulting emergence of a larger middle class, while also appreciating the profound consequences this created for workers and peasants. Additionally, this volume examines the development of the dominant class which remains a defining feature of China's political economy and the Party-state.

Providing an in-depth analysis of class as understood by the CCP in conjunction with sociological interpretations of socio-economic and socio-political change, this study will be of interest to students and scholars of Chinese Politics, Chinese History, Asian Politics, and Asian studies.

Marc Blecher is James Monroe Professor of Politics and East Asian Studies at Oberlin College, USA.

David S. G. Goodman is Professor of Chinese Politics and Director of the China Studies Centre at the University of Sydney, Australia.

Yingjie Guo is Professor of Chinese Studies at the University of Sydney, Australia.

Jean-Louis Rocca is a professor and researcher at the Center for International Studies, Sciences Po Paris, France.

Beibei Tang is Senior Associate Professor in the Department of China Studies at Xi'an Jiaotong-Liverpool University, China

CLASS AND THE COMMUNIST PARTY OF CHINA, 1978–2021

Reform and Market Socialism

Marc Blecher, David S. G. Goodman,
Yingjie Guo, Jean-Louis Rocca,
and Beibei Tang

LONDON AND NEW YORK

First published 2022
by Routledge
2 Park Square, Milton Park, Abingdon, Oxon OX14 4RN

and by Routledge
605 Third Avenue, New York, NY 10158

Routledge is an imprint of the Taylor & Francis Group, an informa business

© 2022 Marc Blecher, David S G Goodman, Yingjie Guo, Jean-Louis Rocca, Beibei Tang

The right of Marc Blecher, David S G Goodman, Yingjie Guo, Jean-Louis Rocca, Beibei Tang to be identified as authors of this work has been asserted in accordance with sections 77 and 78 of the Copyright, Designs and Patents Act 1988.

All rights reserved. No part of this book may be reprinted or reproduced or utilised in any form or by any electronic, mechanical, or other means, now known or hereafter invented, including photocopying and recording, or in any information storage or retrieval system, without permission in writing from the publishers.

Trademark notice: Product or corporate names may be trademarks or registered trademarks, and are used only for identification and explanation without intent to infringe.

British Library Cataloguing-in-Publication Data
A catalogue record for this book is available from the British Library

Library of Congress Cataloging-in-Publication Data
Names: Blecher, Marc J., author. | Goodman, David S. G., author. | Guo, Yingjie, 1957– author.
Title: Class and the Communist Party of China, 1978–2021 : reform and market socialism / Marc Blecher, David S G Goodman, Yingjie Guo, Jean-Louis Rocca, Beibei Tang.
Identifiers: LCCN 2021044976 (print) | LCCN 2021044977 (ebook) | ISBN 9781032185323 (hardback) | ISBN 9781032185293 (paperback) | ISBN 9781003255017 (ebook)
Subjects: LCSH: Social stratification—China—History. | Middle class—China—History. | Mixed economy—China. | China—Economic policy—20th century. | China—Economic policy—2000–
Classification: LCC HM821 .B554 2022 (print) | LCC HM821 (ebook) | DDC 305.5/50951—dc23/eng/20211104
LC record available at https://lccn.loc.gov/2021044976
LC ebook record available at https://lccn.loc.gov/2021044977

ISBN: 978-1-032-18532-3 (hbk)
ISBN: 978-1-032-18529-3 (pbk)
ISBN: 978-1-003-25501-7 (ebk)

DOI: 10.4324/9781003255017

Typeset in Bembo
by Apex CoVantage, LLC

CONTENTS

Authors		*vii*
Preface		*ix*
Abbreviations		*xi*
Glossary		*xii*

	Introduction: class, stratification, market socialism David S. G. Goodman	1
1	Classes in themselves and classes for themselves: social consciousness divorced from social existence Yingjie Guo	25
2	Class and social mobility: stratification and social change since 1978 Beibei Tang	43
3	The performance of class: lifestyles and behaviour Beibei Tang	64
4	The peasantry under the impact of industrialization, urbanization and household registration Yingjie Guo	81
5	Economic growth and working-class decline: structural reform and social change after 1978 Marc Blecher	104

6 The middle class in reforming China: the dream
  of a classless society   125
  Jean-Louis Rocca

7 The dominant class after 1978: elite persistence
  and the ironies of social change   158
  David S. G. Goodman

Bibliography   *178*
Index   *212*

AUTHORS

Marc Blecher is James Monroe Professor of Politics and East Asian Studies at Oberlin College. He has also served as Senior Research Fellow at the UC Berkeley Center for Chinese Studies, Visiting Professor of Political Science at the University of Chicago, and Visiting Fellow at the Institute of Development Studies of the University of Sussex (UK). His most recent book is *Politics as a Science: A Prolegomenon* (Routledge), co-authored with Philippe Schmitter. He has published five books and dozens of articles on local politics, popular participation, and political economy in China. His research has been supported by the American Philosophical Society, the Ford Foundation, and the National Endowment for the Humanities.

David S. G. Goodman is Professor of Chinese Politics and Director of the China Studies Centre at the University of Sydney. He is a Fellow of the Academy of Social Sciences, Australia; and an Emeritus Professor at both Xi'an Jiaotong-Liverpool University, Suzhou, China; and the University of Technology, Sydney. Recent publications include *Class in Contemporary China (2014), The Handbook of the Politics of China (2015),* and (with Shigetsu Sonoda) *China Impact: Threat Perception in the Asia-Pacific Region* (2019).

Yingjie Guo is Professor of Chinese Studies at the University of Sydney. His research is related to nationalism in contemporary China and class discourses in the post-Mao era. His recent publications include *Local Elites in Post-Mao China* (2018) and *Handbook of Class and Stratification in the People's Republic of China* (2016).

Jean-Louis Rocca is a professor and researcher at the Center for International Studies, Sciences Po Paris, France. A specialist in the study of Chinese society, he is the author of *The Making of the Chinese Middle Class* (2017), *A Sociology of Modern China* (2015), and co-author (with Françoise Mengin) of *Politics in China: Moving*

Frontiers (2002). Rocca is a member of the editorial board of *The China Quarterly*. He has spent 10 years in China and in particular 6 years as a full professor at Tsinghua University.

Beibei Tang is Senior Associate Professor in the Department of China Studies at Xi'an Jiaotong-Liverpool University. She has undertaken extensive ethnographic research across different localities in China, with particular focuses on local governance, social stratification, and state-society relations in urban China. Her research is published in high-impact journals such as *The China Quarterly*, *The China Journal*, and *Journal of Contemporary China*. She is the author of *China's Housing Middle Class* (Routledge 2018), the co-editor of *Suzhou in Transition* (Routledge 2021), and the winner of the 2015 Gordon White Prize.

PREFACE

This is the second of two volumes that examine the role of the Communist Party of China in bringing about social change in China during the hundred years since 1921, through a focus on class and inequality. The first volume *Class and the Communist Party of China, 1921–1978: Revolution and Social Change* concentrates mainly on the period from the establishment of the Communist Party of China in 1921 to the decision to change the development strategy of the People's Republic of China at the end of 1978. This second volume is concerned more with contemporary developments since the end of 1978.

Continuing conversations between and among researchers are an essential part of the process from which (one hopes) understanding develops. So it is with these two volumes which have emerged from a series of conversations among colleagues over several decades, primarily among those who are the authors but also with others. The China Studies field has grown considerably over those decades, and the full cast of those whose scholarship has influenced these two volumes is best reflected in the bibliographies to each volume.

At the same time, in particular, the authors would like to acknowledge the influence of and conversations with Joel Andreas (Johns Hopkins University), Viviane Bertrand (University of Lyon), Shaun Breslin (University of Warwick), Antonella Capelle-Pogacean (Sciences Po, Paris), Lowell Dittmer (University of California, Berkeley), Mihaela Hainagiu (Social Sciences, Paris), Jane Duckett (University of Glasgow), Li Chunling (CASS Sociology), Francois Mengin (Sciences Po, Paris), Nadege Ragaru (Sciences Po, Paris), Tony Saich (Harvard), Dorothy Solinger (UC Irvine), Sun Wanning (University of Technology, Sydney), Shen Yuan (Tsinghua

University), Zang Xiaowei (City University, Hong Kong), and Zhou Xiaohong (Nanjing University).

Marc Blecher
David S. G. Goodman
Yingjie Guo
Jean-Louis Rocca
Beibei Tang

ABBREVIATIONS

ACFTU	All-China Federation of Trade Unions
CASS	Chinese Academy of Social Science
CCP	Communist Party of China
CGSS	China General Social Survey
CHIP	China Household Incomes Project
CPPCC	Chinese People's Political Consultative Conference
DDR	German Democratic Republic (former East Germany)
ENGO	Environmental Non-governmental Organization
GDP	Gross Domestic Product
GMD	Nationalist Party of China, Guomindang (Kuo-min-tang).
MoE	Ministry of Education
NGO	Non-governmental organization
NBS	National Bureau of Statistics
NPC	National People's Congress
PLA	People's Liberation Army
PRC	People's Republic of China
RMB	*Renminbi* 人民币 PRC currency
SOE	State-Owned Enterprise
UEE	University Entrance Examination

GLOSSARY

1 *jin* 斤 = 0.5 kilos = 1.1 pounds
1 *mu* 亩 = 0.06 hectares = 1/6 acre
1 *yuan* 元 = a dollar. 1 US$ = 6.8 dollars in China's People's Currency
Comintern = The Communist International, established in 1919 by the Communist Party of the Soviet Union to develop world revolution.
Danwei 单位 = Work unit
Dazhuan 大专 = Three-year higher education college
Guanxi 关系 = Influence (relationship)
Guomindang 国民党 = Nationalist Party of China
Hukou 户口 = Household registration
Jiang Jieshi = Chiang Kai-shek
Jiating chushan 家庭出身 = Family background
Mantou 馒头 = A type of steamed bread bun
Mao Tse-tung = Mao Zedong
Modern Standard Chinese = Mandarin
Nomenklatura = The table of ranks, official state-supported positions in a Communist Party-state
Renminbi 人民币 = People's Currency
Shequ 社区 = Residential community
Tizhinei 体制内 = 'Within system', within the Party-state
Xiaokang 小康 = Prosperous, well-off
Xiaoqu 小区 = Neighbourhood

INTRODUCTION

Class, stratification, market socialism

David S. G. Goodman

1 July 2021 has been celebrated in China as the hundredth anniversary of the founding of the Communist Party of China (CCP). From the beginning, the CCP has been committed to the social, economic, and political transformation of China. How that project has been implemented is the subject of this and the previous volume (*Class and the Communist Party of China, 1921–1978: Revolution and Social Change*) that together constitute a history of social change in China's past hundred years.

Class is at the heart of this enquiry because the CCP's commitment to transformation has been explicitly expressed in terms of class and class conflict. In Europe, Communism had developed with the emergence of an industrial working class in the nineteenth century. Its starting point was class conflict and the potential political power of the proletariat. In China, the experience of revolutionary activists had been somewhat different before 1921 with the main focus on national salvation, regeneration, and modernization, not least because of foreign encroachment into China. As a result, although the CCP was founded with the aid of the Soviet Union through the Communist International [Comintern] as part of the latter's revolutionary outreach, the goals of the CCP have often included political nationalism alongside or as part of other goals. Nonetheless, the role of the proletariat and class conflict was then and has remained an essential part of the CCP's appeal. The CCP describes itself as 'the vanguard both of the Chinese working class and of the Chinese people and the Chinese nation' (CCP Constitution 2017). The People's Republic of China (PRC) remains an explicitly class-based political system: according to the Preamble to the state constitution, it is a

> people's democratic dictatorship led by the working class and based on the alliance of workers and peasants, which is in essence the dictatorship of the proletariat' and while 'The exploiting classes as such have been abolished in

DOI: 10.4324/9781003255017-1

our country . . . class struggle will continue to exist within certain bounds for a long time to come.

(*PRC Constitution* 2018)

In addition to the ideological constructs of the CCP, class and stratification in terms of the institutionalized inequalities of wealth, power, and status are the keys to explaining social change more generally. Societies may be differentiated by how in this more general sense class and the composition of specific classes are understood; how the interactions between and among classes are both conceptualized and mediated; and necessarily the degree of class consciousness in each society, and its manifestation. Of course, as this volume and *Class and the Communist Party of China, 1921–1978: Revolution and Social Change* provide considerable evidence, the CCP's political project of class is not necessarily the same as that of the analysis of the social historian, even where those two approaches are necessarily interrelated.

There are clear points of both sociological and political interests that have resulted from the CCP's development of its approach to class, stratification, and social change. The search for a proletariat on which to found a revolutionary class-based movement during 1921–1949 led eventually to the CCP seeing the peasantry as the inseparable allies of the proletariat. Having won political power and socialized the means of production, the CCP then declared (in 1956) the end of class conflict between landlords and poor peasants in the countryside, and between the bourgeoisie and the proletariat in the cities. The exploiting classes were declared vanquished though within 2 years the leadership declared that there was still a bourgeoisie (this time shorthand for all reactionary classes) to be struggled against. More recently, with the introduction of structural reform since the early 1980s, the importance of the middle class as the principal agent of both social change and stability has increasingly been emphasized: an unusual development in a Marxist environment where class polarization and conflict have more often been the norm.

An examination of the evolving relationship between the CCP, on the one hand, and the theory and practice of class in China, on the other, is then important for understanding the dynamics of social change. At the centre of this analysis are concerns with the interactions of structures of wealth, status, and political power. The sources for study are inevitably dominated by the CCP. At the same time, there is the danger of employing the CCP's socio-political categorizations as if they were a rigorous, precise, and invariable articulation of class that reliably and predictably links wealth, status, and power. It has been clear that the CCP's classification has often been unsystematic and very much of the moment. Even in the revolutionary period, allocation to a specific 'class status' was deliberately variable, not consistent, and usually determined by local factors (Jerome 1973: 74). One consequence of those environmental influences is a need to inquire behind the rhetoric. The CCP's socio-political categories were those employed at specific times and under particular circumstances. They do not just chart the process of change; the categorizations themselves were the drivers of that social change. Class analysis was and remains fundamental to the CCP's organizational and political behaviour. It determines how the CCP recruits as well as how it conceives and implements social reform. Changes in its class analysis go together with the development of its programme of social change and reflect the adaptive process of policy implementation entailed in that attempt.

There are several hypotheses that may be tested in the process of understanding the changing relationship between class and the CCP. The most obvious is that perhaps the national revival goal of an internationally strong China able to take its 'rightful place' as a world leader has (and almost always had) precedence over the goal of proletarian world revolution. The second is that (partly in consequence) domestic revolutionary social change may only have ever been a mobilizatory device rather than an end in itself: the goal was to rally 'the people' – the majority of the populace – behind the CCP. Often, though not always, this was towards economic growth and a higher standard of living. A third and related hypothesis is that the meaning and use of class vary in accordance with competing and shifting visions within the Party in respect of present and future directions of social change in the PRC. Even more interesting perhaps is the possibility that the CCP's discourse of class has become inherently self-subversive. Were that to prove so, then the consequences include a range of possibilities, from the emergence of different class configurations (socially and politically) to new forms of class rule, and even to the CCP's need to revise the theoretical basis of its own position in the state.

The investigation of these hypotheses continues the approach adopted in *Class and the Communist Party of China, 1921–1978: Revolution and Social Change*. It considers the CCP's conceptual treatment of class and class relations in the period since 1978, alongside providing an understanding of the evolution of the relationship between the CCP, on the one hand, and various classes and social categories, on the other. In addition, it outlines the development of specific classes and social categories in China after 1978. Any account of class and indeed social change in China during the last century almost necessarily highlights the discontinuities apparently represented by both 1949 and 1978: 1949 because of the establishment of the PRC and 1978 because of the decision to replace an economic development strategy based on state socialism with one predicated on market socialism. At the same time, it is also clear that especially from the point of view of class there are continuities in Chinese society through both 1949 and 1978. Although the establishment of the People's Republic came justifiably clothed in the rhetoric of revolution, in practice 1949 also institutionalized not only the rule of the new revolutionary elite but also to a large extent the social continuation of the immediately pre-1949 social structure. Indeed, one key determinant of class profiles both before and after 1949, as well as before and after 1978, would seem to have been a high degree of path dependence, to which education, wealth, political power, and social status all contribute.

Class and stratification

Class is a central concept in the social sciences not least because of its role in the writings of Marx and Weber. While Weber did not agree with Marx about the importance of class as the predominant determinant of social and political change Weber had considerably more to say about class in general (not least of course because Marx never finished laying out his theory completely). Differences between Marx and Weber, their subsequent intellectual followers, and later social scientists have meant that the concept of class should perhaps sometimes be seen more as ubiquitous than fundamental. As Raymond Aron observed more than sixty years ago 'Sociologists disagree on the meaning of the term "class" – either they do not all use it to denote the same reality or they have different views of the reality to which it applies' (Aron 1960: 260). At the same time, while class may not provide an exclusive and comprehensive explanation of society and change, it certainly provides a framework for understanding social change, not least precisely because of the variations and differences in interpretation.

Conceptualizing class

Class has been a highly contested concept with a vast range of meanings including economic interest, social status, occupation, political correctness, consumption, taste, and, most recently, identity (Edgell 1993: 38; Wright 2005; Le Roux et al. 2008: 1050). Edgell provided a fairly useful guide to the different understandings of class by describing them in terms of three dimensions: by conceptual approach, of which the most important would be that between social class and occupational class (largely a distinction between Marxian and Weberian approaches to the problem); by unit of analysis, whether the focus should be the individual or the family; and by degree of coverage, whether class analysis applies to everyone or only the economically active (Edgell 1993: 42).

Sometimes, because of the association of class with Marx and a Marxist political agenda, social stratification has been used as a euphemism for class; and sometimes, remarkably even on occasions for the same political reasons, class is used to refer to any kind of social stratification. In North America in the middle of the twentieth century, it became more usual for social scientists to talk about status and elites rather than class (Mills 1956), though towards the end of that century and into the Twenty-first Erik Olin Wright (in the USA) and Mike Savage (in the UK) led a determined attempt to restore academic interest in the concept of class (Wright 1989; Wright 1997; Savage 2000). An equation of status and class is something of an intellectual irony given that Weber's formulation of status was intended as a counterpoint and to some extent a foil to Marx's notions of class (Gerth and Mills 1946: 180–195).

Given the difficulties in consistently defining and operating a concept of class in social analysis, one might well argue that class is generally a more mobilizatory concept than a precise or reliable analytical tool. This aspect of the concept of class is clearly apparent in practical politics, especially but not exclusively where revolutionary left-wing parties that are part of or draw on the Marxist tradition, such as the Chinese Communist Party, are concerned. It is also apparent in the business world where class differences not only assist producers and marketeers in their search for target audiences but are an essential part of advertising to consumers (Lu P X 2008; Silverstein et al. 2012; McKinsey 2019).

At the same time, the usefulness of the concept of class as a mobilizatory device in an intellectual context should also be appreciated. As Rosemary Crompton argued, for all the debate about the definition of class, and all the imprecision in its measurement, focusing on class draws attention to the fundamental inequalities that constitute society.

> It is not possible to develop a *single*, over-arching, approach to the topic. It is argued that 'class' makes a significant contribution to structured social inequality in contemporary societies. 'Class', however, is a multifaceted concept with a variety of different meanings. There is no 'correct' definition of the concept, nor any single 'correct' way of measuring it.
>
> *(Crompton 2006: 658)*

Class is then certainly important as a concept for drawing attention to inequalities generally: of power, wealth, social standing, lifestyle, culture, and opportunities. But it does more than that. It also draws attention to the relationships between different kinds of inequality, especially in terms of the development and influence of sources of power and authority in society (Savage 1995: 25). Erik Olin Wright summarized the concern with class in terms of six questions about these inequalities (to each of which he suggested the answer is 'class'):

1. *Distributional location:* "How are people objectively located in distributions of material inequality?"
2. *Subjective salient groups:* "What explains how people, individually and collectively, subjectively locate themselves and others within a structure of inequality?"
3. *Life chances:* "What explains inequalities in life chances and material standards of living?"
4. *Antagonistic conflicts:* "What social cleavages systematically shape overt conflicts?"
5. *Historical variation:* "How should we characterize and explain the variations across history in the social organization of inequalities?"
6. *Emancipation:* "What sorts of transformations are needed to eliminate oppression and exploitation within capitalist societies?"

[Wright 2005: 180]

It has been a long and sometimes tortuous journey that has led from Marx and Weber to these more complex, and sometimes contradictory understandings of class. In the end, the obvious alternatives are either methodological pluralism or to accept that society has become so diverse and fragmented – characterized by 'complex inequality' – that it has in fact become 'classless' not because there is no property or inequality but because there is no longer the possibility of wider social and political organization beyond short-term alliances in issue-based politics (Pakulski and Waters 1996; Pakulski 2005: 178). The pluralist approach is, in Wright's words, to recognize that

> Different frameworks of class analysis may provide the best conceptual menu. One can be a Weberian for the study of class mobility, a Bourdeiuian for the study of the class determinants of lifestyles, and a Marxian for the critique of capitalism.
>
> *(Wright 2005: 192)*

The influence of Marx and Weber

The search for explanation of class within the social sciences began, as indicated, with Marx and Weber. They both saw class as all about economic interest, and indeed the ownership (or otherwise) of (for Marx, mainly productive) property. They both also were primarily concerned with the analysis of the capitalism of contemporary advanced industrial society of their day. But there, the agreement and similarities essentially end. Marx was a working revolutionary and a critic of capitalism, who saw it as morally unjustifiable. His approach to understanding class was designed to explain both how society would change and why it should. Weber was a social scientist who saw the rationality of capitalism as not only desirable for running a society but also the only guarantee of individual freedom. In complete contrast to Marx, he viewed socialism as undesirable because it would merely hasten the dehumanizing aspects of bureaucracy and provide disincentives for the individual to work.

Class was the central concept in Marx's analysis of society and change. Remarkably, given the impact his ideas have had on the social sciences (which clearly speaks to the mobilizatory potential of class as a concept), Marx never completed a coherent explanation of class or class analysis and was often inconsistent in his application of the terms (Bendix and Lipset 1967). The third volume of Marx's *Capital* is unfinished and stops where it might just start discussing the topic in detail. Much later and from a very different political standpoint, Ralf Dahrendorf (1959) attempted to reconstruct what might have been the fourth volume of *Capital* with the focus on class and taking into account the changes that had emerged in the organization of capitalism in and after the end of the nineteenth century.

Despite any lack of clarity, Marx's ideas have bequeathed three important points of departure for later discussion of the dynamics of class and social stratification. The first and possibly the most important is that for the most part Marx was an economic determinist. In terms of class analysis, this meant that an individual's class position would determine their political behaviour, and that a class as a social group could be expected to behave in line with its economic interest. This though is not to say that class action is guaranteed. While there is always the assumption that the capitalist class will act to protect its interest, the working class (of whom much is expected, for it is their 'historical mission' to overthrow the capitalists) will need to acquire a high degree of class consciousness in order to act. Marx distinguished between a class 'in itself' and a class 'for itself' with only the latter entailing organization towards common interests (Marx 1847: 173). Marx seemed sometimes a little unsure, but for later Marxists there was and has been a major difference between working-class action and proletarian consciousness, with only the latter being identified as the political act that drives the dialectic of history.

The development of a proletarian consciousness among the working class is part of the second important point of departure bequeathed by Marx to discussion of class. Marx was an arch radical dichotomizer. History was driven at every stage in its development by the struggle between two antagonistic classes. This is not quite to say that there were only two classes at any stage of historical development, but rather that there were only two that mattered. In the capitalist stage of development, these were the capitalist class, who owned property, and the propertyless proletariat, forced to sell their labour for wages. As the class conflict between them heightens with the development of capitalism, and as the proletariat's consciousness rises, so does the potential for revolutionary change. Of course, ideology and consciousness work both ways, and Marx was well aware that the capitalist class controlled the world of ideas as well as of production. It would always seek to present its interests as those of the whole community, which Marx regarded as a manifestation of 'false consciousness'. For Marx, only the proletariat had the potential to speak for the whole community, as would occur after revolution and the establishment of socialism. This was the origin in the hands of later Marxists of the call to establish 'the dictatorship of the proletariat'.

The third point of departure for later debate was Marx's emphasis on ownership of property. Marx was faced with a world of capitalist owner–entrepreneurs, and it was their ownership of capital and the proletariat's absence of ownership that he invested with political significance. He had no experience of the corporate world that was to develop later with its share-based public companies where directors and a chief executive officer might be accountable to shareholders, let alone the development of state-owned enterprises of any kind. Direct ownership of property (or its total absence) was important because it assisted class polarization and conflict. The capitalist class would increasingly seek to take advantage of those with only labour power who would in reaction become politicized by that process.

In contrast, class was not the central concept in Weber's analysis of society and change, though he did have much to say about both class and indeed even about Marx on class, whom he referred to critically as 'a certain talented author' (Weber 1924: 185). For Weber, status was considerably more important than class and much more at the heart of his main concern, which was social stratification. Weber agreed that class was all about economic interest and indeed the ownership of property, but he was not simply an economic determinist:

> "Economically conditioned" power is not, of course, identical with "power" as such. On the contrary the emergence of economic power may be the consequence of power existing on other grounds. Man does not strive for

> power only in order to enrich himself economically. Power, including economic power, may be valued "for its own sake." Very frequently the striving for power is also conditioned by the social "honor" it entails. Not all power, however, entails social honor.
>
> *(Weber 1924: 180)*

Weber identified classes as 'not communities' but as potential groups existing in society: people whose personal experiences, market situation, and life chances are causally shaped by the same economic assets and interests. These he contrasted with status groups, which he saw as 'normal communities' determined by 'a specific, positive or negative, social estimation of honour' (Weber 1924: 190). The interaction between class and status groups then delivered for Weber the beginnings of a more complex understanding of both class and social stratification than the polarization described by Marx. Weber identified two broad positively privileged classes: the owners of property and the commercial classes, including all those with services and skills to be hired such as merchants, bankers, professionals, and even 'workers with monopolistic qualifications and skills'. Weber also described three negatively privileged property classes (the unfree, the declassee, and paupers) and three negatively privileged commercial classes (skilled, semi-skilled, and unskilled workers). In between, there were the middle classes – peasants, artisans, officials, teachers, and intellectuals (Edgell 1993: 12–13).

Weber's legacy to the later discussion of class and social stratification was then largely antithetical to that of Marx, not least because he did not share the latter's view of history and its progress. While accepting that class was about economic interest, Weber did not see economic interest as the sole or even major determinant of social and political change. Weber described a more detailed and complex social stratification, with an emphasis on class fragmentation rather than class polarization. He also drew attention to additional kinds of social stratification other than economic inequalities, in particular, ethnicity. Weber also employed a dramatically less economically deterministic approach to the analysis of social change. In particular, he highlighted questions of esteem and self-identification, which have become increasingly important to the understanding of class and indeed social stratification.

The sociology of class and stratification

The subsequent sociology of class has been very rich, and any attempt to summarize is bound to overgeneralize and to do a disservice to the debates that have taken place (details may be found in Edgell 1993; Savage 2000; Wright 2005). There have though been a number of major developments that in particular impact on the consideration of class in the PRC: questions about the primacy of the ownership (or otherwise) of property; issues related to the growth of the middle classes; the greater salience of gender; the emergence of the 'cultural turn' centred on the work of Bourdieu, which building on Weber's ideas has disaggregated the factors determining class positions and emphasized self-reflexivity and embedded social action; and a growing if general agreement on an overall class structure.

For both Marx and Weber, positioning as owners of property or being property-less was at the heart of their understandings of class. This distinction clearly does not take account of the full range of economic forms that have developed with industrial society. Shareholding and the development of management practices have made for structural change. Large corporations may own economic activities, but it is sometimes far from clear who owns the large corporations, let alone who decides how they will operate. When those large corporations are themselves state- or publicly owned questions of ownership as means of determining class become even more confused. In discussing Communist Party-states, as they developed in the Soviet Union and Eastern Europe to the late 1980s, this led some observers, especially Neo-Marxist critics, to argue that with the socialization of property or at least ownership it was the relationship to the control of the means of production that determined class (Ticktin 1981). Milovan Djilas, who had been a leader of Yugoslavia until 1954, described the emergence of the 'new class' in Communist Party-states who ruled by virtue not of their control of the economy but of their political positions (Djilas 1957). Szelényi and others have long pointed out that in both a state socialist and market socialist political economy (as the PRC has variously been since 1949) the ownership of capital is often less important than the Party-state's direction of redistributive economics and the effective control of capital and resources (Szelényi 1978; Szelényi 2008).

These later understandings of class in Communist Party-states have resonances more generally with the views of C. Wright Mills (Mills 1956) describing the 'Power Elite' in North America in the middle of the twentieth century, and on a larger scale with the later views expressed by critics of the neo-liberalism that emerged during the 1990s (Harvey 2007). The relationship to the control of the means of production, rather than ownership, also became a dominant theme in analysis of capitalist industrial societies from both Marxists (Poulantzas 1979) and Weberians (Dahrendorf 1959). Moreover, in describing a newly emergent technocracy, Burnham went even further seeing managers as a new class completely supplanting the authority and control of capitalist owners (Burnham 1941), a view echoed albeit in a non-Marxist framework by Galbraith somewhat later (Galbraith 1968).

Neither Marx nor Weber in their various class analyses provided for the emergence of the middle classes in the numbers and in the ways that they later manifested in industrial societies. Yet the growth of the 'white-collar' professional and managerial middle classes had fast become the hallmark of advanced industrial societies (Mills 1951). While research on the working class had historically been privileged in the sociology of class (Savage 2000: 152), it was the growth of the middle classes and the possibility of the emergence of new and separate identities that posed the greatest intellectual challenges. From the Neo-Marxist side, Wright described the empirical evidence of its size as growth as the 'embarrassment' of the middle class, since this seemed to deny the case for an increasingly polarized class structure

(Wright 1984). Inevitably, because of the pluralism inherent in their approach to stratification, Weberian sociologists were more easily able to accommodate the conceptual expansion of the middle classes (Goldthorpe 1980; Edgell 1993: 13).

Discussion of the respective merits of Marxist and Weberian approaches to class and class analysis reached their height in assessing the nature and roles of the middle classes and in developing schema that dealt with the consequences of more and more varied middle classes – those who were not clearly of the property-owning ruling class or the propertyless working classes – and sometimes these debates even became quite heated (Savage 2000: 7). Weberians focused on occupational class and Marxists on social class. Weberians emphasized hierarchy, and Marxists stressed the relational nature of class. Weberians highlighted social order, and Marxists conflict. Weberians stressed the centrality of the market and life chances and Marxists of production and exploitation (Edgell 1993: 36–7; Wright 1997: 31).

Gender is clearly a very different kind of social stratification to class. All the same, the extent to which the early analysis of class and social stratification avoided consideration of gender was only understandable in terms of the mores of society at the time. As increasingly from the end of 1950s on, women found their public voice this situation started to change (Watson and Barth 1964). It rapidly became apparent that class analysis and indeed any consideration of stratification needed to take account of gender, including eventually the very definition of work and the workforce that excluded housework. For some time, a key issue for debate was whether gender or class should be regarded as the primary determinant of individual or social change, though more recent research has concentrated on the interdependence of influence (Heath and Britten 1984; Crompton and Mann 1986; Wright 1989; Pollert 1996).

The 'cultural turn' in the social sciences is the name given to various ways in which culture has come to be seen as a fundamental part of economic, social, and political analysis. The culture in the term is not just a reference to high or popular culture, but equally to the ideas and values that may be embodied in cultural manifestations. The emphasis on culture as ideas and values is significant because the cultural turn also focuses on the importance of ways of thought as a primary reality. Thus, for example, not only lifestyle but also identity have become areas for considerable research. Pierre Bourdieu's work (notably *Distinction*, Bourdieu 1984) has been at the centre of this change in the social sciences. Through extremely detailed and technically and theoretically sophisticated research Bourdieu has concentrated on the processes of how social collectives, including but not exclusively classes, are formed mainly through the performance of consumption and lifestyle. (For a detailed account, see Weininger 2005.) Building explicitly on Weber, Bourdieu links the determination of occupational classes in their social space – in the process of identifying cultural and social capital in addition to economic capital – to symbolic practices of social classification.

Remarkably, since the end of twentieth century, sociologists appear to have generally reached a degree of agreement on a basic three-class division of society in industrial society, which can be reached if the Marxist view of history is (at least temporarily and for academic purposes) put aside (Wright 1997: 29). There are three main sources of class power: property, qualifications, and labour (Giddens 1973). These have led to the identification of three broad classes that are to be found in all societies: 'a dominant class based on the ownership of capital, an intermediate class based on the acquisition of educational and/or organizational assets, and a subordinate class based on the possession of physical labour' (Edgell 1993: 81). In addition, there may also be constituent classes or sub-classes within each of these three main classes, as well as one or more underclasses completely outside consideration of class position. The differences between societies are then seen in the relationships among the three broad classes, and the specific constituent classes and sub-classes of which they are comprised.

Class and social change in the PRC

The CCP's understanding of class since the establishment of the PRC in 1949 has been shaped by its experience on the road to power; and the CCP's understanding of class since 1978 has additionally and equally been shaped by the political conflicts from 1949 to the late 1970s. The former highlighted the centrality of land, and land ownership to China's political economy and hence to the CCP's programme and appeal for change, alongside opposition to industrialists and entrepreneurs. The latter eventually bequeathed an intense aversion to and rejection of class conflict, which extended to a hesitancy to use class as a political tool to some extent.

China's social structure

Well into the twentieth century, China's social structure had for centuries been dominated by the gentry, the landowning class who not only formed the local elite but also provided the scholar–officials for service in the imperial system of rule. Dynastic families might have appeared, ruled, and been overthrown, but there was greater longevity to the gentry, though necessarily gentry families waxed and waned in importance in each locality. Land was central to the definition of the gentry, but it was not the only source of their power. This was a single local elite that effectively monopolized political, economic, and cultural power. In the words of one commentator, albeit describing the situation in the late Qing:

> China's social and economic elite gained status from education and passing civil service exams, wealth from land and commerce, and power from government positions and leadership roles within local communities. They formed large and complex families that had interests in land and commerce and maintained residences for extended families simultaneously in villages and towns or cities. At the heart of the elite reproduction were scholars who after passing the civil service exams staffed the world's largest state bureaucracy . . . Families producing scholars often gained wealth from land ownership, commerce or some combination of both.
>
> *(Wong 2009: 236)*

It is estimated that by the 1940s the gentry were less than half a per cent of the population: fewer than 2 million people (including families) in a population of about 400 million (Chang C 1970: 116; Eberhard 1975). Some guide to the scale of the gentry can also be gained from Yung-Teh Chow's study of a county in Southwest China during the 1930s and 1940s. There were then about 2,200 counties in China. Chow in his county study identified 26 gentry families in a population of just under 70,000 people, who over time competed for power and influence. Social mobility occurred within classes, but across class distinctions it was low. The local elite maintained its position not only through economic means but also by regularly replenishing its ranks, not least by supporting people (often through adoption) from lower-class backgrounds to sit for examinations and enter official service. This though was very variable over time (Chow 1966). It is estimated that in the Tang Dynasty (618–907) only 13.8% of officials were from 'humble' (i.e. not gentry-born) backgrounds, whereas during the early Song Dynasty (960–1279) this rose to 46.1% (Ho 1962: 260).

In the Republican Era across most of China, there was little challenge to the dominant local position of the gentry. As the imperial system collapsed, they had flexed their muscles through the development of provincial assemblies, and the various experiments with representative local government that were attempted during the Republic. The warlord regimes that replaced the imperial system in many places, as well as the Republic itself as it developed, either worked closely with the local elites or ran the risk of confronting the power of the entrenched local gentry. In Shanxi Province, for example, opposition from local elites to his plans for modernization and democratization led warlord Yan Xishan to ally with the CCP whom he thought he could use to counter the local elite's influence (Gillin 1967: 51; Jiang and Li 1990: 1973). Even the Japanese regimes established after invasion, from 1931 in the Northeast and after 1937 elsewhere accepted and worked through the local gentry (Duara 2003; Brook 2005).

This is of course not to argue that there was no socio-economic change in the first half of the twentieth century. Modernization and industrialization proceeded, if fitfully and unevenly across China before 1949, especially in urban areas and treaty ports. Despite problems of national unification, war, and civil war, there was the development not only of industry and capitalist enterprises but also of a modern state and many of the institutions associated with those processes, including schools, health services, postal services, financial institutions, and a state administration. Though social differentiation was limited in scope and scale, and highly concentrated spatially, these years saw the emergence of a capital-owning bourgeoisie; as well as professional and managerial middle classes, including intellectuals associated with the new education system and mass media of communication; and the beginnings of a working class. There were many social connections among these new developments and the earlier social structure, but equally there were opportunities for ordinary people to join the economic elite on occasion (Bergère 1989: 45ff).

At the same time, land ownership and relationship to the land were clearly crucial for the vast majority of the population who lived outside the major metropolitan areas. Despite a growing interest in the social sciences during the Republic, there is unfortunately little reliable information available about land distribution. Research from extant contemporary surveys suggests a dramatic inequality. Four per cent of rural households were landlords who owned 39% of the land. Six per cent of households were rich peasants who hired labour to help them farm the 17% of the land that they owned. Twenty-two per cent of rural households were owner-farming middle peasants who owned 30%of the land. Thirty-six per cent of rural households were poor peasants who owned 14%of the land. Twenty-four per cent of rural households were tenant farmers, and 8% of rural households were agricultural labourers. These figures provide only the most approximate of guides, and there were in any case intense local variations. Tenancy was greater in the south than in the north of the country; and there were areas of the north where there were few if any landlords, though in the north, the landlords were often absentee landlords (Esherick 1981).

From its first congress in 1921, the Communist Party of China was committed to a programme of ensuring national unity, economic development, and social change. The nationalist agenda was shared with the Nationalist Party and led to cooperation until 1927, and again when faced by the threat of Japanese invasion during 1936 and when this actually occurred in and after 1937. At such times the more revolutionary aspects of the CCP's objectives were put temporarily on hold, but the commitment to economic development, class preference, and class conflict were never abandoned. The first attempts to establish Communist Party areas of government after 1927, based on peasant mobilization, were relatively short-lived and resulted in retreat and the Long March (1934–5) from Southeast China first to the West and then to the North, where the CCP regrouped around Mao Zedong and other leaders. More successful were the base areas established to resist Japanese invasion (1937–45): these included not only Yan'an where the CCP capital was established in the north of Shaanxi Province but also the behind-the-lines governments of North and East China. These not only mobilized the local population politically but also experimented with programmes of economic development and even revolutionary social change, such as land reform and the development of farming cooperatives. At the heart of these developments were the highlighting of class differences and class antagonisms (Goodman 2013).

Classification and class levelling

With the establishment of the PRC in October 1949, the CCP had not only a clear agenda but also some considerable experience in knowing how to proceed to implementation of policies designed to bring social change. Certainly, the revolutionary experience before 1949 was to play a central role in the PRC's development during the next 30 years, not least because of the legitimacy it gave Mao Zedong, who had not only led the CCP after 1942 but also so often proved to be right where others were wrong. Mao's disproportionate influence was to prove unsettling for the first 30 years of the PRC for while there was no disagreement among the CCP's leadership about the need for national unity and social change, there was considerably less certainty about how economic development should be pursued, and unfortunately as the years passed, these debates became entangled in elite level conflicts that often started with Mao Zedong.

National unity was signalled by the establishment of the PRC, first through military control commissions at local levels as institutions of government for a number of years, and then through the promulgation of a new state constitution in 1954 and the development of a new system of government, based on two parallel hierarchies: a state administration supervised by the CCP. The implementation of revolutionary social change was more complex and took longer to effect. Social control and a process of class levelling – destroying the power of the privileged in the earlier society and its replacement by a specific state-sponsored system of stratification and discrimination – came in three stages, directed at the rural areas, the urban areas, and the intelligentsia.

Central to the establishment of social control was a process in which everyone was required to have a specific household registration that included details of their class background. Regulations assigned two class labels to each individual: class origin (*jieji chengfen* 阶级成分) and class background (*jiating chushen* 家庭出身). There were some 62 class descriptors. Class origin was determined by a person's activities during 1946–9; class background by their father's activities when the individual in question was born. These class descriptors were shaped by economic and status factors, as well as an assessment of political reliability to the new regime, and dramatically influenced life chances under the PRC. Individuals with a 'good' class description – those from the working classes or the politically reliable – were favoured in education and employment over those with a 'bad' class description, who were often scapegoated in later political campaigns (Kraus 1981).

Land reform was the first stage in class levelling, designed less to redistribute wealth than to eradicate the power and influence of the old (local) ruling class and to establish the new regime's processes of social control. Certainly, there was land redistribution: landlordism and landlessness were both abolished. The poorest 20% of the rural population doubled their income compared to the Republican era, and two-thirds of the peasantry became middle peasants (Selden 1988: 9). At the same time, politics dominated these acts. More land was redistributed (700 million *mu*) than was owned by landlords (Esherick 1981), and land reform was itself a political performance. Work teams organized villagers to attend struggle meetings to denounce the local landlord or landlords. Landlords had to be found by the Party-state even where the pattern of landholding might be otherwise, with cadres often being allocated quotas in order to identify local 'landlords' (Huang 1995: 105). The political imperative for change was followed up relatively quickly during the mid-1950s with peasants being organized into lower stage cooperatives and higher stage collectives on the path to larger units of collective farming after land reform, a process largely completed by the end of 1956.

The second stage of class levelling was a similar process of state control being extended and the socialization of the means of production in the urban areas.

The urban environment was politically and organizationally complex in 1949, not least because much of the economy in the coastal provinces had been dominated by foreign investment and involvement. The Party-state developed its reach into enterprises in a two-pronged offensive, empowering workers under CCP leadership at factory level and national political campaigns from the top-down, appealing to the patriotism of the capitalist class on the one hand and being prepared to use more force on the other (Andreas 2012: 108). At first, the Party-state worked in cooperation with private owners to establish economic stability, but starting in 1952 the urban equivalent of land reform, the 'Five Anti' Campaign (against bribery, tax evasion, fraud, theft of government property, and the stealing of state secrets) led to struggle sessions, confession of economic crimes, and ultimately the collectivization of businesses (Gardner 1969). By the end of 1956, almost the entire urban population was assigned to a state-regulated work unit so that housing, welfare (including education for children), and security were provided at the point of employment. By this stage, almost all economic activities in urban areas had come under either direct or indirect state control through (respectively) state-owned enterprises or collectives, and from 1955 on there was a wage system for state staff and workers with 26 grades of officials, 17 grades of technician and 8 grades of workers (Korzec and Whyte 1981). By the 8th CCP National Congress of 1956, it was possible for Deng Xiaoping (then Secretary General of the CCP) to announce the end of the exploiting classes and class conflict with the emergence of a single working class that united everyone (Deng 1956: 213–214).

The final stage of class levelling occurred in 1957 with control being exercised over the intelligentsia. The new regime had been keen to maintain the support of the intellectuals, not least as a significant number had supported the CCP. At the same time, there were concerns about control and discipline. The CCP set out to adapt existing institutions in order to develop new professional intellectuals who it hoped would be both politically reliable and technically advanced (Andreas 2012). In May 1956, Mao Zedong had encouraged professional intellectuals to voice their concerns about social and political change. In reminding his audience of the pre-imperial practice, he had said 'let a hundred flowers bloom, a hundred schools of thought contend'. This did not eventuate on any large scale until after February 1957, but in the following weeks criticisms of the PRC and the CCP were sometimes more than the leadership thought acceptable. The result was the Anti-Rightist Campaign which started in July with many professional intellectuals not simply being criticized but also losing their jobs and being sent to 'Reform through Labour' camps, often until the 1970s or 1980s. It is estimated that some 300,000 were adversely affected by this campaign (Mu 1962: 173).

Never forget class struggle

Mass mobilization and campaign politics were very much the order of the day for the PRC during its first 30 years, and this too clearly has its roots in the experiences of the CCP before 1949. Faced though with the tasks of developing the economy, there was less certainty about the way to proceed. During 1953–57 with direct assistance from the Soviet Union, it basically followed that country's model of a centralized socialist economy, privileging workers and urban areas, developing heavy industry first, concentrating on the areas of industrial and economic development already established (before 1949), and emphasizing investment in machinery. By 1955, Mao and other leaders had begun to express doubts for both economic and political reasons about the wisdom of following this line of development. The high degree of centralism involved in the Soviet Model was sitting uneasily with China's economic diversity, managing the peasantry presented a more sizeable problem than in the Soviet Union, there were growing tensions between the PRC and the Soviet Union that eventually culminated in the Sino-Soviet Split in the early 1960s, and Mao Zedong himself was somewhat impatient. The result was considerable debate within the CCP leadership about the ways to be followed, which led to both experimentation and elite conflict in which Mao Zedong and his views played a central role, not only during the mid-1950s but until the issue was finally resolved after his death in September 1976.

The major issues at stake in the various discussions that took place about the appropriate path to development were summarized by Mao Zedong in a speech delivered in April 1956. They included debate about the speed of development, the spatial distribution of economic development as between the coastal provinces and the interior, the ordering of importance to be given to the development of specific sectors of the economy, the degree of decentralization to be encouraged in economic development, and the extent to which technical transformation should be the driver of change or socialization (Mao 1956a). Though other ideas were formulated at the time, and many, such as those associated with Chen Yun, were to see the light of day in the Reform Era that started in the late 1970s (Solinger 1984), the immediate debate really centred around Mao Zedong. Mao had acted unilaterally, though to some extent successfully, to increase the speed of development in 1955 and 1956. Faced with the opportunity again in 1958, he persuaded the CCP to adopt a series of programmes that became The Great Leap Forward, designed to catch up with the rest of the economically developed world as quickly as possible through increased grain production, mass mobilization, rapid industrialization, and collectivization. One slogan of the times was 'Catch up with the United Kingdom's 150 years [of advanced economic development] in fifteen years: make every one of our days count as ten of theirs'.

These policies were followed until a halt was called in 1961, with the recognition that severe problems had arisen. The encouragement of speed had resulted not so much in increased production as the reporting of increased production with the further catastrophic result that later plans had been laid on the basis of nonexistent goods and food. Mass mobilizatory farming methods and other attempts to increase yields, such as terracing and working with often friable topsoil, proved counter-productive in many parts of the country. In place of the attempted economic boom came mass starvation and an absolute drop in population numbers by the early 1960s, with some provinces (notably Anhui and Qinghai) reporting severe famines. Some of the leaders of the CCP were aware of the problems resulting, and led by the long-term military leader and then Minister of Defence, Peng Dehuai, attempted to rein in the Great Leap Forward at the Lushan Meeting of the CCP leadership in 1959. Mao reacted badly, which led to Peng's dismissal and was to have later ramifications for elite politics.

With the retreat from the Great Leap Forward came the inevitable inquiry into the reasons for its failure. Mao Zedong put the weight of his interpretation on the lack of appropriate political consciousness by the CCP and its cadres, without surrendering the general outline of his approach to economic development. He pursued this line of argument through the early 1960s, and it eventually developed into a criticism that the CCP and the PRC had been taken over by forces who were not simply opposing him, but also the entire socialist project. In 1962, this became a call to 'Never forget class struggle'. Increasingly, he came to the view that there was opposition in the elite and in society to his ideas and that this opposition represented the manifestations of a new bourgeoisie and other counter-revolutionary classes.

There is a clear problem in attempting to identify opposition to Mao at this time. It was not just a question of Mao refusing to accept possibly helpful criticism, but more complicatedly that he was always at the centre of debates and other leaders for the most part attempted to either influence him or do his bidding. As a result, because things were frequently uncertain they often found themselves caught flat-footed (Teiwes 1984: 93). By the mid-1960s, Mao Zedong came to believe that the CCP had been captured by 'Those in authority taking the capitalist road'. To remove them and their influence, he launched the Great Proletarian Cultural Revolution (1966–1976) relying on support from the head of the People's Liberation Army [PLA] Lin Biao and the four members of the Central Cultural Revolution Group (who became celebrated as the 'Gang of Four') Jiang Qing (Mao's wife), Zhang Chunqiao, Wang Hongwen, and Yao Wenyuan. At the height of the Cultural Revolution and its most violent phase (1966–1968), Mao Zedong called on those who supported his views on class and class conflict, as well as university and high school students as Red Guards, to overthrow the organizations of party and state and remove those designated as 'capitalist-roaders' from office. Those who lost their positions, who were imprisoned, and some of whom died included not only the majority of senior officials in the CCP and the state administration, and many professional intellectuals, professors, and teachers, but also most notably the President of the PRC, Liu Shaoqi, and the Secretary-General of the CCP, Deng Xiaoping.

The Ninth Congress of the CCP in 1969 provided a display of unity and agreement on the way forward that was rapidly to prove illusory. Lin Biao was nominated as Mao's chosen successor, but in 1971 he died mysteriously in a plane crash, allegedly after having plotted a coup against Mao. This development essentially left the political arena open to the influence of the Gang of Four. Other leaders and possibly even Mao himself were concerned about their influence, indeed that precise description reportedly came from Mao who instructed the group 'Don't become a Gang of Four'. After Lin Biao's demise, in the mid-1970s, the debate on economic development that had started in the mid-1950s started up again albeit in a somewhat muted way. Deng Xiaoping was restored to the leadership for a short while with the support of the Premier of the State Council, Zhou Enlai (who had managed to survive the Cultural Revolution) but when the latter died in January 1976. Deng was removed from office again. Mao Zedong himself died in September 1976, which triggered the arrest of the Gang of Four, Deng's eventual return to leadership, and a complete re-evaluation of the PRC's strategy on economic development, and indeed the CCP's approach to class and class conflict.

Reform and market socialism

Change came with a series of political events that culminated at the Central Work Conference of the CCP in October–November and later at the Third Plenum of the Eleventh Central Committee of the CCP in December 1978. Here, the Party leadership, with Deng at the helm, committed itself to the most significant shift in development strategy since the foundation of the PRC. The CCP opted for a programme of 'Reform and Openness' that prepared the ground for a move away from the model of state socialism that had developed since the mid-1950s and returned to many of the ideas on economic development formulated at that time. The main economic objectives were to reduce the role of government in economic management, introduce marketization into the domestic economy, and open up the domestic economy to global interactions.

Equally fundamental were the political objectives of the change in strategic direction: in relatively short order, it rejected the experience of the Cultural Revolution on a grand scale and attempted to ensure the restoration of the CCP's norms of operation. The reaction against the politics of class was immediate: at the beginning of 1979, 'bad' class labels were removed from those so identified. In June 1981, a CCP Conference adopted the 'Resolution on certain questions in the history of our party since the founding of the People's Republic of China'. The Resolution criticized Mao Zedong for his actions during 1962–1976, held him responsible for 'leftist' errors in those years, and castigated him for ignoring the principles of collective leadership within the CCP. Moreover, the 1981 CCP Conference vindicated those political leaders who had been the victims of the Cultural Revolution, and in the majority of cases restored them to office (Goodman 1994: 89). Class conflict and references to class or specific classes did not disappear immediately or totally from public discourse, but such expressions were increasingly limited and of lesser importance. Society was now seen as having two classes and a stratum: workers, peasants, and the intelligentsia, respectively.

In contrast to the first 30 years of the PRC, the following decades were marked for the most part by political stability. For the CCP, the goal was domestic political constancy, the development of the Chinese economy, and the restoration of what was seen as China's leading role in world affairs. Necessarily, these goals have gone together though there was both an experimental and a developmental approach towards these goals over those years. The first decade of 'Reform and Openness' was the most uncertain as the CCP debated how to proceed, and it was not without difficulties, not least of which by the end of the decade was inflation; disagreements within the leadership, if without the intense conflict of the Cultural Revolution era; and a degree of popular unrest. Elite unity, however, was provided by Deng Xiaoping in the early 1990s firmly fixing the legitimacy of the regime to its ability to deliver growing prosperity. Successive CCP leaders – Jiang Zemin (1989–2002), Hu Jintao (2002–2012), and Xi Jinping (since 2012) – delivered on the promise that China can grow prosperity and world status through an emphasis on market socialism.

Unsurprisingly, the Reform Era's emphasis on introducing market forces to the development of China's economy and China's integration into the world economy brought major changes to the CCP's perspectives on class and social change. After the mid-1950s, when the private sector of the economy was to all intents and purposes closed down, until the end of 1990s, businesspeople had been regarded with some suspicion, even after the early 1980s when the development of small- and medium-sized businesses was being encouraged by official economic policy. This all started to change towards the end of 1990s as businesspeople became more officially recognized as 'advanced' social elements, culminating with their ability to join the CCP openly from 2002 on'. (Some had been members already by virtue of previous occupations and some more surreptitiously.) This was clearly a major change for the CCP (Goodman 2014a).

The emergence of businesspeople as an approved social category was associated with the growth of the non-state sector of the economy in which many of them operated, and the reduction of the state sector of the economy. Although the non-state sector is often referred to as the private sector, activities are quite frequently the result of various different kinds of public–private interaction as much as if not more than of private investment, ownership, and operation (Naughton 2010: 437). This shift in resources and emphases had major impacts on other social classes besides just those engaged as entrepreneurs in business development.

In the first place, the urban working class who had previously worked in the highly protected state sector of the economy was greatly reduced in size and indeed political importance. Some 60 million urban workers were laid off by economic restructuring between 1993 and 2006 (Hurst 2009). In their place, a new working class was created by economic reform. Migrant peasant labourers moved from rural to urban areas to take up the new manual labour opportunities being created in manufacturing, construction, and retail. Unlike the former (and to a lesser extent), the remnant state sector urban working class though the new migrant working class was denied urban welfare privileges, especially in the larger metropolitan areas. Household registration provided every individual with either a rural or an urban identity, and migrant peasant workers were initially excluded almost absolutely from the wider urban benefits. Their trade-off was said to be their ownership or share of ownership in land at their rural domicile (Solinger 1999). While there have been elements of reform to this polarization, elements of class rigidity remain (Solinger 2018).

The growth of the economy generally and especially its increased complexity and technological development have also resulted in the growth of the numbers of professionals, technologists, and managers. This expansion is almost always associated with the growth of the non-state sector of the economy, but it applies equally to the state sector. The latter has been increasingly expected to operate in response to market demand for its outputs and market prices of supply for its inputs, especially labour. The result is the growth in the middle classes responsible for sustaining social and economic development including in health and education as well as in business, manufacturing, and other service industries. While the existence of the middle classes was not a new phenomenon either in China or in the PRC, economic restructuring and the introduction of market socialism have increased the numbers in the middle class, if not quite by the numbers imagined sometimes by both the Party-state and commentators outside the PRC (Goodman 2014c: 55).

The growth of the middle classes, and even more the development of a political discourse of support, has been one of the more remarkable aspects of China's social and political change in the twenty-first century, necessarily associated with the beginnings of a reconceptualization of class and reflecting the disquiet about domestic political conflict associated with class struggle. In his valedictory speech as General Secretary at the CCP Congress in 2002, Jiang Zemin, though recognizing the achievements of economic development pointed out that while the upper classes had grown in wealth, there was a need to increase the size of the 'middle strata' and to decrease the numbers of those who were in less well-off social categories (Jiang Zemin 2002). A variety of government agencies responded by setting targets for the growth of the middle classes: 40% of the workforce by 2010 (*Xinhua* 2005) and 55% of the population by 2020 (Wu Jiao 2007). This discourse has been high profile ever since towards the goal of creating a 'moderately prosperous' society. The logic is clear: if people are encouraged to become and aspire to be middle class, it will fuel economic growth, and if the majority of the population becomes moderately prosperous, then the regime's continuing performance legitimacy will ensure social instability is minimized. The State Council's Development Research Centre in its joint report with The World Bank acknowledged that the objective is to emulate the experience of other industrial countries in ensuring 'a large middle class that acts as a force for stability, good governance, and economic progress' (World Bank 2012: 16).

Domestic discussion of the growth of the middle class was for a while somewhat controversial. The policy lead in promoting the middle classes was taken by Lu Xueyi and colleagues at the Institute of Sociology in the Chinese Academy of Social Sciences and its Research Group for Social Structure in Contemporary China. Starting in 2002, they developed a theoretical framework for describing and interpreting change in China's social structure, which have been used in the Institute's annual reports on social stratification. It provided for ten strata derived from survey work, originally grouped into broader categories of 'upper, upper middle, middle, lower middle, and lower' (Lu Xueyi 2002: 9) though these broader categories were later reduced to 'upper middle, lower middle, and workers' before broader categorization was eventually abandoned (Lu Xueyi 2012: 403). The ten strata are state and social administrators; managers; private entrepreneurs; individual business owners; professional and technical personnel; office workers; employees of commercial services; industrial working class; agricultural labourers; and the urban and rural jobless, unemployed and semi-employed. Politically, it was argued that all but the last strata could be regarded as or had the potential to become middle class. Possibly of even greater importance, the framework permits a typology of class by occupation to exist alongside the previous orthodoxy of class by ideology (workers, peasants, intelligentsia).

In Chinese, class (*jieji* 阶级) and stratum (*jieceng* 阶层) are clearly differentiated not least because of the particular role of class in the CCP's Marxism-Leninism. Lu Xueyi and his colleagues commented on their use of stratum/strata instead of class differently though. He and they were seeking to draw a distinction between the situation in the twentieth century and class as interpreted by Mao Zedong, specifically as applied in China's revolutionary era before 1949, and under state socialism before 1978. In addition, in his own words 'As to the ten major social strata in the classification of this study, the theoretical meaning of the term "stratum" is close to that of the term "class" in English'. There are clear echoes of the then-recent sociological discussion and developments outside China related to the interaction of class and stratification and the subsequent development of broad agreement about the class structure of society, and indeed the influence of Goldthorpe, Giddens, and Erik Olin Wright is explicitly acknowledged (Lu Xueyi 2005: 419).

Xi Jingping's elevation to the leadership of the CCP in 2012 rapidly saw the push for the development of a middle-class China being folded, not unnaturally, into the drive to realize the 'China Dream': prosperity at home, recognition abroad (Xi Jingping 2013; Gallelli 2018). At the same time, the last decade has seen revival of a CCP class description of society in terms of the 'two classes and a stratum' – workers, peasants, and the intelligentsia – a formula that was first identified in the mid-1950s and resurrected in the 1980s. The period of Xi Jinping's leadership has been characterized by increased urbanization and marketization of business practices, though somewhat paradoxically also by a greater emphasis on the role of state-owned enterprises in economic development. In time, it may be that the paradox is explained by increased market-responding practices even in state-owned enterprises, though this has not noticeably been the case since such a specific development was announced at the 3rd Plenum of the 18th Central Committee in September 2013. Either way, it is likely that the emphasis on growing the size and importance of the middle classes, or perhaps better described as middle strata, will continue.

Class and the CCP: 1978–2021

The chapters in this volume centre on the decades since the introduction of reform into the PRC's version of state socialism that started in 1978. It contains chapters on the CCP's understanding of class and the socio-economic consequences of its development of performance legitimacy. In particular, despite the rigidity in the understanding of class as a Marxist-Leninist construct social structures and stratification have changed substantially through the 40 years since the change in economic development strategy began at the end of 1978. One consequence is that both by design and by practice the performance of class has become more high profile. In addition, to the general views of social change, the volume addresses specifically the development of specifically the dominant class, the middle classes, the working classes, and the peasantry.

In Chapter 1, Yingjie Guo examines how the Chinese Communist Party and Chinese social scientists have approached class and class analysis in the reform era. From a discursive viewpoint, the Chinese Communist Party is right to insist that social classes exist in the People's Republic of China, as in all class societies, but both the objectivity and subjectivity of the classes in its class maps are questionable. So is the objectivity of its notions of inevitable class antagonism. In fact, discursive fixing is the only way to determine whether structurally determined antagonism exists between exploiting and exploited classes, whether some classes are more 'progressive' than others, and whether the exploited classes are bound to acquire the right consciousness required for their liberation from exploitation and oppression by the exploiting classes. Before 1978, the CCP bestowed meaning upon and thus produced social classes as friends and enemies of the Party and as agents and targets of the Chinese Revolution. A major discursive shift began to take place in its class identification after 1956, when objective classification criteria gradually gave way to subjective criteria. Since 1978, the CCP has turned classes into empty signifiers, retaining the class concept for ideological purposes but trying to erase the meaning that was bestowed upon the classes identified before 1978. In this endeavour, they have been supported by a range of Chinese social scientists, who while they may not agree on an appropriate class analysis are united by their opposition to past theory and practice.

The opening up of the Chinese economy and the introduction of market socialism have resulted in major changes to social structures and stratification. In particular, the introduction of sectors of the economy beyond the state has led to not simply the growth of entrepreneurialism and business but also the expansion of the middle classes and significant changes in the working class. These and the consequences for inequality and social mobility are examined in Chapter 2 by Beibei Tang. While highlighting the changes in structures afforded by economic change, she also highlights the importance of path dependence that follows from the associational influence of the Party-state and the household registration system. As a result, occupational mobility may have increased due to marketization and urbanization, but income inequality may not have changed and social mobility has become more rigid.

There is more though to class and social stratification than fundamental inequalities of wealth, status, and power. In particular, as Chapter 3 by Beibei Tang demonstrates, different kinds of inequalities reinforce privilege and disadvantages that have developed with China's market reforms and urbanization. A range of social relations interact to result in lifestyles and behaviours for various groups through which their class identity is rehearsed and presented. This performance of class is both related to and intertwined with understandings of class as ideological formulation and class as socio-economic structure. Here too the role of the Party-state remains a constant, and despite differences in detail among various classes, all provide support for the Party-state and the CCP's leadership in their social and political behaviour. Consumption and lifestyle are key components in the various class identifications, but the inequality of opportunity explains the CCP's successful management of social stability despite economic changes on the individual and social levels. Class differentiation builds on aspirational upward social mobility rather than class antagonism.

The role and status of Chinese peasants have changed significantly over time in the CCP's meta-discourse of the Chinese Revolution as the latter has been re-articulated again and again. The class became the principal subject of the Chinese Revolution between 1927 and 1949, and its members were further elevated in the PRC's status order and represented as 'masters of the country', together with the industrial workers, in official Party-state discourses from 1949 to 1978. Yet they were at the same time subjected to the imperatives of the PRC's socialist industrial development and treated as a reserve labour force which could be conveniently drawn into urban areas when necessary or sent back to the villages as the need for cheap labour decreased. In Chapter 4, Yingjie Guo charts that background and how it continues to determine the role of the peasantry since 1978, but unlike in the past, they have been turned into an object of capitalist urbanization. Moreover, their socio-political status has declined now that they are no longer a major part of the subject of the Revolution, which the CCP has abandoned except in rhetoric, re-orientating the PRC from socialism and communism towards economic development, and combining socialist and capitalist modes of production. The most important direct source of impact on the peasantry in the past seven decades has been household registration (*hukou* 户口), which, together with political and occupational criteria, has played a decisive role in making and unmaking classes by maintaining and removing the boundaries between rural and urban categories. Over the last seven decades, it is *hukou* which defines the peasants' official class identity, while occupation and residence are of no more than secondary importance, as the class membership of the peasants who do not obtain urban *hukou* remains unchanged even if they move into other occupations or live in the cities for extended periods of time.

In Chapter 5, Marc Blecher analyses how the structural reforms that began in 1979, and which in industry went into high gear in the early 1990s, have produced significant social change for the Chinese working class. Economically, many urban-resident workers including even rural migrants have seen their incomes and standards of living rise, but many others – especially those who have become unemployed or have had to find new work due to industrial restructuring and the rise of the labour market – have not. Those who remain employed in state industry have lost the social welfare benefits that came with their jobs in state-owned firms. Socially, the working class expanded exponentially, diversified radically, became subject to capitalistic wage labour, moved out of its tight-knit workplace-based residential communities, and lost both its high social status and any political influence it had achieved in enterprise operations. Its ideas about itself and its place in the world were transformed to reflect its new subordinations. The economic and social changes were brought about mainly by the Party-state and China's new capitalistic forces without much worker participation, and workers have not been able to resist them, though they have managed to reverse a few of the worst effects. Workers played a bigger role in forging their own ideational adaptations rather than adopting them from government propaganda.

The appearance in strong policy terms of the middle class is one of the more intriguing aspects of social change since 1978. In Chapter 6, Jean-Louis Rocca examines the emergence of the new intermediate social strata. Many Chinese researchers have seen in this phenomenon parallels with the emergence of 'middle classes' during phases of economic growth in developed countries. Some have even gone so far as to foresee a transformation of the political system under pressure from the middle classes assumed to be naturally liberal and democratic. In China, as elsewhere, the middle class is a collection of diverse groups whose only unity is the desire for a comfortable and increasing standard of living. Structurally though the Chinese middle classes resemble the middle strata of the Maoist era from which they have emerged. Party and government cadres, professionals, and a substantial proportion of workers and employees in former and current state enterprises have been able to maintain their social status through opportunity hoarding. They have little interest, at least for the time being, in calling into question the supremacy of the Party even if some of them are sometimes ready to protest or criticize specific policies, decisions, or actions in both politics and society.

In Chapter 7, David S. G. Goodman examines the development of the dominant class since 1978. The introduction of first 'opening up and reform' and then a socialist market economy since that date might reasonably be expected to lead to a class structure dominated by wealth. An examination of the social backgrounds of the political and economic elites suggests that while a community of interest may have developed between the two, the PRC remains far from a system dominated by capitalists. It is the existence and operation of the Party-state that remains the defining feature of China's political economy and its dominant class. At the same time, somewhat ironically, the dominant class of 2021 would seem to result to a considerable extent from the intergenerational transfer of politics, wealth, and social capital with roots not only in the PRC's political system after 1949; the economic restructurings of the late 1980s, the mid-1990s, the late 1990s, and the early 2000s; but also from the pre-1949 political economy.

1
CLASSES IN THEMSELVES AND CLASSES FOR THEMSELVES

Social consciousness divorced from social existence

Yingjie Guo

The meaning of class, like many other things, is conferred by historically specific chains of signification or discourses that constitute the identity and significance of class as a social reality. Much of the conceptual purchase and explanatory power of class will then be lost when it is taken out of the theories in which it is embedded. Moreover, its established meaning and significance will be altered when detached from one discourse and attached to another. This is exactly the case with the use of class in the PRC during the last two to three decades, when Marx's approach has been rejected and 'forgotten' by social analysts and the CCP – even though the latter continues to pay lip service to Marxism – in favour of alternative concepts, methodologies, and theories that sidestep class relations and therefore do not lend themselves to postulations of class struggle. The point of departure for the CCP is not so much sociological as political-ideological.

What is particularly striking about the current class discourses in the PRC is the extent to which class has become a nominal category or an aggregate of population defined by means of objective criteria. As a consequence, classes appear to be largely empty signifiers either in the form of objective aggregates, which are at best classes in themselves, or social categories with subjective attributes only, or classes for themselves. This class-making and class-unmaking practice flies in the face of Marx's class analysis, to which the CCP is obliged to adhere. From Marx's viewpoint, the objective existence of classes is not simply based on verifiably economic conditions but also encompasses class subjectivity or consciousness. In other words, classes that exist objectively must be at the same time both classes in themselves and classes for themselves. However, the Party's claimed class objectivity and subjectivity are questionable; indeed, the two dimensions are often separated or severed in its class discourse.

This does not mean that Chinese analysts do not talk about class consciousness and action or look upon classes as being devoid of subjectivities. On the contrary,

DOI: 10.4324/9781003255017-2

they seem more interested in class consciousness and propensities for action than class entities. Some of these writers seek to identify the subjective attributes of objectively defined classes but find little that can be considered class consciousness. Others speak of class subjectivities alone, as if class entities simply exist out there and their physical existence and identity are unquestionable. Still others ascribe putative class attributes to occupational or educational categories, sectors of the population, and so on, taking it for granted that these categories and sectors are classes capable of taking collective action.

Equally striking is the social analysts' preoccupation with the middle class variously defined and the shift of the CCP's primary concern from the working class to the middle strata of society. Without a doubt, the new class par excellence in China is the middle class instead of the industrial proletariat. As the former is named, created through classification, and privileged over other classes, the PRC's existing class map has become outdated and must be redrawn, the established status order in society reorganized and the polity re-defined. This is a significant political development in so far as classes express the fundamental identity of society while major changes in the socio-political status order entail the reorganization of the polity and society (Giddens 1977: 29). The development is also noteworthy in that it is part and parcel of China's ongoing systemic transformation and an important piece in the jigsaw puzzle.

Although some of the class analyses are hampered by conceptual confusion, methodological difficulties, or slackness on the part of the analysts, their ideological orientations are nonetheless apparent. The analyses debilitate Marx's class concept and break up the structure–consciousness–action (S-C-A) chain which underpins Marxist and other class theories and gives these theories explanatory power and ideological significance. Disrupting the S-C-A chain facilitates the political-ideological use of class as it allows the advocates of model classes to make them by projecting desirable attributes onto objectively defined groupings and proceed to make claims about their progressive role in socio-political change. This is what the CCP did in the past and what the advocates of new model classes in the PRC are doing now. Their major difference lies in the class that is promoted, the status order to be created and the polity to be designed.

Economic structure, class consciousness, and class action

Class discourses in the PRC have accentuated a number of basic questions about the class concept, class analysis, and class theories that have been the subject of recurrent debates in the social sciences in the last several decades, although some aspects of the discourses are quite unique. To begin with, what constitutes a class? What are classes capable of doing and what do they actually do? Are they social forces or collective actors? If they are either, what galvanizes them into action or makes the action possible? Is it class consciousness, collective identity, common interests, predispositions, antagonism, solidarity, or something else? How do these things come about? Above all, what is the point of class analysis? Answers to these questions shape and even dictate conceptualizations of class, analytical methodologies, and explanations of social relations and trajectories of change.

Marx's class discourse has been at the centre of debates on class not only in the PRC and but also in many other parts of the world due in part to the comprehensive analysis of capitalist society that Marxists provide with a view to effecting its transformation and in part to the centrality of class in their analysis and explanations of the transformation. In China, the move away from Marxist theories is also consistent with general trends in the English-speaking world, although it has resulted from a different set of factors. These debates and trends, as well as the specific political and intellectual milieu in China, provide the theoretical and political-ideological contexts of class discourses in the country and are pertinent to their analysis.

From a Marxist perspective, and the standpoint of other theorists who treat structure, consciousness, and action as facets of the same phenomenon, the point of class analysis is above all to give an account of the role of social classes in sociopolitical change. This mode of analysis is predicated on the assumption that classes cannot be discussed independently of consciousness (Thompson 1968: 10), which classes as social realities must manifest in the formation of common patterns of behaviour and attitudes and differentiated 'class cultures' (Giddens 1977: 111 and 134). Consequently, class theories consist of two analytically separable elements: 'the theory of class formation and the theory of class action' (Bendix and Lipset 1959: 153). Analysts therefore turn their attention to links between formation and action (Dahrendorf 1959), objective and subjective dimensions (Braverman 1974), aggregational and relational aspects (Stark 1980), or look upon structure and agency as one (Thompson 1968; Giddens 1973; Bourdieu 1987).

What is of uttermost importance in Marx's accounts of the role of classes is the proposition that conflicting class interests may be identified corresponding to the dichotomous structural location of individuals and groups, and that class action is then likely to emerge from these interests and relations. This unity between structure, consciousness and action is the essence of what Pahl (1989) calls the S-C-A model. It might be thought to be a characteristically Marxist progression, but there are non-Marxists (e.g. Lockwood 1958; Dahrendorf 1959; Bendix and Lipset 1967; Parkin 1979; Goldthorpe et al. 1987; Erikson and Goldthorpe 1988), who also accept this model, implicitly or explicitly. If it is taken out of Marx's framework, his theory will become untenable and his conceptualization of class will be disabled as well. The same can be said about non-Marxist class theories and conceptions informed by some version of this model.

The most widely adopted alternative approach in class analysis is one that pursues empirical investigation of class structure, or classes in themselves, which may be labelled the 'structure model' for the sake of convenience. Here, the term class is used to describe structures of material inequality or groups ranked in a hierarchical order; classes mean groupings unequally rewarded in material and symbolic terms. More often than not, occupation takes precedence over income as a marker of class in the English-language literature.[1] Indeed, class structure and occupational structure are widely taken to be synonymous – a convention which has emerged from practices established by statisticians of dividing up the population into occupational groups and labelling them 'classes' (Crompton 1993: 77). The classes thus labelled are objective entities which can be empirically investigated, and class analysis essentially means the sorting of individuals and more often aggregates of populations into unequal positions.

This way of identifying classes resembles what is to Charles Tilly (2001: 361) a basic model of how inequality comes about, except that the positions are considered class positions in this analytical model. In its simplest versions, the model contains just three elements: a set of unequally rewarded positions which are demarcated by objective, gradational indexes of a more or less particular quantity (such as income, prestige, and social standing); a sorting mechanism that channels people to different boxes; and individuals who vary in objective characteristics that the sorting mechanism detects, whereas subjectivities are not taken into account in the classification. It is as though individuals and groups are brought to the scanner, evaluated, and sent to an appropriate position. The occupants of a position or a cluster of positions become a class.

An important divergence has developed between the structure and S-C-A models (Crompton 1993: 12), which predominate in class analysis. Three major differences set the models apart. One, the structure model concentrates on class formation and composition, while the S-C-A model is concerned with class consciousness and action as well as formation. Thus, classes in the former are predominantly objective groupings, but they are considered objective entities with collective consciousness in the latter. Two, the structure model is gradational in which it investigates indexes of a quantity, while the S-C-A model is relational because it is sensitive to relations of exploitation, domination, and so on. Stated differently using Abercrombie and Urry's terminology (1983: 109), the concept of class refers to positions within the technical division of labour in the structure model and social relations at work, or positions within the social division of labour, in the S-C-A model. Three, the structure model tends to produce a larger number of classes and much more diverse class schemes than the S-C-A model.

Both are problematic on several accounts. Above all, the former lacks theoretical depth and has little to say about consciousness or action. That is not a problem if collective consciousness is not the object of analysis or of no interest to the analyst. The principal value of the structure model lies in the fact that the identified classes are among the most useful indicators of material advantage and disadvantage in modern societies and are widely used in social policy, market and advertising research, and so on (Crompton 1993: 10). It may also give one some idea about the shape, composition, and trajectory of society. In comparison, the S-C-A model has much more explanatory power and compelling quality, but it is a theorem that must be confirmed or falsified theoretically and empirically.

Revisions and criticisms of the Marxist approach to class over the greater part of the last century have led to a decline of interest in it and the watering down of Marx's class conception and the S-C-A model. Criticisms levelled at

Marxist discourses explicitly on ideological grounds are probably best exemplified by Margaret Thatcher's comment that 'Class is a communist concept. It groups people as bundles and sets them against one another' (*Guardian*, 22 April 1992). Other critics stress the class concept's loss of ideological significance and political centrality as a result of the decline of Marxism, the collapse of Soviet communism, and the waning appeal of socialist ideologies and class radicalism (Pakulski and Waters 1996). That, they suggest, at least partially explains why both the Right and the Left are abandoning their preoccupation with class issues, with the former turning its attention to morality and ethnicity while the latter, to issues of gender, ecology, citizenship, and human rights.

Sociological critics who focus on class as a social reality typically argue that class is an increasingly redundant issue (Holton and Turner 1989). The cited reasons for this are many. One set of reasons is that the importance of class cleavages has declined since stratification in the industrialized West has become increasingly pluralistic, multidimensional, and shaped by factors located outside the workplace, while the old class divisions based on them are decomposing under the impact of the welfare state, occupational differentiation, rising affluence, changing political dynamics, market fragmentation, and the rise of institution-based divisions (Clark and Lipset 1991; Clark et al. 1993). Another, overlapping set of reasons is that classes are dissolving, class divisions are losing their self-evident and pervasive character, class identities are challenged by new associations and new social movements, and most advanced, post-industrial societies are no longer class societies (Pakulski and Waters 1996).

A second, related cluster of criticisms is concerned with the utility of the class concept and insists that the ability of class to explain social and especially political processes has declined (Clark and Lipset 1991; Clark et al. 1993), or that class as a concept is ceasing to do any useful work for sociology (Pahl 1989: 710; Pakulski and Waters 1996). The most rigorous theoretical critiques focus on questions of structure, consciousness and action. Some of these critiques contend that class action is not inevitable, as classes merely represent possible bases for common action (Weber in Gerth and Mills 1948: 181), and as the differentiation of property classes need not result in class struggles and revolution (Giddens and Held 1982: 69–70). Others stress the indivisibility of structure and action (Giddens 1987: 220–221) and the difficulty of applying Marx's 'abstract' or 'theoretical' conception of class to 'concrete' classes.[2] Still others question the objectivity of interests pursued by diverse actors in various sites of struggle and conclude that classes are simply not and cannot be collective actors or social forces (Hindess 1987).

A similar decline of interest in Marx's class theory began to become apparent in the PRC in the late 1970s paradoxically as a result of collaboration between a Party-state which continued to allege loyalty to Marxist ideologies and social analysts who sought to subvert these ideologies. It must be stressed, however, that the move away from class in the PRC by no means echoes the criticisms found in the English-language literature. In fact, few Chinese analysts and commentators deny the relevance or utility of the class concept and class analysis. What they reject is the Marxist approach to class. Their case against it has nothing to do with the theoretical validity or invalidity of the Marxist and the alternative approaches; nor is it based on critiques of Marxism or empirical findings that contradict it or support the alternative approaches. By and large, it is driven by abhorrence of a class struggle that has traumatized many Chinese and of Mao's radical Chinese Revolution, as well as the yearning for a desirable model of polity and society or preferable modes of socio-political life.

Throughout the greater part of the 1980s, the slogan of 'farewell to revolution' – specifically to the violent act of one class toppling another – rang loud. The thrust of the slogan was, first and foremost, the rejection of the theory of class struggle and historical materialism, which posit dichotomous class relations and take the antagonism between the 'warring classes of society' (Engels 1934: 37) to be the motive force of history. It is the Marxist theory of class struggle, as is widely believed in China, that caused the loss of countless lives and suffering to millions of Chinese. Therefore, it must be rejected in toto; whether class was a useful concept or a social reality that must be understood and whether class analysis had any sociological value was not an issue.

Unsurprisingly, the rejection of class in Chinese academia and society at large met with little obstruction from the CCP. After all, the Party had already abandoned class struggle and 'continuous revolution' by the late 1970s in favour of economic development through marketization. All the same, class is not a redundant issue to be ignored due to its place in the Party's ideology, and its allegiance to Marxism, spurious or not, prevents it from openly renouncing Marx's class concept and class theory. Additionally, class is a political reality that cannot be dismissed, as the PRC's class structures, class composition, and class relations have changed dramatically over the last three decades, and these changes must be explained and justified without contradicting the Party line. On the other hand, neither the idea of class struggle nor the notion that there is class warfare in Chinese society is acceptable to a party that now stresses the primacy of social stability and harmony. Thus, the CCP would rather take a 'no-discussion' approach to class. Social analysts and commentators, too, are keen to understand those changes, redraw the PRC's class map, and recommend new social configurations to the Party-state. The contest and overlap between the social analysts and the CCP have added a complex political dimension to the class discourses in the PRC.

Consciousness divorced from existence: utility of class to the CCP

Class poses a daunting dilemma to the CCP for the simple reason that it was central to its ideology during the 'new democratic revolution' and the 'socialist revolution', but has become, in the last three decades, an obstacle to reform and the construction of a 'harmonious society'. In the past, the Party looked upon the proletariat and peasantry as the principal agents of revolution and the reactionary classes as its enemies. Part and parcel of 'reform and opening-up' has been the abandonment of revolution in favour of economic development through marketization. In consequence, the CCP's primary concern has shifted from the working class to chief creators of wealth and consumers with ample purchasing power, although it is reluctant to describe the latter in class terms. The dilemma is here to stay as long as the Party does not abandon Marxism in theory as well as in practice. In the meantime, the PRC has a superstructure resting precariously on an economic foundation that neither determines nor corresponds to it. Without the will or the recourse to resolve this fundamental contradiction, the CCP can only paper over the gaping holes in the superstructure.

In fact, the Party's ambivalence towards class has been apparent ever since 1949, especially when it is divided over whether to assign first priority to socialist revolution or economic development. The significance of class fluctuated as the pendulum swung between those poles. This is coupled with ideological inconsistencies and confusion. On the one hand, the class concept has been embedded in the constitutions of the CCP and the PRC as well as the national flag and national emblems. By definition, the CCP is the vanguard of the Chinese proletariat guided by Marxism, Leninism and Mao-Zedong-Thought, while the PRC is a socialist state under the people's democratic dictatorship, led by the proletariat and based on the alliance of the workers and peasants. The PRC's legitimate political subjects, or 'masters of the country', including the CCP, the proletariat, the peasantry, the petit bourgeoisie, and the national bourgeoisie, are represented by the five stars in the national flag and emblems.[3] Thus, there can be no doubt about the class nature of the Party and the state. On the other hand, the Party has often played down class, particularly when economic development took precedence over 'socialist revolution'.

However, these state symbols are out of date as they were designed and adopted in the early 1950s, before the 'socialist transformation of productive property', which eliminated the national bourgeoisie, if not the petit bourgeoisie. But why is it that a party that attaches great importance to names and political symbols has left the national bourgeoisie in the flag and emblems? The CCP's difficulty, of course, is that state symbols need to remain stable, while socio-political change is constant, that the Party cannot update these symbols every time they become obsolete for fear of creating impressions of ideological–political instability and inconsistency. The fear becomes even more acute in the light of entrenched perceptions in China that associate modifications of state symbols with the collapse of dynasties.

Hence, instead of revamping the national flag and emblems, the Party chooses to obliterate their original symbolism and to give them a new meaning. The five stars in the state symbols are now said to stand for the CCP and the 'whole Chinese people': The class nature of these symbols is thus erased and replaced by nationhood (Guo 2004). However, the class identity of the CCP and PRC as defined by their constitutions cannot be erased as easily and unnoticeably; it is therefore downplayed and diluted through the introduction of Jiang Zemin's theory of 'three represents', which transforms the identity of the CCP from a class organization of the proletariat to a national party representing the whole nation. Of course, whether it can protect the interests of all the PRC nationals, including the conflicting interests of the contending parties in a dispute, is another question.

There is even more confusion and contradiction in another class scheme the CCP has devised, which was in circulation in the greater part of the Mao era and beyond. It features the bourgeoisie, landlords, rich peasants, and other 'reactionary classes' in addition to the proletariat, peasantry and intellectuals. Although the CCP declared as early as the 1950s that exploiting classes had disappeared, the Party continued to label the family backgrounds of some members of society as bourgeoisie, landlords, rich peasants, and so on. This practice lasted well into the 1980s, affecting millions of Chinese to varying degrees, although discrimination gradually eased in the reform era. The significance of the labels should not be underrated. Their carriers were relegated to the bottom of the PRC's socio-political status order, deprived of a broad range of civil and political rights and had less favourable life chances and opportunities for upward mobility.

In addition, the CCP has maintained consistently since the early 1950s that class struggle will continue for a long time, and that statement is retained in the current constitutions of the CCP and the PRC. It is inconceivable that the Party will launch another full-blown class struggle without being concerned about its potential impact on the stock market and the Chinese economy. Presumably, the statement is retained in the constitutions in part because the Party – or some of its leaders – sees it advantageous to use the idea as a deterrent to political opponents or as a pretext under which to crush political opposition, and in part because the statement accords with Marx's proposition that class struggle pervades all class societies. Thus, the Party pays lip service to Marxism by acknowledging class struggle, but only as a latent or theoretical possibility that it can manipulate, while disabling the theory by denying the existence of exploiting classes and class antagonism.

The two classes (the proletariat and peasantry) in the CCP's current class map can be rolled into one working class or working people. Although the Party acknowledges the emergence of new social groups in the reform era, such as businesspeople and private entrepreneurs, it does not treat these groups as classes separate from the working class but as part of the latter or as transitional groups that do not belong to any existing class (Jiang 2001: 169). Even those who work with large volumes of capital and rank among the richest in the country and in the world are placed in the working class 'because they were originally members of the working class and now work under a political system opposed to exploitation' (*The People's Daily*, 17 February and 25 April 2001). In this milieu, the CCP has thrown open its doors to private entrepreneurs and businesspeople and, indeed, prioritized their interests (Jiang 2001).

That class scheme and its justification are not convincing, to say the least, and they are refuted by overseas authors and members of the Left in China. Dickson (2004) and So (2003: 478), for example, have pointed to a class of 'red capitalists' and 'a cadre-capitalist class' which 'has emerged to monopolize economic capital, political capital, and social/net capital in Chinese society'. Deng Liqun (1991; cited by Lam 2001) argued in the early 1990s that the bourgeoisie had already taken shape as a class and that there was acute class struggle in Chinese society. Numerous other commentators on the Left continue to make the same point,[4] although their comments are not well known in China despite the fact that they are allowed to circulate relatively freely. The Party can only deny the emergence of a bourgeoisie, because 'we will not allow a new bourgeoisie to take shape' (Deng 1993: 172) and because 'if a bourgeoisie has emerged, we must have gone astray' (Deng 1993: 110–111). But these statements are meaningless in the absence of proper class analysis.

Evidently, the CCP's various class schemes are not related to the actualities of class structures and class consciousness; nor are they the result of sociological investigation. What mattered to the CCP in the past was a general judgement on the extent to which classes or strata of classes were supportive or opposed to the CCP. Classes were treated as friends and enemies, while the point of class analysis, as Mao Zedong (1926) reiterated, was to ascertain who were the friends and enemies. The value of the judgement was best seen from political outcomes instead of sociological evidence. What matters in the reform era is the maintenance of a class scheme which conforms to the constitutions of the CCP and the PRC but which is largely unrelated to existing class structures or actual class consciousness and action. The nominal status of the industrial workers as the leading class, in particular, does not square with the fact that over 61% of the class are now employed in the private sector (Lu et al. 2010), while the rest are only nominal owners of China's public property or unemployed.

In either case, the Party's class schemes are devised and maintained for political-ideological purposes more than anything else. Little attempt is made to establish the unity of class structure, consciousness, and action; on the contrary, while the unity is assumed, consciousness and action are often detached from structure, or ignored altogether to allow the arbitrary labelling of classes. A consequence of this is the creation of classes or class elements without the matching class consciousness and class consciousness independent of class structures. This is advantageous to the CCP on several accounts. For one thing, the Party is able to deal with class conditions and consciousness separately. For another, there is little benefit for the Party to lock individuals into classes so that members of the 'good' classes need not exert themselves while the rest despair of ever escaping from the 'bad' classes. Thus, class membership is manipulated in such a way that it functions as an incentive structure, and individuals are rewarded and punished with membership in the good and bad classes on the basis of consciousness alone.

In the past, for example, the CCP analysed classes at two levels. Consciousness was not used as a criterion for classification at the macro-level, as the analysis began with the designation of a number of abstract or theoretical class positions based on property ownership, relations and occupation. This was followed by the sorting of large aggregates of population, instead of individuals, into these positions. Judgements on the subjective attributes of these positions, not the individual occupants, were formed on the basis of detected or perceived characteristics related to ownership, relations, occupation and conditions. The judgements provided a general guide about the revolutionary and counter-revolutionary potential and propensity of the various classes and recommended ways of dealing with the classes.

At the micro level, the analysis focused on individuals rather than groups and on consciousness and action instead of structures. This time, individuals who had been sorted into class positions in aggregates were screened one by one, to correct any errors that might have occurred in the sorting of aggregates. The criteria for sorting aggregates were considered secondary to the individuals' subjective attributes or 'political performance'. Indeed, the latter could trump the former. For example, a designated member of the bourgeoisie could be allowed to join the proletariat and even the CCP if he/she demonstrated proletarian consciousness or behaviour. Conversely, somebody who belonged to the proletariat might be relegated to the bourgeoisie if he/she was perceived to talk, think or act in a bourgeois fashion. The reclassification of individuals was a simple political decision to be made by Party officials.

In all those cases, class structures on the one hand and class consciousness and action on the other are invariably separated and manipulated for political purposes. What matters is consciousness and action, whereas structure is rendered meaningless. In fact, the focus of the CCP's 'political thought work' throughout its history has been placed on examining individuals' subjectivities, instilling the right ideas and values, and turning them into loyal followers of the Party and new Chinese with a socialist consciousness. That is to say, socialist consciousness is neither a criterion by which the progressive classes are defined nor something that derives automatically from their relations to the means of production, but something to be nurtured or instilled. Similarly, the separation of structure and consciousness enabled the CCP to assert in the Mao era that there were still exploiting classes long after the elimination of what made these classes exploiters and indeed classes. The Party could also claim that the proletariat remained a proletariat even after it had become part of the ruling class who owned all the means of production in the PRC, although its preferred term seemed to be the 'class of workers'.

In the reform era, the CCP has not only shied away from Marx's class theory but also gone to great lengths to de-class Chinese society and to cover up the actualities of class structures and relations. The proletariat and peasantry are nothing but occupational categories that serve a perfunctory ideological function, while the class map is altered drastically by placing the intellectuals in the working class and by eliminating the nominal categories of exploiting classes. These alterations have nothing to do with changes in objective class structures but are justified purely on grounds of ascriptive consciousness and action or artificial labelling criteria. In other words, the CCP makes believe that there are now no expoited or exploiting classes in the PRC because there is no exploitation.

Paradoxically, the alterations have taken place at a time when many intellectuals have parted company with the proletariat and peasantry and when there have emerged new social groups which may well be classified as the bourgeoisie by Marx's criteria. The position of the working class, too, is no longer the same as in the Mao era, as it is now differently related to the means of production and has lost the status and most of the privileges it once had. The CCP simply ignores every dimension of the class concept when it asserts that the working class remains the 'masters of the country', that there is not a bourgeois class in China, and that every social group in the PRC belongs to the working class.

Whether or not this is the case can best be ascertained through class analysis, and if the CCP really adheres to Marxism, as it asserts, there is no reason why it should resist a Marxist analysis of the class conditions in the PRC. The only reason it refuses to undertake such an analysis is that it will inevitably lead to the identification of a bourgeoisie with a considerable amount of productive property, a proletariat deprived of the means of production and class exploitation, among other things. Similar conclusions may emerge even if China's class structures and relations are analysed from numerous non-Marxist perspectives. Such developments are not something the Party wants to highlight or acknowledge not least because it cannot square them with its claims about its adherence to Marxism, the socialist nature of the PRC, or its relationship with the proletariat.

Classes in themselves: hegemony of the structure model

It is not just the CCP theoreticians who insist on the two-class structure of Chinese society; many Chinese academics follow suit. This particular framework has two variants: one takes all social strata to be constituent groups of the existing classes; the other treats some strata as free-floating or transitional groupings which neither belong to the classes nor form separate classes. An alternative approach, which has prevailed in Chinese academia in recent years, is to break up the two-class structure and rearrange all identified social groupings into a new hierarchy of strata or consider the identified occupational categories as 'interest groups'. In all these schemes, the structure model predominates, and classes and strata are defined almost exclusively by objective indexes such as occupation, education, income, and consumption and sorted into a gradational hierarchy.

In the CCP's two-class structure, for instance, both the proletariat and peasantry are occupational categories, as previously mentioned. The new social groups that have emerged in the reform era are classified into occupational categories too, including managers and technical personnel in private enterprises and foreign-owned enterprises, individual-operated business proprietors, private entrepreneurs, employees of intermediate social organizations, and independently employed professionals (Jiang 2001: 169). An example of the second variant of the two-class framework is the scheme of Zhu Guanglei and his fourteen co-authors (2007[1998]).[5] In this case, the proletariat consists of blue-collar workers, white-collar workers, intellectuals, public servants, and retired workers, while the peasantry includes all agricultural labourers. The free-floating or transitional groups include private entrepreneurs, company managers, individual-operated business proprietors, workers of township and village enterprises, rural cadres and intelligentsia, rural migrant workers, military officers and soldiers, and university students. As these groups do not form new classes, the two-class structure remains intact. Consequently, there are no class antagonisms to talk about, and all conflicts of interest – if there are any – can only be interpreted as easily manageable 'contradictions within the people'.

The 'stratum analysis' approach is best exemplified by the work of Lu Xueyi and some twenty colleagues of his at the Chinese Academy of Social Sciences (CASS).[6] In an influential series of three volumes on social stratification, mobility, and structure in Post-Mao China, Lu et al. (2002, 2004, 2010) divide China's 'occupied population' totalling 700 million, into ten occupational strata. These include state and social administrators, managerial personnel, private entrepreneurs, professional and technical personnel, clerical personnel, individual-operated business proprietors, commercial and service personnel, industrial workers, agricultural labourers, and the unemployed and partially unemployed. Another kind of 'stratum analysis' centres on perceived common interests of occupational categories to be ranked on explicit or implicit scales indicating the extent of benefit (for example, Zhang Wanli 1990; Gu et al. 1995; Li Qiang 2002; Li Peilin 1995; Zhang Houyi 1994).

These examples represent the prevailing paradigms in class analysis in the mainstream Chinese-language literature. Other class schemes may differ from these in terminology, the number and typology of categories or the combination of classification criteria,[7] but the identified classes, strata and groups are commonly defined with reference to occupation. It matters little in the classification whether or not the classes and groups share other characteristics, as nothing but occupation determines their group or class membership. Other causal components of life chances, such as income, education, or political, economic and cultural capital, mainly affect the individuals' ranking within the groups and the groups' ranking in the overall hierarchy, or the totality of classes.

In the CCP's class scheme, for example, a private entrepreneur who has a PhD degree and owns a fair amount of productive property and a blue-collar worker with no means of production, little education, and meagre wages may become members of other strata or groups if, and only if, they move into other occupational groups, but they both belong to the same class irrespective of their group membership. In the case of Zhu et al., despite their claim that the classes and groups are defined with composite criteria including, in addition to occupation, production relationships, education and income, it is not explained how these criteria are actually operationalized in their classification. It is even hard to imagine how they can be, for the identity of individuals who are sorted into occupational classes and groups is fixed regardless of the other criteria. This is also the case with the class scheme of the CASS team, although this is by far the most sophisticated and influential of all class schemes in the Chinese-language literature and therefore deserves more attention.

One of the essential questions to ask here is whether or not any of the aforesaid categories can be called classes, and if so, what kind of classes they are and for what purpose the class schemes are constructed. Certainly, many social analysts in the PRC speak of strata or groups instead of classes, and the terminology, as well as the analytical methodology, is politically charged and contested (Guo 2008). In the class scheme of Lu et al. (2005: 419), no sharp distinction is made between these terms, although they opt for 'stratum' in Chinese publications 'in order to indicate that the groups in our classification are different from "classes" which were defined according to political criteria in the civil war and the Cultural Revolution', but use stratum and class interchangeably in English publications. It is also possible that they do not want to be seen in China to be openly challenging the official class scheme. In manipulating the terms this way, they reject the Marxist class concept and theiry without noticeably overstepping official boundaries of permissible dissent.

In any case, by 'strata' or 'groups', Lu et al. mean 'classes', except that their classes are conceived consciously in opposition to Marxist varieties. As a matter of fact, their versions not only differ from Marx's; they are not classes at all in the eyes of Marxists. Nor can they be seen as such from the perspective of a broad range of non-Marxist class theories which hinge on relations and conflict. The reasons for this are many, but two are particularly crucial. To begin with, their classes might be considered (objective) classes in themselves but not (conscious) classes for themselves. Not that they made no attempt to investigate subjectivities; in fact, they asked their respondents questions about their own class identification and their attitudes towards China's reforms, their general satisfaction, and so on. But they found little that could be seen as class consciousness. Their failure to give a satisfactory account of class consciousness and action is largely a result of their occupation-aggregate class analysis and other problems. This approach is not well suited to the exploration of the links between structure, consciousness, and action (Goldthorpe and Marshall 1992). For they conceive of class in respect of positions in the technical division of labour in contrast to relational schemes that consider classes to be rooted in mutually exclusive relationships which produce such deep and fundamental cleavages that they constitute enduring bases for conflict and struggle.

In Marx's analysis, for example, the development of classes is a non-resolvable source of conflict which splits society into 'two great hostile camps': the propertied and the propertyless. These classes are placed in a situation of reciprocity such that neither can escape from the relationship without losing its identity as a distinct class (Giddens 1973: 29). This theorem underpins Marx's S-C-A model. From a Weberian perspective, classes derive from social relations of exchange, and though the links between class relations and action are probabilistic rather than deterministic, classes are nevertheless located in paired relationships of domination and subordination. All relational class theorists define or describe classes in similar terms. It is such relations of exploitation and domination which, these theorists believe, generate class identities, awareness of class interests, group coherence, class values and common patterns of behaviour – in short, class consciousness. In other words, relations grounded in deep and fundamental cleavages of one kind or another are what turns population aggregates into classes and supports the S-C-A model.

To be sure, the classes in the CASS scheme are not entirely unrelated to one another. For example, the private entrepreneurs who own companies and their employees, including professional and technical personnel and industrial workers, may be differently related to the means of production and, if they are in the same company, may occupy different positions in the authority structure as well.

But these relations are obscured or rendered insignificant as individuals and aggregates are taken out of their actual socio-economic situations and sorted into multiple occupational categories. It is not immediately obvious, for instance, how professional and technical personnel, individual-operated business proprietors, commercial and service personnel, industrial workers, agricultural labourers, and the rural and urban jobless are related to each other.

The relations are obscured further when the organizational, economic, and cultural capital of class members is represented in numerical scores and when the classes are placed into gradational hierarchies according to the class average score on these three scales (Lu et al. 2010: 402). As can be seen from Table 1.1, the 'upper middle tier' of the overall hierarchy encompasses the first six classes (state and social administrators, managerial personnel, private entrepreneurs, professional and technical personnel, clerical personnel, and individual-operated business proprietors). The 'lower-middle tier' comprises the commercial and service personnel, industrial workers, and agricultural labourers. And the bottom tier includes the unemployed and partially unemployed. There is an upper tier vaguely termed the 'wealthy tier' or 'economic elites' (Lu et al. 2010: 408–409), but it is not specified which classes fall into this tier.

The only notable relationship between the classes can be seen in their ranking on the three scales. Thus, it can be said that state and social administrators possess more organizational capital than the other classes; private entrepreneurs and managerial personnel receive higher incomes than industrial workers, agricultural labourers, and the unemployed and partially unemployed; and professional, technical, and clerical personnel have more cultural capital than the rest. That relationship may be characterized by inequality but not exploitation or domination. In fact, the occupational classes are stripped of all deep and fundamental cleavages and antagonistic relations, while the multiple-class hierarchy does not represent a common social field of relevance where classes struggle along a single line of division or

TABLE 1.1 The CASS class scheme

Tiers	*Classes*
Upper Tier	?
Upper Middle Tier	State and social administrators
	Managerial personnel
	Private entrepreneurs
	Professional and technical personnel
	Clerical personnel
	Individual-operated business proprietors
Lower-Middle Tier	Commercial and service personnel
	Industrial workers
	Agricultural labourers
Bottom Tier	The unemployed and partially unemployed

Source: Lu et al. 2010: 408–409.

around a common causal component of life chances, such as ownership of productive property in Marx's class analysis or market capacity in the Weberian approach.

One explanation of this methodological choice is that there are no relations of exploitation and domination in Chinese society. Another explanation is that Lu and his colleagues, like most social analysts and commentators in the PRC, refrain from delving into social conflict and construct social structure and social classes in such a way that fundamental class cleavages, irreconcilable class conflicts, or warring classes are evaded or concealed. The second explanation is more plausible in the light of the Party-state's emphasis on social stability and harmony. Class and antagonistic class relations, as well as analytical methodologies that capture these relations, have little place in the Party-state's utopia of 'harmonious society' simply because these will undercut images of harmony or add to the challenge of building a 'harmonious society'. In fact, Lu Xueyi states explicitly that stability and harmony are important considerations in 'stratum analysis' as opposed to 'class analysis':

> There is a view among Chinese sociologists that class analysis and classification was a practice of the revolutionary epoch, which was associated with class struggle. Stratum analysis, on the other hand, is advantageous to social harmonization and integration . . . The purpose of classifying China's 1.3 billion people into strata is to bring out the enthusiasm of the whole society, harmonize the relations between the social strata, and build a relatively harmonious and stable society.
>
> (Lu 2006: 21)

To that end, conflicting social relations are circumvented in the ten-class scheme. What is more, social mobility is conceived to be intra-occupation mobility or trans-occupation mobility, which can be achieved without drastic socio-political change. Social stratification, similarly, means gradational gaps which can be narrowed between members of the same class, the classes, and the tiers of the overall hierarchy. Another way of putting this is that class members, classes, and tiers are by and large differentiated by the technical division of labour and demarcated by gradational indexes of a more or less particular quantity. It is surely easier to increase that quantity than to change productive relationships and to alter technical divisions of labour than social relations of exploitation and domination. It is also easier to justify gradationally unequal material rewards resulting from the technical division of labour than class exploitation, domination, and antagonism.

From the viewpoint of the Party-state, social inequality with the potential to destabilize society can be addressed through the social policy of 'controlling the growth of the top strata of society, expanding the middle strata, and reducing the bottom', which was adopted at the 15th CCP congress in 1997. The Party-state can also address the issue through limited redistributive intervention without having to deal with inequality-generating productive processes and relations. Indeed, it is not desirable to alter existing productive processes and relations in favour of equality, for China's 'reform and opening-up' is intended, first and foremost, to promote efficiency at the expense of equality, or egalitarianism as it is negatively labelled in official communications. China's social scientists may not see eye to eye with the Party-state on everything, but they are united in their common desire to maintain the momentum of 'reform and opening-up' and to construct a stable and harmonious society.

Needless to say, the investigation and analysis of occupational hierarchies have been closely associated with theoretical models of society that stress the importance of the social harmony and functional interdependence associated with the division of labour in complex societies. Liberal functional theories of stratification, in particular, typically see the structure of social inequality as a mechanism through which the most appropriate and best-qualified persons are allocated to the functionally most important positions in society. As a consequence, the question of individual status attainment instead of socio-economic mechanisms and social relations has been a key topic in stratification research. It is not in the least surprising, therefore, that functional class theorists, especially Davis, Moore, Blau and Duncan, are cited more frequently than conflict theorists in the Chinese-language literature.

Despite the lack of convincing evidence about class consciousness, however, social analysts and commentators rarely refrain from making claims about the subjective attributes of largely objective classes, although most of the complimentary remarks are reserved for the middle classes or strata. Zhu Guanglei et al. (2007: 78), for example, claim that the white-collar workers are one of the most important strata of Chinese society and a positive force for social development. Lu Xueyi (2006: 23; cited by Zhou Zhaojun 2009) asserts that the middle classes are 'a politically and economically stabilizing force', 'a social stabilizer', 'promoters of advanced culture', 'a natural opponent to violence and dictatorship', and 'represent moderation and rationality'.

With these writers, it is at least possible to figure out which middle classes or strata they are talking about; more often than not, putative qualities, values, and propensities for action are ascribed to a taken-for-granted middle class that appears to be no more than a figment of the imagination. The result is the creation of a subjective middle class that is not grounded in an unspecified or unidentifiable structure (Guo 2008). Still, it is commonplace for analysts to suggest that the consciousness derives from actual structures. Although they reject Marx's class theory, many proceed from the S-C-A model, habitually assuming that classes, however defined or identified, are conscious collectivities and agencies, and they freely use a combination of elements of structure and S-C-A models. In this respect, they differ little from Party-state officials who are steeped in the deterministic view that the consciousness of people as social forces and political actors are determined by their social existence, except that they realize the new universalising class whose historical mission to transform society is no longer the proletariat but the middle class.

Conclusion

It is evident, then, that class has not become a redundant issue in China; nor do Chinese analysts and the CCP believe that the concept of class and class analysis is no longer of much use. It is equally evident that the utility of class in China is more political-ideological than sociological. While the Party has abandoned Marxism in favour of economic development and social harmony, it remains important for the CCP to make believe that it has not betrayed its own class base or abandoned its Marxist-Maoist ideology. In this sense, it is left with a dis-synchronized ideology and a dis-synchronized ideology–practice nexus. The former is exemplified by glaring ideological inconsistencies and the latter by the ideology's failure to legitimize the class structure and class relations to be found in Chinese society. These contradictions significantly affect the ways in which class structure, consciousness, and action in China can be described and analysed.

The Party's move away from Marxism has enabled Chinese social analysts and commentators to abandon the Marxist class concept, class analysis and class theory; yet, few go so far as to openly challenge the CCP's official position on the issue and most prefer to beat around the bush and challenge the Party line within permissible boundaries. The widespread condemnation in the 1980s of the theory and practice of revolution, ranging from the Communist revolution to the French Revolution, has been translated in the last two decades into class analysis methodologies that circumvent the kind of class conditions and relations that give succour to Marx's class theory, especially class struggle. This is coupled in recent years with the imperative of building a harmonious society. Thus, most Chinese analysts are theoretically aligned with functional class theories which not only go against the grain of Marxism but also highlight social harmony and integration. In both respects, they have little quarrel with the CCP.

What is rather ironical is – although perfectly in keeping with general trends in the social sciences all over the world, particularly in Europe and North America – that, in the wake of the farewell to class, interest in class, particularly the middle class, has soared in the last two decades or so. In fact, the preoccupation with the Chinese middle class inside and outside China has evolved into something like an obsession. The rise of this class contrasts with the fall of the proletariat, which is now rarely mentioned in the mass media or Party-state communications. The obsession also contrasts with the silence on the bourgeoisie, which cannot be named legitimately. Even though members of the Left continue to write about these classes, their writings do not make it into the mainstream mass media or the academic literature. This has less to do with the lack of the freedom of speech or Party-state censure and obstruction than with the fact that what they have to say is deprived of legitimacy in the PRC's current discursive field.

It is ironic too that the construct of the Chinese middle class has not been subjected to the same sort of critical scrutiny as Marx's class concept, even though the construct also illustrates the limitations of class analysis when it obfuscates social relationships or lacks rigorous empirical grounding. The middle class should be no exception if classes are indeed dissolving, if class identities are challenged by new associations and new social movements, or if class as a concept has lost its ability to explain socio-political processes, and has declined to the point where it is ceasing to do any useful work for social analysis. Similarly, this class cannot be thought to be a social force and collective actor if classes as a whole cannot be considered as such. However, these criticisms of class analysis should be critically examined too. There is little reason, for example, to deny the possibility of classes becoming social forces or collective actors, for this is both a theoretical and empirical question. In contrast to political-ideological uses of classes, the sociological utility of class lies in conceptual clarity and sound analytical methodology.

Notes

1 Blau and Duncan (1967: 6–7), for example, believe that occupation has become, for the majority of the population, probably the most powerful single indicator of levels of material reward, social standing, and the life chances in general in modern societies. Reid (1981) defines social class as 'a grouping of people into categories on the basis of occupation'. Parkin (1972: 18) asserts: 'The backbone of class structure, and indeed of the entire rewards system of modern Western society, is the occupational order'.
2 Anthony Giddens (1973: 30, 1987: 220–221), for example, believes it is difficult to apply Marx's 'abstract' or 'pure' conception of class to specific, historical forms of society or connecting the former to 'concrete' classes. Similarly, Bourdieu (1987: 7) writes that 'the movement from probability to reality, from theoretical class to practical class, is never given' in Marxist class theories.
3 The national flag and national emblems of the PRC were designed and adopted in the early 1950s, before the national bourgeoisie disappeared as class following the state's takeover of all productive property from private owners. They were therefore out of date between then and the reform era, when social groups have emerged which can be classified as national bourgeoisie.
4 Such writings can be found, for example, at Wuyou Zhi Xiang (Utopia) <www.wyzxsx.com/> and Mao Zedong Qizhi Wang (Mao Zedong Flag) <www.maoflag.net/?action-viewthread-tid-1469882>.
5 For similar class schemes, see Li Shenming et al. 2002, Yan Zhimin 2002, Duan Ruopeng et al. 2002 and Zhou Luogeng et al. 2002.
6 Other writers who take the same approach include Li Lulu (2003) and Yang Jisheng (2000). Li Chunling (2005) takes this approach too, although, unlike Lu et al., she often uses 'class' instead of 'stratum'.
7 A rare exception is Li Chunling's early class scheme (see, for example, 2002), which comprises 16 classes defined with reference to both technical and social divisions of labour drawing on the neo-Marxist approach and neo-Weberian approaches. However, she follows the ten-strata scheme of Lu Xueyi et al. in *Cleavage and Fragment* (2005). One can only surmise that she moved on from the 16-class scheme, which was rarely mentioned by other authors.

2
CLASS AND SOCIAL MOBILITY
Stratification and social change since 1978

Beibei Tang

This chapter examines the transformation of class structure and social mobility patterns in China during the Reform Era. The analysis covers three periods: the early Reform Era in the 1980s, the market reforms of the 1990s and the 2000s, and the period since characterized by the further development of the market economy and urbanization. The exploration of the transformation of class structure and social stratification proceeds by examining class formation as structure as well as a process of class in the making. It identifies key changes in structure and the emergence of new classes since the reform, as well as the driving forces for those changes. The transformations of structural and related opportunities in the Reform Era include both changes to class definitions and labels in the Maoist era, and emerging new classes which did not exist in the Maoist era. In addition, the chapter also explores the social mobility patterns and identifies the opportunity structures that lead to the coexistence of mobility and rigidity in Chinese society, as well as a more polarized society in terms of both wealth and opportunities.

China's changing class structure is situated in its multifaceted economic transformation in the past four decades, especially in terms of marketization, industrialization, urbanization, and rural-to-urban migration. As David S. G. Goodman points out, class mobility in China is best understood in terms of 'the intergenerational transfer of compound inequalities of wealth, status and power, rather than solely in terms of ideas of class and stratification drawn from the experience of socio-economic development elsewhere' (Goodman 2014a: 7). In this chapter, the analysis of class structure and mobility goes beyond static categories and explores the dynamic interactions of complex social relations shaped by market economy and the socialist state. In addition to economic mechanisms, it examines the role of the Chinese Party-state in shaping class structure and social mobility patterns, through (re)distribution mechanisms and inequality discourses, which further lead to impacts on various dimensions of class-making and the expanding heterogeneity within class during China's economic reform.

DOI: 10.4324/9781003255017-3

Social class is thus defined in a broad way, reflecting multiple dimensions in the Chinese context, including economic structures, income, consumption patterns and lifestyles, and perceptions and values (Goodman and Zang 2008: 6). It also includes dimensions such as education level, occupation, social status, and taste and aesthetic values (Donald and Yi 2008), and collective action (Tomba 2005; Zhang 2010). The terms social class and social strata are here used interchangeably. According to Ann Anagnost (2008: 501), the use of social strata to reference social inequality in the Chinese context 'does not assume social antagonism'. Class analysis in reform-era China has largely focused on 'life chances' which is essential in Weberian class analysis and emphasizes the importance of resources to an individual offering opportunities for social mobility. From the perspective of intergenerational mobility, life chances usually are related to parents' socio-economic situation in the market. When it comes to intragenerational mobility, life chances then refer to opportunities and limitations of individuals' moving horizontally or vertically in the social hierarchy throughout their life course (Wright 1997). In this sense, social class then results from both 'individual and generational mobility' (Weber 1978). Here, analysis first examines how the market and the Party-state intertwine to exert impacts on individual life chances, transform opportunity structure, and (re)produce social inequality. Analysis of intragenerational and intergenerational mobility further reveals how the life chances of individuals and groups are determined during China's economic transformation. Since education is often considered an important mechanism in shaping social stratification and mobility, by mediating the influence of family background on individuals' status attainment, especially in Western industrialized societies. Then, the chapter explores in what ways and to what extent education mediates existing social inequality and influences social mobility in reform-era China.

Transformation of class structure

Social stratification before the Reform Era was characterized by an immobile system featuring ascribed factors, including family background (*jiating chushen* 家庭出身) defined according to the class categories employed by the CCP, and the household registration (*hukou* 户口) system which divided the country into two societies. Class categories under Mao were determined by the CCP's political ideology largely reflected in 'class labels', such as 'counter-revolutionary', 'capitalist', 'the stinky ninth' (for intellectuals who were seen as the Ninth Category of Counter-revolutionaries), 'landlord', and 'rich peasant', as well as the more general 'rightist'. When the CCP decided to initiate reforms, those class labels were removed or adjusted. And class structure associated with these class labels was replaced by a new class structure of 'two classes and one stratum', namely, the working class, the peasant class, and the intellectual stratum (Lu 2003). This new class structure also served more as an ideology-orientated official doctrine than the complicated class structural changes occurring in society.

Quite a few social groups emerged during the reform and were not included in the official summary of 'two classes and one stratum'. Li Peilin (2018) summarized these emerging new groups including rural-to-urban migrant workers, a middle class largely composed of professional technicians (high academic qualifications and intellectual labour, equivalent to the white-collar class elsewhere), and private entrepreneurs. More importantly, the social structural change under China's reform has been a dynamic process rather than a fixed official script. It includes new groups being consistently formed and existing groups being continuously adjusted. As Li Peilin (2018) pointed out, the designation of 'two classes and one stratum' did not specify the unprecedented expansion of the workers, as well as the large-scale decrease in the peasant population with growing differentiation and ageing trends. In reality, Chinese class stratification has been transformed from a rigid status hierarchy under Mao to a more open, evolving class system in the post-Mao period (Bian 2002).

Change in the 'two classes and one stratum'

After the economic reforms started in the 1980s, one major policy initiative launched to reinstitute the social structure was to recognize and accept the differentiation of individuals' economic status and private property ownership. One way of doing this was to encourage the private business owners from before the 1956 socialist transformation to re-enter the non-public sector. According to Li Qiang (2019: 38–39), the previous business experiences and skills of this group of people helped a speedy recovery of the social structure with economic stratification after 1978. Along with the development of market economy in the 1990s, the Chinese working class has been further expanded and become more diverse. First of all, the service sector has become the largest concentration of China's working class. According to the National Statistics Bureau, by 2016 the working population in industries reached 220 million, nearly 29% of the total 770 million working population, while around 43% of the working population were in the service sector. In the meanwhile, the proportion of workers in state-owned enterprises (SOE) also dropped significantly. In 1978, the SOE workers made up about 75% of the total working population and collectively run enterprises workers made up around 25% of the total working population. By 2015, there were over around 30 million SOE workers and 4 million workers in collectively run enterprises. While workers in non-SOEs reached nearly 200 million, more than half of them were employed by private enterprises. Another survey suggests that by 2015, the country's private sector employed 128 million workers. And 74% of the private enterprises were in the service sector (Li 2018).

Second, there has been a significant rise of the so-called professional technicians – those with high academic qualifications and engaged in intellectual labour. According to Li Peilin's study (2018), this group increased from 4% of workers in 1978 to 12.5% in 2015, constituting the majority of the middle class in China. This trend is a continuation of the rise of 'the red engineers' before the reforms, when the CCP shifted its class differentiation based on political capital, and decided on cooperation after 1949 between the new political elite and the old educated elite

(Andreas 2009). As the market economy developed in the 1990s, a higher return to human capital occurred and the CCP promoted a trend towards meritocracy in China, since it desired to foster a more efficient and dynamic bureaucracy. The emphasis on educational credentials resulted in the rising importance of higher educational achievement in both administrative and professional elite position recruitment (Walder et al. 2000; Li and Walder 2001). Within the government system, as Xiaowei Zang (2004) observes, there have been and remain two distinctive career paths. Those on paths to government positions are screened more vigorously for human capital, whereas, for those on paths to the CCP hierarchy, political loyalty is evaluated more strongly. And university education increases mobility rates for those in the government system.

The third substantial change is the emergence of private entrepreneurs. Li Qiang's (2019: 92) analysis suggests that from 1992 to 2015, the number of private business owners increased nearly 3.5 times, exceeding 51 million. And the number of employees in private business was 10.5 times greater in 2015 than in 1992, reaching 260 million. Chinese official statistics show that by the end of 2015, there were 35.6 million private entrepreneurs (investors) in China and nearly 60% of private entrepreneurs were concentrated in the East (Li 2018). According to a survey organized by the All China Industry and Business Association in 2004, the average education level of private business owners increased significantly in the previous decade. More than 20% had university or higher education, 31% had junior college (*dazhuan* 大专) education, and 33% had high school or vocational high school education (All China Industry and Business Association 2005: 30).

The expansion in urban worker numbers has been accompanied by the decrease of agricultural labourers. National statistics show that agricultural labourers constituted nearly 28% of the total working population in 2016, decreasing from 44% in 2000 and 82% in 1978. By 2015, there were more than 500 million labourers with rural household registration. About 20% of them were working at village and township enterprises, and 35% of them were working in the urban areas. Technically speaking, they belonged to the group of workers rather than peasants. Like their 'working-class' counterparts, the 'peasant class' also experienced diversification characterized in their case by the emergence of rural-to-urban migrant workers and landless farmers. The registered number of migrant workers with rural household registration but engaging in non-agricultural work reached 282 million in 2016, and the great majority were in service sector enterprises. And in the meantime, the urbanization of the Chinese countryside has expropriated rural land for commercial and urban residential projects. It has been estimated that this process produced at least 52 million landless villagers between 1987 and 2010 (Ong 2014), and by 2014, this number was estimated to have reached 112 million (Zhao 2015). The *Blue Book of Cities in China* (CASS 2013) argues that landless villagers made up nearly 30% of China's urban population by 2012. The national urbanization rate rose from 18% in 1978, to 36% in 2000, to 59% in 2017, with the urban population reaching 813.47 million in 2017 (NBS 2018).

Emergence of new classes

Development of marketization and urbanization has directly resulted in the emergence of new social classes, including private entrepreneurs, the urban middle class, rural-to-urban migrant workers, and landless farmers. Those groups all experienced changing political and economic status and diversification of income sources. And the Party-state has played an essential role in their status attainment, in addition to the market mechanisms widely observed in other societies. The development of private entrepreneurs is a good example. Along with the growth of the private entrepreneurs' group as just discussed, there has been a gradually changing CCP discourse reflected in government policies between 1980 and 2001 to allow, accept, and co-opt private entrepreneurs. Previously considered as a 'tail of capitalism' to be eliminated, the individual economy was considered as a 'supplement' and 'complement' to the public economy in the 1980s. Private entrepreneurs went through being 'permitted to exist and develop' by the end of 1980s, to 'a new social stratum making significant contributions to the country's development and modernization' (Jiang 2001), and therefore deserving of a place in the CCP by the 2000s. Private entrepreneurs today are considered to be an important component of the Chinese economic elite and the new middle class.

With the introduction of the market reforms in the early 1990s, the Party-state realized that to a certain extent, a growing middle class would help to stabilize social structure in China, by continuously maintaining a consumption market through middle-class lifestyles, and buffering conflicts between the subordinate classes and the dominant class through having another group in between. Moreover, a large middle class would also bring a non-confrontational ideology, as well as provide perceivable channels for upward mobility for the lower classes. According to Chinese academics, the Chinese middle classes share a few common characteristics: their income, wealth, consumption, and living standard are equivalent to or higher than the officially prescribed 'comfortably well-off' (*xiaokang* 小康). In terms of occupation, they occupy the middle range in the occupational status hierarchy, largely equivalent to the white-collar class elsewhere. This group includes civil servants, company managers, technicians, and private business entrepreneurs (China Daily 2006). As to education, in general, they have received more than 13 years of education (Li Chunling 2003, 2010a). According to the Chinese General Social Survey (CGSS) 2013, about 21% of the entire population achieved polytechnic school (*zhongzhuan* 中专), or university-level education or higher-level education. This was equivalent to the size of the middle class measured by occupational status and income (Li Qiang 2019: 294–304). The 2010 Census also showed similar results: nearly 20% of the population belonged to the middle class, with more than 40% of the urban population and 12% of the rural population being considered as middle class (Li Qiang 2019: 279). According to CGSS 2005, 2010, and 2013, more than half of the middle class were in the East Region, and more than 60% were in tertiary industry by 2012. And the gap between the numbers of the middle-class population found in the East

Region compared to other regions was growing larger over the years (Li Qiang 2019: 297–301).

Scholars seem to agree that the common features of the Chinese middle class include a good education, a prestigious career, a decent income, and social influence. All the same, the definition and measurement of the new middle class in China is a matter of some debate. There is little consensus about whether and to what extent the Chinese middle class should be defined or measured by income or occupation. Researchers have adopted various criteria to define the Chinese middle class, including income, home ownership, car ownership, education, managerial positions, and urban household registration (Tsang 2014).

Studies have shown heterogeneous family background including farmer or worker families (Li Chunling 2010a) and diverse occupations of the Chinese middle class including professionals, managers, and officials (Wang and Davis 2010). Due to this multidimensional composition of the Chinese middle class, the understandings of this group go beyond an over-simplified, one-dimensional interpretation of co-optation by the Party-state. This may be more reflected in the aspect of the middle classes' relations with the Party-state. The pathways that took urban citizens to this status are diverse, including marketed-oriented trajectories, socialist-state-sponsored trajectories, and a mix of both (Tang 2018). For example, during the housing reform between the 1990s and the early 2000s, privatization and commercialization of urban public housing had produced a nation of homeowners who purchased apartments heavily subsidized by their socialist work units. In addition, Lin and Sun (2010) argue that the Party-state's initiative in expanding higher education has created a potential massive middle class with higher education in China today cultivating the masses rather than the elites for the potential of middle-class status. And this well-educated middle class is assumed to have ramifications for China's future economic and political development and trajectory.

In the meanwhile, there has been a consistent increase in the number of rural-to-urban migrant workers. In 2011, there were 230 million internal migrants to Chinese cities. The number rose to 253 million in 2014 and 291 million in 2019 (also see discussions in Chapter 5 by Blecher). According to the National Health Commission of PRC, between 2011 and 2016, the employment rate of migrant workers was between 85% and 89%. Male migrants are more likely to find a job than female migrants. Among the employed migrant population, 26.4% were self-employed and 66.2% were employed by others. 59.2% of the employed migrant population had signed fixed-term contracts. And 26.8% did not sign any contract. The higher educational level one had, the more likely he/she would sign a fixed-term contract. Only 6.2% of the migrant workers became employers themselves, among whom nearly 64% had no more than three employees (National Health Commission of PRC 2018). A recent study shows that by 2017 the Yangtze River Delta had the highest employment rate for its migrant population, at slightly over 90%. The statistics in the Pearl River Delta region and Jing-Jin-Ji region (Bejing, Tianjin plus Hebei province) were 89.2% and 86.6%, respectively. In those three regions, over 75% of the migrant population concentrated in four top-ranked industries, ranging from manufacturing, followed by retail, accommodation, and restaurant services, to other services such as repairs. More than half of the migrant populations were in business and services jobs, and around 30% were manufacturing/transport workers. Private enterprises took over 35% of the migrant workers and private business owners employed over 33% of them (National Health Commission of PRC 2018).

After over 30 years of officially endorsed internal migration, migrant residents in Chinese cities have become more diverse and exhibited a rather different profile from the early years of movement. First, migrants to urban destinations are not entirely transient as they used to be, with one 2010 estimate by the State Council putting the average length of stay at 5.3 years. In addition, younger generations have become the majority of this population group. According to a 2017 report, the average age of the migrant population was 30, among whom 21.9% were under the age of 15, 74.5% were between 15 to 59, and 3.6% were over 60 years old (National Health Commission of PRC 2018). Moreover, some migrants commit themselves to their place of residence in ways other than the transfer of household registration. By 2017 nationwide around 40% of the migrant populations had lived in their current cities of residence for more than 5 years, and more than 20% had lived there for more than 10 years. According to a national survey in 2017, for the long-term migrant residents who had stayed in their city of destination for 6 years, 63.5% of them moved because of job opportunities, 24.9% of them moved due to land appropriation and relocation, and 8.5% of them were born at their current city of residence. Nearly half of the long-term migrant residents were in the tertiary sector, among whom 42% were in the retail industry, 2.4% and 4.3% higher than the entire migrant population, respectively. And around 28% were in the manufacturing sector, 2.6% lower than the whole migrant population. Approximately, one-third of them were self-employed, 4.3% higher than the entire migrant population (National Health Commission of PRC 2018). To date, in the existing class analysis in China, migrant residents still form an analytical category separate from local residents (i.e., those residing in the place of registration), due to disparities in access to public welfare and in governance.

China's urbanization has also produced a new group of urban residents who have entered urban life not through migration, but through transferring nearby peri-urban–rural residents into urban residents in an organized and managed way as cities expand and spread. The common practices of China's nationwide urbanization campaign have been expropriations of rural land for commercial and urban residential projects. The area of land requisition in 2016 amounts to 1,714 square kilometres, 45% of which was farming land (Ministry of Housing and Urban-Rural Development 2016). This process usually took place together with a top-down process of administrative transition, the so-called 'transforming villages to (urban residential) communities' which granted urban household registration to the farmers in exchange for rural land. Despite local variations, this process has been carried out consistently in terms of separating villagers from their farming land, providing urban services and social security to landless villagers, and instituting urban grassroots governance structures in the former rural residential communities. Across different places and at different stages of urbanization, compensation deals have varied greatly which has caused stratification among the landless farmers (Song et al. 2020). In some areas, the landless farmers became a new group of urban poor due to inadequate compensation (He et al. 2009; Liu et al. 2010), while in some places such as big cities and certain coastal areas, they were more adequately compensated, especially in the late 2000s and the 2010s (Chung and Unger 2013; Wen 2013). As a result, Chinese urban residents have changed from largely homogenous urban public-sector employees to diversified socio-economic groups, including rural-to-urban migrant workers and landless farmers who have lost their farmland during urbanization.

Social stratification and class inequality

Social stratification and inequality patterns are important not only in identifying class structure through between-group differences such as those associated with region, section, system, and generation, but also in revealing differences within the same group due to access to resources. Under Mao, as a socialist regime the Chinese society had less class-based stratification observed than in liberal capitalist societies, due to the absence of private property, less differentiated reward structures, and more egalitarian social policies (Parkin 1979; Giddens 1973). Private property ownership and inheritance property which plays a significant role in social stratification in capitalist societies were replaced by inheritable 'class labels'. In addition, the household registration system determined different life chances of rural and urban population, through distributing economic and social welfare resources considerably favouring urban employees. In Chinese cities, the socialist redistributive economy served as the economic foundations of class stratification through the work unit (*danwei* 单位) system and its largely egalitarian reward distribution and resource allocation (also see discussions in Chapter 6 in Vol. 1 by Blecher). As the public-sector employer organizations and the key institution of a socialist redistributive economy, the work units dominated the organizational hierarchy of economic and social life. The work units guaranteed their employees a variety of perquisites denied to peasants in the countryside: secure jobs, affordable housing, inexpensive medical care, a range of subsidies for everything from transportation to nutrition, and generous retirement pensions, as well as a permanent 'work unit membership' of workers with lifetime employment (Whyte and Parish 1984; Walder 1986; Lin and Bian 1991; Logan and Bian 1993; Bian 1994; Lü and Perry 1997; Logan et al. 1999).

Thus, class labels, household registration, and work units became three key institutional pillars supporting China's rigid social stratification until the end of the 1970s. Those social stratification mechanisms have gradually experienced fundamental transformations under China's economic reform, especially since the market reforms in the 1990s. During this period, a number of key socialist institutions including work units went through marketization and, in turn, altered their resource distribution mechanisms into a hybrid regime where the market also plays a key role. Since then, there has been improvement in the living standard of Chinese citizens and increasing freedom and opportunities for individuals to move up in the social hierarchy. Marketization has also produced social groups who have achieved success due to their individual ambition, merit, and hard work. On the one hand, the interplay of the socialist state and a market economy has altered reward distribution compared to the era of the planned economy. On the other hand, the influence of socialist institutions has not disappeared. Some socialist institutions continue to shape Chinese social structure through modified mechanisms that generate inequality between social groups, in terms of rewards, opportunities, and hierarchies of prestige.

Income and wealth inequality

To date, inequality has been measured mainly through variations in income and welfare distribution. Since the market reforms, inequality in China has increased enormously (Wu and Perloff 2005; Ravallion and Chen 2007; Chen et al. 2010). Especially income inequality experienced a consistent increase between the 1980s and the late 2000s. Between 2009 and 2016, the great majority of data collected by academics in China suggested China's Gini coefficient was no lower than 0.5. Between 1989 and 2011, rural income per capita experienced three and a half times growth and urban income grew fivefold (Sun et al. 2007). And existing studies have consistently found that income inequality in rural areas is higher than in urban areas. Comparing the 2000 Census and 2010 Census, the gap between rural and urban areas had become larger with the increase in middle-level occupations in the cities being almost double the increase in the countryside (Li Qiang 2019: 230). Although income rose substantially for the entire population, the income increased more rapidly for the richer, which became the main cause for China's 20-year-long increase in income inequality after the late 1980s (Li et al. 2018). Chen and Cowell (2015) found that around 2000, the process of generating income distribution in the previous years during the Reform Era moved in a different direction. Since then, it has been easier for the rich to stay where they are on the economic ladder but more difficult for those at the bottom to move up. At the same time, income variations have been continuously growing. As a result, Chinese society is becoming more polarized in income distribution: the rich continue to become richer though not the poor.

In addition to the widening overall income inequality, income gaps between different workers groups have also been observed. With the rapid growth of exports came increasing demands for unskilled workers largely drawn from China's rural surplus labour. Wages of unskilled workers and migrant workers have increased more rapidly than the wages of other workers in recent years (Li et al. 2018). In 2017, the reported average monthly income of the migrant population was 4,872 yuan, an 8.2% increase from 2016. The business owners' average monthly income was 9,550 yuan. The self-employed made 4,626 yuan a month and those who were employed by others received a monthly income of 4,191 yuan (National Health Commission of PRC 2018). There was a significant increase in the monthly average income of the migrant population, from 2,535 yuan in 2011 to 4,872 yuan in 2017. Especially between 2014 and 2016, the annual increase reached 15%. Cohen and Wang's (2009) study revealed that the gender gap in income had increased sharply among urban Chinese employees, and women were consistently more likely to take lower-paid jobs. Their study also suggested that the gender gap was smaller in the state sector and larger in more developed cities.

The two decades since 2000 have been a period of wealth accumulation for the rich, when inequality in Chinese society has gradually shifted from income inequality towards wealth inequality. There has been a growing concentration of asset wealth and income, due to the incomplete transition of property rights (Li et al. 2018). Those with existing properties, connections, or administrative power have managed to take advantage of China's incomplete market transition through high-income inequality, the rapid rise of housing prices, privatization of SOEs and other state assets, and corruption of certain government officials. As a result, wealth inequality has increased substantially (Li and Wan 2015; Knight et al. 2017). Since the late 2000s, Chinese citizens have experienced an important shift from agriculture-based or wage-based income to assets-based income, generated largely by urban housing assets. Although the housing reform was carried out nationwide, the distribution of benefits from the housing reform was not equal. The housing reform only benefited workers with formal urban employment, not informal workers or migrant households. And urban employees who were located in work units that had more resources or that were located in more favourable districts or cities, and individuals who had more status, seniority, or power within their work units, obtained a larger proportionate transfer of housing wealth.

China's growing inequality is also characterized by unequal regional development. Government policies have led to the gradual development of different regions when carrying our market reforms. These included the establishment of 'Special Economic Zones' and prioritized strategies for the eastern coastal areas during the 1980s, the development of key cities such as Shanghai and Tianjin on the eastern coast in the 1990s, and the 'Western Development Programme' proposed to deal with the staggering geographic inequality between East and West China in 1999. Through analysis of the CHIP data, Li et al. (2018) found a two-decade-long increase in the income gap between urban and rural China, East and Central China, and East and West China from the late 1980s to 2007.

China's unequal regional development and rural–urban divide has also been considered a key factor structuring inequality in ethnic minority regions (Gustafsson 2016), since most minority communities are in rural areas, especially in the rural northwest and southwest. Some scholars argue that ethnic inequality is not only because of location and geography but also because of the ways their home regions and their population have been perceived and treated over long periods (Giersch 2020). For example, Emily Yeh (2013) argues that the CCP's development policies in ethnic minority regions were largely driven by the beliefs in lack of capabilities of local population and the perceived need to use Han Chinese experts and migrants from outside the region to implement the development schemes. As a result, in those areas, Han Chinese have dominated development in terms of economic and social opportunities, while local minority populations who are considered backward and underdeveloped have been marginalized. Andrew Fischer (2014) also argues that the exclusion of local minority people from decision-making in resource and development has resulted in high dependence on outside power holders and resources and disempowered development of local communities.

Socialist distribution

As important as it has been, income inequality has only partially reflected social inequality in China. Before the market reforms, differences in salaried income were concealed by omitting non-wage welfare provision through the work units (Szelenyi 1983), artificially compressed by the socialist egalitarian distributional policies (Wang 2008). For state socialism, the greater social inequality actually lies in the higher non-wage compensations for the 'redistributive class' (Szelényi 1978; Konrad and Szelenyi 1979), such as housing, access to higher education, subsidies for certain commodities, health, and pension provision. Given the importance of non-material rewards such as in-kind subsidies and even the prestige obtained through positions and employment, income distribution alone does not provide a comprehensive measure of overall inequality. How resources are allocated to whom has been the core question of social stratification. In the history of PRC, state intervention has been the most powerful mechanism of resource allocation. Administrative power, work units (associated with institutional administrative ranks), and individuals' networks of influence (*guanxi* 关系) have also become key factors shaping resource allocation and reward distribution in China, in addition to the rising market competition and the emergence of a nascent civil society.

Rooted in its Marxist-Leninist ideology, the Party-state system operates the Chinese economy with strong emphases on socialist redistribution through interactions with and state intervention into activities of the market economy. After four decades of economic reform, the public sector still dominates the urban economy in China, in terms of its control of key economic resources, its advantaged operations backed up by the Party-state, and its impacts on employees' socio-economic wellbeing. In addition, the socialist redistribution through which resources and rewards are distributed as collective benefits continues to operate along with the development of market competition. As David S. G. Goodman observes, the dominance of the Party-state and redistributive economy has maintained its political superiority, because the Party-state believes 'There may be a need for economic resources to be allocated through the market, but it is the role of the state to intervene to correct "the imperfections of the market"' (Goodman 2016: 4). Therefore, unlike inequality dynamics observed in Western industrialized societies where success in market competition plays a more determinant role in individuals' social status, in China today, the impact of socialist institutions on inequality dynamics is too important to ignore.

Despite market reforms, the workplace-generated inequality patterns in the Reform Era have been mainly reported through income differences (Nee 1989, 1991, 1996; Parish and Michelson 1996; Xie and Hannum 1996; Bian and Logan 1996; Zhou 2000; Wang 2008). A few studies have pointed out that for much of China's urban population, differences in subsides across workplaces greatly exceed differences in nominal salaries within a particular workplace (Cao 2001; Davis et al. 2005; Wang 2008). Moreover, public-sector employees continue to hold entitlements for rewards that are usually not in terms of fixed wages, but in subsidies and other fringe benefits (Logan and Bian 1993; Li and Niu 2003). Market allocation per se has no clear implication for this kind of reward distribution (Walder 1996; Xie and Wu 2008). Housing and other in-kind subsidies are now incorporated in the monthly salary of employees from some public sectors, not as rewards for market competition but as redistributive benefits (Tomba 2004).

More recent studies have shown that the embeddedness of socialist practices in the hybrid economy generates boundaries that cut across class divisions (Davis and Wang ed. 2009). In particular, Feng Wang's studies reveal that instead of market rewards for individual merits, socialist institutions contribute largely to group-based inequalities in post-reform urban China, with variation in ownership type, industry, locale, and work organization (Wang 2008). Some work units that used to receive favourable investment under the planned economy continued to receive preferential investment and taxation policies during the reform era. And in turn, those profitable work units significantly influenced a high level of rising income inequality in the late-reform era, mainly through high bonus distribution among the employees (Wu 2002; Wang 2008; Xie and Wu 2008). More importantly, as part of the socialist legacy, the institution-based group effects under the socialist market do not aim at maximizing the benefits or profits through market competition, but through maintaining the collective interests and benefits that are equally distributed within the group (Wang 2008; Xie and Wu 2008).

Life chances and intragenerational class mobility

The market transition thesis (Nee 1989, 1991, 1996) has largely influenced social stratification research in reform-era China. According to this theory, market transition leads to a transfer of power favouring direct producers, higher returns to education, and rising opportunities for market activities, accompanied by declining socialist redistributive powers. As a result, the emergence of market institutions would become the determinant factor for changing social inequality mechanisms during the market transition. Market reforms have profoundly transferred intragenerational mobility in China, in terms of changing life chances, through, in particular, higher return to education and market competition in generating economic welfare (Bian and Logan 1996; Xie and Hannum 1996; Zhou 2000; Wu and Xie 2003; Song and Xie 2014). During this process, a mix of market rewards and the persistence of distributive power and privilege together contribute to changing life chances of different groups through their relations with the market and the

Party-state. The structural reform aimed at stimulating on-the-job motivation and greater productivity introduced market competition to state-owned enterprises and gradually generated new reward schemes, redundancies, and shifts to the market as the service provider (Naughton 1997; Bray 2005).

Meanwhile, socialist institutions, especially Household Registration and the work unit, have been continuously generating crucial distinctions between different reward systems and influencing intergenerational mobility under China's market reforms. This is an extension of unequal distribution of resources and opportunities among work organizations which used to exert significant impact on urban worker's status attainment and social inequality under the planned economy. Until the end of 1980s, those closer to the redistributive authority, especially those large state-owned enterprises that provided crucial products for ministry, provincial, or municipal plans, were richly endowed with housing, medical facilities, dining halls, and other amenities (Walder 1986; Bian 1994). In contrast, collective firms and especially private firms were excluded from central planning and hence received no redistributive benefits. Under China's marketization, the differences in resource distribution between work units continue to shape the segmentation of Chinese urban society, by offering a differential opportunity structure for rewards. Although a diversified labour market and increased social mobility brought by the market economy reduced the importance of work units in the promotion of the individual's life chances, a conventional trend remains very visible today: better-off work units manage to provide more and better quality rewards to their employees.

As reforms have deepened, workers and staff have become increasingly dependent upon their employers distributing extra income, openly or under the table, more than compensating for their lower basic salaries (Wu 2002; Chan and Unger 2009). Healthcare benefits have also been increasingly linked to employment status, sector, and type, and those with higher wages are also likely to enjoy better health benefits (Gao and Riskin 2009: 35). Within the same industry or sector, increasing disparity in income and other benefits have become visible between employees from better-off public work units and less successful employers. In the reform era, despite work units having lost partial control of their employees' everyday life, both 'where you are working (one's *danwei*)' and 'what you are doing (one's job)' still matter for the individual's life chances. Membership of 'The Party-state system' has then become more desirable for many urban residents, especially among the urban middle class (Tang 2018).

Since the 2000s, China has carried out urbanization nationwide, together with the continuous development of marketization which took off in the early 1990s. China's urbanization, as a state-led nationwide campaign, has reinforced the involvement of the socialist state while the emergence of the market economy has deepened its development. The importance of involvement and engagement of socialist redistribution in market activities has continued in shaping individual's life chances and social structure during urbanization. On the one hand, urbanization has created opportunities for the rural population to move from agricultural occupations to non-agricultural occupations rewarding market incentives and merits.

The urbanization of the countryside has resulted in variations in collective welfare provision due to the profitability and resource ability of the village collectives. Zhou Feizhou (2009) argues that local governments play a significant role in creating wealth in rural China through expropriation of rural land for urban development projects, as well as for creaming off the bulk of the monetary compensations made to the farmers. Xueguang Zhou (2009) found that for rural residents, their life chances are still largely determined by the rural corporate governance institutions which play an essential role in resource allocation.

On the other hand, the state has dominated the arrangements for welfare distribution and governance, which has significantly influenced the social hierarchy in Chinese cities. By 2017, there were 245 million migrant residents in Chinese cities who did not enjoy the welfare associated with local household registration. According to the National Health Commission (2018) data, in 2017, 30.6% of the migrant population joined urban workers' medical insurance and only 4.6% joined urban residents' medical insurance. Participation in urban workers' medical insurance in the city of residence dropped from 26.3% in 2011 to 22.3% in 2016, and participation in urban residents' medical insurance dropped from 4.5% in 2013 to 3.7% in 2016. Less than 40% of the migrant children were enrolled in public schools by 2016.

Opportunities and intergenerational class mobility

One thesis about industrialism suggests that as a society industrializes, there are higher social mobility rates and more equal mobility opportunities (Lipset and Zetterberg 1956; Lipset and Bendix 1959), as well as the rising importance of individuals' achievement in terms of education and occupation in obtaining higher social status (Blau and Duncan 1978). Comparative mobility literature suggests there are upward trends in social mobility over time along with the development of industrialization (Featherman et al. 1975; Featherman and Hauser 1978). In the context of China, the focus of the question is in what ways and to what extent a market transition lowers economic, institutional, cultural, and geographic barriers between occupational classes. And more importantly, in what ways and to what extent occupational mobility leads to class mobility.

Social mobility studies in Western industrialized societies tend to present the concept of social mobility as a unidimensional concept featured with the overall openness of occupational structure, and relatively homogeneous influences of industrialization on different occupations. However, the socialist market economy and its industrialization and urbanization in China do not necessarily share the same features. Zhou and Xie's (2019) study, in particular, suggests that under China's economic reform, although rural residents are more likely to switch to non-farming jobs, generally speaking, their class status has not changed much with urban classes still being dominant. Comparing data collected from the 1996 survey of Life Histories and Social Change in Contemporary China and five waves of the Chinese General Social Survey (2005, 2006, 2008, 2010, and 2012), they found that intergenerational mobility between the agricultural and non-agricultural sectors has increased substantially during recent decades. However, the link between class origin and destination has significantly strengthened during China's transition from state socialism to a market economy. Other studies have also shown, generally speaking, that Chinese society has become more stabilized or even more rigid in terms of social mobility since the 2000s (Chen and Cowell 2015; Ding and Wang 2008; Sun et al. 2007), following an increase in mobility between the 1980s and the 1990s especially in rural areas.

Thus, increasing occupational mobility in reform-era China does not necessarily result in a more open class structure where there are more equal opportunities for children from various class backgrounds to achieve different class destinations. The deepened market reforms and urbanization have altogether further produced the so-called second generations of the wealthy and powerful. Through the previous '*dingti* 顶替' practices in work units, class reproduction was carried out by letting a child replace a parent in a state-owned enterprise or part of the Party-state (including education and health) inheriting the group membership of the parent. Under marketization, although there is a more diverse labour market and more occupational options, jobs within the Party-state system are still favoured due to job security, better welfare coverage, stable income, and higher status. The parents 'within-the-system' still manage to pass on their advantages through mobilizing resources if their children want to have a job also 'within-the-system'. If their children prefer to join the private sector, they can still inherit their parents' economic and social capitals accumulated through their 'within-the-system' networks.

In the Chinese countryside, the household registration system has weakened its control on labour and geographical mobility of rural residents. However, this institution still limits access to resources, especially the public welfare of rural-to-urban migrant workers. The migrant children are still denied access to public schools in Chinese cities and the migrant schools they attend have become a reproduction of their parents' social status of being migrant workers. Through urbanization, the Household Registration system also has created a rapid upward mobility of some landless farmers and produced the second generation of those who became wealthy due to adequate compensation of land expropriation. For some landless farmers, in exchange for their land, the switch of their rural household registration to an urban one brought urban welfare and administration arrangements and urban residency, although many of them do not have urban employment. Their children, in turn, have become urban household registration holders. But they are unlikely to be accepted by those urban classes who are still dominant.

Education inequality and class mobility

In comparative social stratification research, how and to what extent education mediates the influence of family background on status attainment is a key research agenda (Ganzeboom et al. 1991). Some believe that education contributes to upward social mobility which promotes higher social equality (Lenski 1966; Breen and Jonsson 2005). Some consider education as a tool used by social elites to monopolize the better professions and exclude other social classes, and further reproduce social class and reinforce previously existing inequalities in the society (Bernstein 1975; Willis 1981; Bourdieu and Passeron 1990; Shavit and Blossfeld 1993; Collins 2009). To date, sociological studies across different societies have been trying to find out whether and to what extent educational expansion has provided more opportunities of access to children from disadvantaged backgrounds and therefore reduced social inequality or mainly benefited those from advantaged backgrounds, thus exacerbating social inequality (Shavit and Bloassfeld 1993).

In Western industrialized societies, some scholars consider that students' performance and behaviour would replace income and race for shaping stratification (Coleman 1992). Nonetheless, much scholarship has suggested that education is more of a mechanism for perpetuating social inequalities rather than an institution to equalize opportunities (Lareau 2003; Collins 2009). More specifically, not all social groups in the educational market are equal due to the unequal distribution of different types of capitals among classes and groups (Collins 1979), and socio-economically advantaged groups can utilize their social and economic capitals to convert social advantages into academic advantages through today's educational system (Bourdieu and Passeron 1990). As a result, to a large extent, education reproduces rather than transforms existing structural inequalities (Bourdieu 1984; Ishida et al. 1995). The Maximally Maintained Inequality (MMI) model argues that socio-economic factors impact more on educational attainment at the higher level than at the primary level, and socio-political circumstances also affect a particular level of expansion of opportunities. The Effectively Maintained Inequality (EMI) model argues the persistence of the effect of social origin on educational attainment. That is, when a given level of education becomes universal, socio-economically advantaged classes will seek quantitatively equal but qualitatively better education.

And then in what ways and to what extent will education mediate the impact of class origin on class destination in reform-era China? State policies have certainly determined education stratification in China (Bian and Logan 1996; Deng and Treiman 1997; Zhou et al. 1998; Zhou 2004). There were two periods in the PRC's history for equalization of education opportunities and universalization of school education. One was from the 1950s to the 1970s when China's education policies at the time reflected an egalitarian ideology favouring the children of peasants, workers, and soldiers; expanded primary and secondary education in the countryside; and emphasized a family's 'class labels' and students' political performances rather than academic ability for university admission (Deng and Treiman 1997). As a result, students of socially disadvantaged groups, such as rural youth, women, and the urban poor, obtained enhanced educational opportunities (Hannum 1999; Zhou et al. 1998). The other was the 2006 amendment of Compulsory Education Law which made school education (until Year 9) free of charge to all school-age children and adolescents without taking any examination.

School education

Although school education (the 9-year compulsory education) has been made free of charge for almost one and a half decades, there is an imbalance in development with a limited number of popular schools which are considered to bring qualitatively better experiences for the students. As a result, competition has been fiercer among the parents for sending their children to the schools they favour (Liu 2018), although this kind of activity is not supported by government policies for compulsory education. In addition to students' academic performances, admission criteria for popular schools also include local household registration, additional payments for enrolment, special talents in non-curriculum activities, donations from powerful work units, and recommendations from reputational pre-admission training agencies (Liu 2018: 3). All those factors are largely determined by the parents' income, occupation, and social network (Liu 2015; Wu 2017). As a result, the competition for getting into a popular school has gradually become a tool for the privileged groups to keep advantages for their children. Parents' educational level, education style, and interaction between home and school all make a difference in cultural capital during the students' schooling.

Parallel to China's official education system with schools (both public and private) approved by the government, there also exists an unofficial education system which consists of private migrant schools many without school licenses. The emergence of those schools is a direct outcome of China's rapid growth of rural-to-urban migrant workers who have brought their children to the cities to live with them, rather than leaving them behind in the countryside. According to China's 2010 Census, it was estimated that there were 20 million migrant children and more than 58% were school age by 2010. Because of the household registration system and limited seats available in public schools, migrant children face additional charges to public schools and most of them have to attend privately run, profit-driven migrant schools with poor facilities, and inferior teaching (Kwong 2004; Lan 2014). In 2001, around 76% of migrant schools operating in Shanghai had no official approval. In this kind of unofficial education system, the impact of education in facilitating upward mobility is being restricted due to institutional exclusion associated with local household registration (Lu 2008; Goodburn 2009). Through a study of a private migrant school in Shanghai, Yihan Xiong (2015) found a counter-school culture in private migrant schools, and both the access to public school and learning experiences in migrant schools restricted the upward social mobility of the migrant children. In other words, not only the school type impacts migrant children's academic achievements (Chen and Feng 2013) but also the manner and mechanisms within the school affect students' learning experiences and outcome. Most migrant school students hoped to find work immediately after graduation rather than returning to their home cities to continue their senior high school education (Xiong 2015: 171). Like their parents, the migrant school students' social network tends to be small in scale, high in homogeneity, exhibits a significant degree of exclusiveness, and typically consists of other migrant workers with low socio-economic status.

Not all students, especially among rural students and migrant school students, will go to high school after the 9-year compulsory education. Studies in the countryside found that barriers to quality education include constraints of economic resource, poor academic performance, and lack of aspirations. And rural families may spend less savings on schooling for their children, due to the increasing fees for social welfare services due to the market reforms (Hannum and Adams 2009). For migrant students and students from poor urban working-class families, secondary vocational school has become a popular choice when they fail the high school entrance test and could not afford private preparation schools for university admission. In her study of a secondary vocational school, Terry Woronov (2011) suggests that this group of students are more upwardly mobile compared to their parents who are normally rural-to-urban migrants and poor urban workers, and their upward mobility leads them to a new urban service sector as semi-skilled workers. 'Structurally, economically, and ideologically, they exist in between the migrant workers and former proletariat on one side and the new middle classes on the other' (Woronov 2011: 82). But their social mobility is more likely to be limited within the class rather than between classes. Although they have obtained opportunities for their occupational mobility in urban service sector, their future upward mobility is also constrained due to their lack of educational qualifications.

University education

When school education has become more universal in many societies, scholars have started to pay more research attention to the impact of the expansion of higher education on social stratification mechanisms (Shavit et al. 2007). As pointed out by Bourdieu and Passeron (1990), instead of changing social inequality, higher education enhances the reproduction of social classes mainly through the transmission of cultural capital in educational attainment. In the meanwhile, higher education has become more differentiated with distinctions between elite universities and second- and third-tier universities. More students from working-class family background are attending second-tier and third-tier universities (Brint and Karabel 1989). In France, children from the middle and upper classes account for more than 60% of the total students in elite universities (Bourdieu 1989). In addition, the threshold for a desirable occupation has been increasing, due to the universalization of higher education in many societies (Shavit and Kraus 1990; Van de Werfhorst and Andersen 2005).

In Reform Era China, university education has been an elite education for the career advancement of the elite class (Walder et al. 2000; Zang 2004). University education provides a distinct institutionalized channel for upward social mobility for those who were born with rural household registration (Wu and Treiman 2007). According to a 1996 national survey, half of those with rural origins achieved an urban household registration at the time by receiving higher education (Wu and Treiman 2004). Also, universities have been a key site for ideological control and the CCP's recruitment of members (Guo 2005), especially after Jiang

Zemin's promotion of the Three Represents, an ideological departure which aims to broaden the class base of the CCP including young and university-educated people. China has expanded its higher education since the end of the 1990s. The universities offering 4-year undergraduate degree programmes had increased from 684 in 2004 to 1202 in 2014 (Wu 2017: 9). By 2013, the gross enrolment ratios reached 30% (MoE 2015). Since the university expansion started at the end of 1990s, university education – which used to be an elite opportunity exclusive to a small group of the population – has become much more accessible for students from various socio-economic backgrounds. Liang et al. (2013) argue that education expansion and the university entrance exam system have resulted in a large number of young people from socio-economically disadvantaged families being able to enter elite universities and become part of the elite after they graduate.

Along with the higher education expansion, channels for university admission have become diverse. A selected group of universities and provinces are granted autonomous admission to recruit students independently through their own exams. This is to emphasize more on the student's all-round competence in university admission, as the Ministry of Education's (MoE's) response to address the criticisms for exam-oriented university entrance exam systems. Thus, the content of diverse channels of university admission strongly reflects the government policy priorities. Students in key-point high schools, with various extracurricular activities, are the target of those student recruitment channels. Parents with socio-economic advantages can use their economic resources, social network, and cultural capital to help their children take advantage of this kind of education reform. An analysis of the admission process of Peking University revealed that this admission policy reform has reinforced the advantages of upper-class students in access to elite education (Liu et al. 2014).

Despite the expansion of higher education, admission into elite universities remains, perhaps even more competitive and restrictive. Elite universities are favoured in resource and teaching staff allocation through the two most famous policy initiatives, the so-called Project 211 and Project 985. Project 985 was launched in 1999 to promote 43 top universities to become China's 'first-rate universities at the international advanced level'. Project 211 was initiated by MoE in 2015 aiming to build 100 comprehensive research universities in the twenty-first century. The two projects have largely determined the prestige hierarchy of Chinese universities today. And the universities included in the two projects receive massive funding from the government on research infrastructure, as well as better quality students: University Entrance Exam (UEE) performance is still a determinant factor for entry into elite universities, regardless of family background. That means the competition starts at schools.

Key-point schools play a crucial role in determining access to those elite universities. Xiaogang Wu's (2017) recent study suggests that key-point high schools and special admissions play an important role for students to get into elite universities, and students from upper-middle-class and upper-class backgrounds are favoured in this process. Through initial selection, experienced teachers, and quality education resources, key-point high schools provide students with better training to achieve higher scores in college entrance exams, leading top performers to gain admission to elite universities. In addition, students in national elite universities are more likely to join the Party. Ye Liu's (2016) study found that students' parental educational level had a more significant influence on the students' performance in UEE than did socio-economic status. Students from professional families tended to achieve better in UEE. And over the years, the social diversity of students in elite universities has declined (Liang et al. 2013; Shavit et al. 2007).

The educational opportunities are also varied for students from different geographic origins. A number of studies highlight geographical disparity as the key 'stratifier' of educational opportunities (Hannum and Wang 2006: 258). Substantial regional differences have been found particularly in terms of educational provision and resources, educational attainment at primary and secondary levels, and educational funding (Hannum 1999; Hannum and Wang 2006). According to the MoE (2011), by 2011 a quarter of the elite universities in China were located in Beijing, and 13% were in Shanghai. But only 15% of the elite universities were in West China provinces. Nearly 80% of the key universities were in East China provinces; home to 77% of the total number of universities. Liu's (2016) study found that students from developed cities such as Beijing, Tianjin, and Shanghai have the strongest advantages in the competition for elite opportunities given the much lower entry requirements, while access to elite opportunities is most selective and difficult for students from provinces such as Anhui, Henan, and Jilin, central provinces seem to be most disadvantaged in the meritocratic selection.

Class, mobility, stratification

In Reform Era China, social stratification based on political status has been replaced by stratification based on socio-economic status. In turn, there was a shift – led by the CCP – from class defined by ideology to class determined by socio-economic status largely through occupation. For Chinese citizens, class labels such as 'landlord' and 'poor peasant' which used to define 'family background' in the official class analysis have lost their meanings and been replaced by socio-economic status measured largely by occupation, income, and wealth. New classes that emerged during this period mainly include private entrepreneurs, the urban middle class, rural-to-urban migrant workers, and landless farmers. There are two major driving forces for the changing structural and relational opportunities. One is China's economic reforms focusing more on industrialization and the tertiary sectors in the 1980s, followed by a development of market reform starting in 1992. The other is China's nationwide campaign of urbanization of the countryside as the market reforms have deepened, especially since the early 2000s. During this process, different population groups have reformed relations with the CCP, as well as with each other.

While experiencing a significant improvement of living standards for all the population, China has also been facing increasing income and wealth inequality and persistent regional inequality. Especially since the first decade of the century, there has been a tendency for the rich to accumulate yet more wealth. And socialist redistribution continues to favour those who are within or close to the Party-state system. Under the market economy, socialist institutions continued to influence individual's life chances through monopolistic control over resources. Institutional boundaries created by the Household Registration system and work units, and the associated reward mechanisms still significantly impact the overall pattern of class mobility, despite more open and fluid occupational mobility.

While income inequality consistently increased between the 1990s and the 2000s, mobility became more rigid around 2000. While the boundaries between rural and urban Chinese society and the socialist and market economy have become less clearly defined, class boundaries have been remarked. Class permeability is restricted by limits on labour mobility associated with restrictions of the Household Registration system, changing conditions in the housing market where housing affordability for the younger generation depends largely on inheritance of their parents' housing, and continuous administrative monopoly and redistributive advantages in key-scale industries. The strong interference of the socialist state, to a certain extent, has mediated the inequality produced by marketization, on the one hand. On the other hand, state intervention has strengthened existing status hierarchy among different classes.

Furthermore, education stratification in China today has presented a 'parentocracy' where educational attainment increasingly depends on the wealth and preference of parents rather than the students' academic ability and efforts (Brown 1990: 65). By sending their children to popular schools, privileged social classes maintain and reproduce their existing cultural, social, and economic advantages. Children of high-rank cadres and professionals, residents of large cities, and men in general are more favoured in access to those opportunities (Whyte and Parish 1984; Zhou et al. 1998). In addition, the financial resource gap between different regions has also led to regional disparities in education where the local governments of the coastal and eastern regions provide more financial resources in the education sector (Hannum 1999). The Party-state, the socialist market economy, society, and the family altogether shape the mechanisms of education in mediating class inequalities. When a certain level of education becomes universal, socioeconomically advantaged classes start to seek quantitatively equal but qualitatively better education.

3
THE PERFORMANCE OF CLASS

Lifestyles and behaviour

Beibei Tang

Chapter 2 examined fundamental inequalities that determine class and stratification in terms of intragenerational and intergenerational transfer of wealth, power, status, and opportunities, largely from the experiences of China's socio-economic development since 1978. Beyond the analysis of socio-economic inequalities, this chapter emphasizes the mechanisms of compound inequalities which reflect how relationship and interactions between different kinds of inequalities reinforce privileges and disadvantages that have developed with China's market reforms and urbanization. Compound inequalities, as key indicators of the development and influence of sources of power and authority in society, provide an understanding of class by exploring the dynamic interactions of complex social relations (Savage 1995: 25). Different social relations interact with each other to produce lifestyles and behaviours of various class groups through which their class identity is rehearsed and presented. Of course, the performance of class is intertwined with the development of class as ideological formulation and class as socio-economic structure. All three aspects contribute to the development of China's complex political economy.

The complex social process involved in China's market reform and urbanization is well reflected in the consumption patterns of different classes. In the Weberian understanding of class, consumption patterns indicate both economic and cultural dimensions of class, including relations to the market, life chances, honour, and lifestyle. The Weberian concept of 'status group' differentiates itself from the economic form of 'class situation' and emphasizes 'honour'. Consumption and lifestyles largely constitute the social estimation of honour:

> With some over-simplification, one might thus say that classes are stratified according to the relations to the production and acquisition of goods; whereas status groups are stratified according to the principles of their consumption of goods as represented by special styles of life.
>
> *(Weber 1978: 937)*

and persistent regional inequality. Especially since the first decade of the century, there has been a tendency for the rich to accumulate yet more wealth. And socialist redistribution continues to favour those who are within or close to the Party-state system. Under the market economy, socialist institutions continued to influence individual's life chances through monopolistic control over resources. Institutional boundaries created by the Household Registration system and work units, and the associated reward mechanisms still significantly impact the overall pattern of class mobility, despite more open and fluid occupational mobility.

While income inequality consistently increased between the 1990s and the 2000s, mobility became more rigid around 2000. While the boundaries between rural and urban Chinese society and the socialist and market economy have become less clearly defined, class boundaries have been remarked. Class permeability is restricted by limits on labour mobility associated with restrictions of the Household Registration system, changing conditions in the housing market where housing affordability for the younger generation depends largely on inheritance of their parents' housing, and continuous administrative monopoly and redistributive advantages in key-scale industries. The strong interference of the socialist state, to a certain extent, has mediated the inequality produced by marketization, on the one hand. On the other hand, state intervention has strengthened existing status hierarchy among different classes.

Furthermore, education stratification in China today has presented a 'parentocracy' where educational attainment increasingly depends on the wealth and preference of parents rather than the students' academic ability and efforts (Brown 1990: 65). By sending their children to popular schools, privileged social classes maintain and reproduce their existing cultural, social, and economic advantages. Children of high-rank cadres and professionals, residents of large cities, and men in general are more favoured in access to those opportunities (Whyte and Parish 1984; Zhou et al. 1998). In addition, the financial resource gap between different regions has also led to regional disparities in education where the local governments of the coastal and eastern regions provide more financial resources in the education sector (Hannum 1999). The Party-state, the socialist market economy, society, and the family altogether shape the mechanisms of education in mediating class inequalities. When a certain level of education becomes universal, socioeconomically advantaged classes start to seek quantitatively equal but qualitatively better education.

3
THE PERFORMANCE OF CLASS
Lifestyles and behaviour

Beibei Tang

Chapter 2 examined fundamental inequalities that determine class and stratification in terms of intragenerational and intergenerational transfer of wealth, power, status, and opportunities, largely from the experiences of China's socio-economic development since 1978. Beyond the analysis of socio-economic inequalities, this chapter emphasizes the mechanisms of compound inequalities which reflect how relationship and interactions between different kinds of inequalities reinforce privileges and disadvantages that have developed with China's market reforms and urbanization. Compound inequalities, as key indicators of the development and influence of sources of power and authority in society, provide an understanding of class by exploring the dynamic interactions of complex social relations (Savage 1995: 25). Different social relations interact with each other to produce lifestyles and behaviours of various class groups through which their class identity is rehearsed and presented. Of course, the performance of class is intertwined with the development of class as ideological formulation and class as socio-economic structure. All three aspects contribute to the development of China's complex political economy.

The complex social process involved in China's market reform and urbanization is well reflected in the consumption patterns of different classes. In the Weberian understanding of class, consumption patterns indicate both economic and cultural dimensions of class, including relations to the market, life chances, honour, and lifestyle. The Weberian concept of 'status group' differentiates itself from the economic form of 'class situation' and emphasizes 'honour'. Consumption and lifestyles largely constitute the social estimation of honour:

> With some over-simplification, one might thus say that classes are stratified according to the relations to the production and acquisition of goods; whereas status groups are stratified according to the principles of their consumption of goods as represented by special styles of life.
>
> *(Weber 1978: 937)*

As Atkinson argues, social classes are about a sense of distinction, and they are 'perceptible social groups with shared ways of life, communities and attitudes, arose from these economic foundations through the restriction of social mobility' (Atkinson 2009: 898). 'Status groups' in Reform Era China are more complex than the Weberian focus on inequality generated in the marketplace, in the sense that the Party-state has been actively intervening in market operations and interacting with market mechanisms, as explained in Chapter 2. As this chapter shows, the CCP plays a critical role in promoting, shaping, and orienting consumptions and lifestyles, especially for the middle class. In other words, the lifestyles and consumption observed in Chinese society today not only result from interaction with the global economy, rising consumerism and growing marketization, but are also heavily influenced by the CCP's agenda which seeks to balance economic liberalization and social stability.

Party-state intervention has also heavily influenced social and political behaviour, as well as values and perceptions towards social inequality, mobility, and social justice for different classes, through a series of state-sponsored discourses which serve as guidance and instruction for expected class behaviour. The exchange of language between people is a process of social construction (Berger and Luckmann 1966; Burr 1995) where in specific contexts language is structured, maintained, and transformed in a discursive practice (Jorgensen and Phillips 2002). Since the 1990s, through discourses such as quality, citizenization, stability maintenance, and self-governance, the Party-state has established strong power relations by constructing language that determines behaviour between state and society, and among different classes. In turn, the Party-state has oriented different classes' understanding and experiences with the construction of those discourses or behaviour. This process has not only established and maintained specific discourses but also managed the power relations that result. These include the identity, perception, and values of different classes, which are related to, but not solely determined by, their economic activities. The examination of the performance of class behaviour offers explanations for how the potential of various classes to become driving forces in China's future social and political changes in China can be best understood.

Consumption and lifestyles

China's new consumers and the 'new rich'

In the 1990s, along with launching market economic reforms, central government policy laid a new emphasis on stimulating domestic demand, replacing planning priority in investment-led economy growth with consumption-led growth. The Five-Year Plan in 1998 advocated 'giving full play to the advantages of our domestic markets which are large and have great potential' (China Daily, 24 March 1998). The Fifth Session of the National People's Congress in 2002 designated expansion of domestic demand as 'a long-term strategic principle' and 'a fundamental plan for realizing a relatively rapid economic growth to further stimulate consumption and investment' (Xinhua, 24 April 2002). After more than one and a half decades of market reforms, China still had a savings rate higher than most other countries, even for middle-class families. About 40% of household disposable income was reported as savings in 2008. In 2006, China's private consumption made up only 38% of its aggregate GDP (Li 2010c: 8–9). A 2014 survey shows less than 5% of families purchased financial products. Another 2014 survey shows nearly 50% of families with annual disposable income between 10,000 and 20,000 yuan had savings. And among those who had savings, nearly 50% of families had chosen fixed-term deposit savings (Li 2019: 344). The high savings rate has been intertwined with a widespread campaign to encourage domestic consumption endorsed and encouraged by the Party-state.

This campaign has directly created what Elisabeth Croll (2006) called China's new consumers whose personhood or identity was constructed through their consumption (Croll 2006: 21–22). According to Croll, consumption has generated more diverse social categories and social relations, and Chinese society is represented by a pyramid-shaped structure, with a small and burgeoning middle class in between (2006: 22). The popular consumption items have shifted from the 'three big' (TV, refrigerator, and washing machine) in the 1980s and 1990s to two key items – housing property and private automobiles since the early 2000s. By the end of 2000s, China had become the world's leading automobile producer and consumer, and the home ownership rate had reached over 80% (Li 2010c: 9; Li Qiang 2019: 342). Along with the rise of new consumers and the aspiration for a middle-class society with continuing economic growth came the emergence of the 'new rich'. The new rich are the beneficiaries as well as the drivers of China's economic transformation, including professionals, managerial staff, entrepreneurs, and businesspeople (Goodman and Zang 2008: 2–3). Their cultural values, status aspirations, and consumption patterns are indicators of whether and to what extent their economic success obtained during market reforms are awarded through compatible social recognition and status. New forms of consumption such as luxury goods and leisure are gradually becoming the focus of the disposable income of the new rich (Goodman 2008).

These new rich largely constitute the middle class in China today. Estimates outside China predicted that the country would have the world's largest middle class with more than 30% of the population by 2016, and that by 2025 this group would account for 76% of the urban population (Li 2010c: 9–10). The Party-state also estimated that by 2020 about 55% of the whole population would be middle class, including around 78% of the urban population and 30% of the rural population (Li 2010c: 11). The rise of the Chinese middle class and a more prosperous and globalized society together have led to the accumulation of higher standards of social distinction and the formation of new modes of consumption particularly among the new urban middle class (Tsang 2014). Their consumption plays a large part in defining who they are or wish to be and signal affiliation to one or more of a range of social categories and cultural values.

Social changes and peer groups shape the behaviours and mentalities of different cohorts (Inglehart 1977, 1990). For the Chinese middle class, consumption and lifestyle are significant in self-identity building and obtaining social recognition (Zhou and Chen 2010: 94). Tsang's study suggests that fashion consumption for the older generation of middle class is largely to show in front of outsiders and to strengthen business interests: their conspicuous spending is more of a way of obtaining social capital for business operations. While for the younger generation of the middle class who is more individualistic, materialistic, and money-making in attitude, consumption forms class distinction, in terms of cultural lifestyles. For them, consumption is not only for utilities but also for producing legitimacy to their lifestyle (Giddens 1990). In addition to peer differences, the Party-state system, in the form of the wider public sector, has also significantly influenced behaviour and mentalities of consumption and lifestyle, especially for the middle class. 'The system' differences – as between those 'within the (Party-state) system' and those 'outside' – have also resulted in great heterogeneities in consumption patterns, social interactions and attitudes, and perceptions among the middle class. Those 'within the system' are in a dominant position in setting the rules of how middle-class members present themselves through consumption and lifestyle, and interact with other classes and the Party-state (Tang 2018). For the great majority, housing consumption has become the most common and distinctive consumption pattern among the Chinese middle class.

Housing reform and housing consumption

One key strategy for stimulating consumption and investment was the privatization and commercialization of housing. Through a series of critical reforms regarding housing ownership between the 1990s and the early 2000s, urban employees were given the opportunity to purchase an apartment heavily subsidized by their work units. The housing reform changed the nature of urban housing from a public welfare provided by the socialist state to a commodity which has become the most important component of family wealth for Chinese urban residents. A survey undertaken by Peking University shows that housing property contributes to 79.8% of the urban families' overall wealth (Xie et al. 2014: 33). Official statistics reported that the home ownership ratio in urban China reached 89% in 2010 (NBS 2011), and another Chinese survey estimated that the home ownership ratio in urban China was 85.4% in 2011 (Yang and Chen 2014). Studies in the Pearl River Delta found that in the mid-2000s, nearly 11% of middle-class households owned two or more properties (Liu 2018). In 2017, residential buildings contributed to around 85% of the total sales of commercialized buildings in the country (NBS 2018).

With the development of a housing market, housing reform also contributed to the growing heterogeneity of the urban population and their relations with the Party-state, through different trajectories of producing homeowners. Official statistics show that around 40% of urban homeowners acquired their housing through housing reform during the 1980s and 1990s and 38% purchased from the housing market (NBS 2011). As a result of housing commodification, urban neighbourhoods have become diverse according to housing affordability and have produced what Li Zhang (2010) has called the 'spatialization of class'. Modern gated communities in the cities – usually exclusive to a small group of super wealth residents in many Western societies – have become a major form of domicile and most popular choice of urban middle-class homebuyers. The gated communities offer a privileged lifestyle characterized by a high-quality life, professional property management services, privacy, and exclusion (Tomba 2004; Pow 2009; Zhang 2012): a status symbol for China's 'housing middle class' (Tang 2018).

In recent years, a new urban class has also become a potential consumption force for urban housing targeted by state policies. The members of this new urban class are largely former members of the agricultural population in terms of long-term rural-to-urban migrant workers and landless farmers whose land has been expropriated during urbanization of the countryside. According to the NBS, in 2016 unsold commodity housing reached 700 million square metres. Central government developed a policy initiative to 'reduce (housing stock)' by encouraging migrant workers to become a major consumer force through the 'citizenization of migrant workers' (Li 2019: 12). For example, in 2010, long-term migrant residents in Guangzhou accounted for 2.3% of the migrant population and 2.11% in Suzhou. At the end of 2016, respectively, 36.7% and 37.2% of the residents of Guangzhou and Suzhou remained as migrant residents. The state-led 'citizenization' scheme (to be discussed later in detail) allowed and encouraged migrant workers to purchase apartments in the city where they reside, gaining in turn, access to urban welfare such as medical insurance and school enrolment. Annually from 2016 to 2020, this campaign was meant to turn 13 million rural-to-urban migrants into so-called new citizens, that is, migrant residents with urban household registration granted by the designated cities of residence. Many landless farmers, for their part, have been relocated to urban housing during urbanization, as Chapter 2 described. In most cases, landless farmers were relocated to urban housing estates specifically developed for relocation projects. Some landless farmers who were adequately compensated traded their compensation housing to upgrade to better quality, newly developed urban housing estates. Although such development is still at the very early stage, this part of the former agricultural population is gradually becoming new urban homeowners.

Education expenses

For the great majority of the urban middle class, their housing consumption is closely related to another major, long-term expense for their families: children's school education. As discussed in Chapter 2, education plays a crucial role in class formation and reproduction. Especially when it comes to the potential for China's middle class to improve their conditions during the market reforms, a high level of education has more significant meaning beyond its actual scale (Anagnost 2008; Wang 2008). Expenditure on children's education constitutes important cultural and consumption practices for Chinese citizens. In particular, for the middle class whose possession of cultural capital in most cases is identified with educational attributes, securing their children's future with similar or even better cultural capital has become the goal for a substantial proportion of family expenditure.

Whether there is a good school in the neighbourhood has become one key determinant of housing consumption in urban China today. As Chapter 2 explained, under the 9-year compulsory education scheme, school enrolment occurs as the result of household registration and residence registration of the students. Subsequently, the so-called school-zone housing area – apartments in a neighbourhood with a good school – has featured greatly in the development of housing market. Those apartments are normally 20% to 30% more expensive. Fieldwork observation offers a vivid example. Neighbourhood A and Neighbourhood B are located on each side of the main street in town. According to administrative zoning, they are subordinate to two different administrative divisions. Children registered with Neighbourhood A administrative zone are not eligible to enrol or start school in Neighbourhood B administrative zone. As a result, despite almost the same geographic location and housing quality and history, the housing price in Neighbourhood A is on average 30% cheaper than that in Neighbourhood B. With more and more young middle-class couples with children moving into Neighbourhood B, Neighbourhood B has become a famous middle-class neighbourhood in town with young, white-collar middle-class families, while Neighbourhood A has become home for farmers who have been relocated and long-term migrants without local household registration. Their children are only eligible to enrol in schools in Neighbourhood A which have a history of receiving students from low-income working-class or landless farmer families. A recent Chinese media report shows that the success rate for getting into a reputable junior high school, and even the end of semester exam scores, had impacted housing prices in the relevant neighbourhood (Xinhua 2021).

Along with apartment purchase in order to achieve school enrolment, come extra expenses for after-school classes and non-curriculum activities. Middle-class parents are anxious because of the limited admission quota for junior high school. In order to help their children to produce a dazzling CV, they sign up for private tutors and after-school classes both online and offline. They also sign up for academic and non-academic contests and competitions, as long as those certificates are recognized for junior high school admission. The weekends are usually fully booked with classes that are believed to increase the chance of getting into a good junior high school. Automobiles, like apartments, are needed for those activities. Once the children start junior high school, University Entrance Exam (UEE)-oriented expenditures become more universal, as discussed in Chapter 2. Lin and Sun's study of the national statistics data shows an 80% increase in higher education enrolment between 1990 and 2002. And the number of universities had increased from 1,075 in 1990 to 1,225 in 2001 to 1,792 in 2005 (Lin and Sun 2010: 221–222). The total enrolment of university students experienced an increase of nearly 9 times from 1997 to 2009, reaching 26 million in 2009. It was estimated that by 2030, half of the age cohort will have university education. For middle-class students, in addition to go to state universities, today their families can also choose to send them to study overseas or at joint-venture universities in China. Compared to the state universities, joint-venture universities in China and overseas university programmes have fees that charge a premium nearly 9 to 10 times higher.

In sum, consumer culture and lifestyles significantly contribute to the cultural determination of class in China. Of course, this cultural dimension is closely associated with the other aspects of class such as the economic structure of society and relations with the Party-state. The consumption and lifestyle of the Chinese middle class is not only a function of their socio-economic position but also a reflection and response to the Party-state's strategies on stimulating domestic consumption, as well as creating a potential large-scale well-educated middle class who are believed to have economic and political ramifications for China's future. As reflection of and response to the Party-state, class performance in China today is not only limited to consumption and lifestyles but also rehearsed through class activities and behaviours largely guided by CCP-led discourses.

The CCP-led discourses

Along with the formation of new class structures in the reform era, the CCP has been clearly aware of and cautious about the potential risks and challenges to its leadership of and relationship to different classes. A twofold strategy has been adopted to secure and strengthen the CCP's core position and leadership among existing as well as new classes. One is to recognize, accept, and co-opt classes produced through non-public ownership, especially in terms of private business owners and entrepreneurs, as shown as resulting from the policy changes discussed in Chapter 2. This has led to the rise of the 'red capitalists' as 'allies of the state' (Dickson 2003; Chen and Dickson 2010). In addition to discourses targeting particular classes, there are also general discourses aimed at guiding citizens' behaviour, ensuring the CCP's leadership at local levels and maintaining social and political stability at large. A few discourses are of particular significance. Although developed at different stages of the market reform, they are interrelated through forming an over-arching state strategy of ensuring the CCP's absolute leadership of the various different classes. These include discourses of citizen quality, citizenization, maintaining stability, and self-governance. Those discourses not only provide guidance and expectations of class behaviours from the Party-state perspective but also reshape the Party-state's strategies for dealing with different classes from time to time, according to class behaviour regulated by those discourses.

The quality discourse and citizenization

The discourse of quality (*suzhi* 素质) was developed in the 1990s. It refers to the formation of human capital and cultivation and is used most of the time with a hierarchical distinction between high and low, or good and poor *suzhi*. High or good *suzhi* has become a social distinction defining appropriate, expected, desired practices not least to ensure upward social mobility. Along with the improvement of citizens' *suzhi* becoming a national goal (Kipnis 2006), the usage of *suzhi* discourse covers a wide range from judging individual and/or group behaviour and attitudes, to assessing neighbourhoods and occupations, and evaluating general population quality closely associated with regional economic development.

In particular, the individual quality (*geren suzhi* 个人素质) has become a class marker where dominant class is considered to have higher or better *suzhi*, while subordinate class to have lower or poorer *suzhi*. More importantly, *suzhi* is considered not necessarily attached to one's economic status. The emphasis on individual quality rests more with the non-economic dimensions of class. That is, those with cultural capital (i.e. university education and professional qualifications) and those closely associated with the Party-state (i.e. occupations within the system) are believed to have higher quality. According to this discourse, rural residents and rural-to-urban migrant workers have lower *suzhi* than urban residents. The urban new rich or middle class has better *suzhi* than the urban poor. Among the middle-class groups, despite variations in wealth, public servants and professionals are considered to have better *suzhi* than private businesspeople without university education. As a result, middle-class people with high *suzhi* are portrayed as role models for appropriate and desired behaviours: pursuing higher education and professional certificates, supporting the development of the nation, being polite, following the rules, disengaging from collective actions, and most importantly supporting the leadership of the CCP.

Similar to university students, certain groups of migrant workers and landless farmers are considered potential members of the middle class by the Party-state (Li 2019: 346–349), largely because of their potential consumption power, especially in urban housing properties as just discussed. Unlike university students, migrant workers and landless farmers are expected to improve their *suzhi* to meet the middle-class standard. As a result, an extension of the quality discourse has been developed in the 2010s, as the most recent guidelines and expectations for migrant workers and landless farmers aim to create a new urban class. This is the so-called 'citizenization' (*shiminhua* 市民化) scheme led by the State Council. The nationwide campaign clearly stated its goal of incorporating the 'former agricultural population' which includes rural-to-urban migrant workers and landless farmers into the economic, social, and political life of cities (State Council 2016). Improving those groups' *suzhi* is one major political task of and evaluation criteria for the citizenization campaign. The citizenization discourse has been developed to guide the management of those groups, especially in terms of their behaviour expected to meet the 'quality' standards of the urban population.

The citizenization discourse is practiced via the 'new citizen' scheme operated through points accumulation. Different sub-schemes – i.e. *hukou* (户口) transfer, local public-school enrolment, and medical insurance coverage – require different points. The *hukou* transfer requires the highest points among the three, and only a very small portion of the migrants are eligible. For the point-based applications for the 'new citizen' scheme, local governments have different specific requirements, but similar structure and content in accordance with central government policies. The Basic Points normally include age, education, professional qualifications, contribution to a housing provident fund and social security, residential property ownership in cities, and the length of time residing in the designated city. The Extra Points permit an emphasis more on the contributions to the local community. They include patent innovations recognized by local municipal government, awards received while living in the designated city, i.e. government awards and sports game awards, volunteering activities including money and blood donation, investment and tax activities, and public health including vaccination of the family members. There are also categories for points deductions, including violation of birth-planning policy, criminal records, and breach of credit mainly in terms of failure to contribute to social security and welfare schemes. In Guangzhou, over 90% of the successful applicants for *hukou* transfer received extra points in technical skills and expertise in 2018. Around 25% received extra points through social services and volunteer activities. The successful applicants were overwhelmingly young and well educated. Eighty-five per cent of them were under the age of 40, and over 90% of them had college (including vocational college) education or higher.

Stability maintenance and self-governance

Rising inequality associated with social and economic transformation has resulted in a trend of unprecedented, widespread social tensions across the country. There has been an impressive surge of 'collective incidents' since the early 1990s and a rapid increase in various types of disputes (Tang 2016). According to the Ministry of Public Security, in 2005 the number of incidents of social unrest and protests reached 87,000, rising from 10,000 in 1994 (French 2007), reaching 180,000 in 2010 (Orlik 2011). In 2010, around 11% of the total population lived in protest-affected regions and about one-third of the 11% were directly or indirectly involved in some form of protest (Tang 2016: 109).

To relieve social tensions and conflicts, the Party-state promoted two key concepts. One is 'harmonious society (*hexie shehui* 和谐社会)' targeting social and political stability, which leads to the development of the discourse of 'stability maintenance (*weiwen* 维稳)'. Supporting and contributing to social stability has become a key performance component of both the quality discourse and citizenization discourse. The other key concept is 'social management innovation' which endorses and encourages non-conventional ways of governance, especially in terms of conflict resolution and local decision-making. One key example is to resolve social conflicts and provide social services and assistance, through considerably large-scale grassroots-level governance networks covering neighbourhoods and Street Offices which is at the lowest level of the official state administration apparatus.

The discourse of stability maintenance constitutes the CCP's crucial response and effort to manage social inequality and social change, which infiltrates almost all aspects of Chinese life. It has been impacting and facilitating local disputes, due to inadequate and ineffective legal conflict resolution methods and the state's ambiguous attitude towards mediation (Benney 2016). Despite being a top-down governance approach, the influential and widespread discourse and practices of stability maintenance are accompanied by increasing freedom for local officials, and in turn, space for local autonomy and flexibility in employing diverse methods for conflict resolution. As a result, local experiments are becoming widespread particularly at neighbourhood level which represents the boundaries for territory and population management under a municipal administration.

In the 1990s, the Party-state introduced so-called community construction as an organizational innovation, which shifted grassroots-level administration and welfare provision to residential communities (*shequ* 社区), especially in urban working-class neighbourhoods (Bray 2006: 537; Shieh and Friedmann 2008: 185). One essential part of the community construction scheme was so-called community self-governance. Community self-governance was designed to replace the previous paternalistic procedures through which the government solved social problems (Heberer and Göbel 2011). In middle-class neighbourhoods, community self-governance was introduced as a new governance tool that in principle encourages urban citizens to be the decision-makers and responsible for neighbourhood affairs. Some scholars argue that this is a deliberate government strategy for middle-class homeowners and their homeowner committees (Tomba 2014). Through social coordination at local level, the self-governance discourse aims at co-opting non-state actors into grassroots governance structure and practices. Regardless of diverse practices, there is a common goal and expectation: maintain stability and support the CCP's leadership, especially at the grassroots level.

Perception, class identity, and political participation

In Marx's class analysis, individuals' socio-economic position determines their political behaviour, and in turn, a class as a social group shall behave according to its economic interest. In its early years, the CCP had strongly emphasized political consciousness led by socio-economic conditions. After the start of the Reform Era, the CCP gradually separated class as socio-economic position from class as political consciousness. The ideational shift was carried out largely through an emphasis on functional interdependence and integration in the social and economic division of labour of an increasingly complex society, mainly through occupational hierarchies. As a result, class identities have been largely oriented towards economic interests and relations which are not necessarily reflected in the political participation of different classes.

During more than four decades of economic reform, there have been heated debates on whether and to what extent the CCP's control of political power will be challenged by different classes, such as peasants, the urban unemployed and laid-off workers, the urban middle class, and private entrepreneurs. All those classes have experienced or witnessed rising inequality, corruption, social tensions, a crisis of ideology, and political repression during the reform era. Somewhat surprisingly, to date most studies have shown that the Party-state still manages to receive strong public support from the majority of the Chinese people and different classes (Nathan 2003; Chen 2011; Tang 2016). In particular, there is consistent empirical evidence indicating that citizens on the whole are satisfied with the central government, which constitutes the source of public support for the CCP. This paradox, to a large extent, is driven by the complex perceptions and values of different classes, their vague and ambiguous class identities, and their state-led experience of political participation.

Inequality and the myth of social volcano

The research on social perception and values in contemporary China suggests the coexistence of two groups of contradictory findings. On the one hand, there is awareness, dissatisfaction, concern, and anger with the extent of inequality and social injustice. Chen and Cowell's (2015) study suggests that along with the rise in income inequality, there has been a rise in inequality of opportunity which contributes to a perception of unfairness in economic outcomes resulted from restrictions on labour mobility, changing conditions in the housing property market and administrative monopoly in key large-scale industries. But for many Chinese citizens, their anger towards inequality is driven more by a perception of unfairness for resource and opportunity distribution (Whyte 2010) than income inequality. More interestingly, the perceptions of unfairness and injustice are more commonly observed among the urban workers and middle classes than the socio-economically disadvantaged classes. The urban workers, the professional and managerial middle classes, and those who are better educated tend to emphasize their concerns about the lack of fairness and social justice (Han and Whyte 2009: 204). The middle class who are associated with political power tend to be critics of social injustice (Lee 2009). However, the most disadvantaged groups are not showing the strongest feelings of distributive injustice (Han and Whyte 2009: 209).

On the other hand, there has been general satisfaction and happiness with the improved living standards among different classes, not limited to those who consider themselves as beneficiaries of the reforms (Han and Whyte 2009: 206; Li Chunling 2013: 28). According to a 2013 survey done by Tsinghua University, the great majority reported that they considered their positions in the social hierarchy had moved up in the past 10 years (Li 2019: 144). And this echoes the results of the 2010 Census, which shows the middle-level socio-economic group expanded significantly compared to 2000, with some of the lower-level group members' upward mobility (Li 2019: 192). CGSS [China General Social Science] 2003 and 2013 also suggest overall satisfaction and stable social order, despite anger and criticism about economic inequality, corruption, and social injustice (Lin et al. 2015). Despite their anger, the middle class tends to have a more positive evaluation of social stability in China than the working class (Hsiao 2010: 258).

In addition, two important social stratification mechanisms contribute to the explanations of China's unerupted 'social volcano' (Whyte 2010). One is the inequality of opportunity during the economic reforms among different classes, as detailed in Chapter 2. Through those opportunities, the CCP has managed to sponsor intragenerational upward mobility of different occupational groups and crafted dependence of those groups on the distribution system led by the Party-state, in exchange for their acceptance of its leadership (Wright 2010). The economic achievement of the reforms generated a widespread optimism about the chances for the upward mobility of ordinary people. For most of them, the differences between individual attributes contribute more to the income gap than the unfairness in the system. Han and Whyte's study (2009) suggest that most urban residents draw conclusions about the fairness or unfairness according to their own recent experiences and their observations of the widening gap between the rich and the poor in their local community. Their perceptions are little shaped by comparing themselves with other groups elsewhere.

The other important mechanism is stratification within the class. Take the working class as an example. With the disempowerment of the old working class in the public sector during the market reforms, a new working class composed largely of rural-to-urban migrant workers and urban workers in the marketized economy sector has yet to lead to cooperation between the two segments of the working class. The public-sector workers and non-public-sector workers, the urban workers and migrant workers appear to be different working classes, with separate labour movements and activisms (Anita Chan 1995: 36; Appleton et al. 2006). The two working classes see each other as competitors for job opportunities and upward social mobility where public-sector workers' status was declining and non-public-sector workers – especially migrant workers – managed to move up (Solinger 2002: 311). Among the middle classes, there are also different upward mobility trajectories for those 'within the (Party-state) system' – public servants and professionals – and those 'outside the system' – private businesspeople (Tang 2018). And each group tends to consider the other group (or groups) as the main beneficiaries of the reforms. The stratification mechanism within a certain class, to a certain extent, has directed the focuses from antagonism among and between classes to competition for different reward mechanisms and benefit distribution within the same class. This is largely accompanied by ambiguous class identity and class consciousness among different classes.

Ambiguous class identity and class consciousness

Through the process of marketization and urbanization, the rural–urban divide has produced a new group in the urban working class: the rural-to-urban migrant workers. The complexity of this group is that it not only blurs the boundaries of the former working class in the public sector but also characterizes its growing diversity as the market reforms deepen. Research on migrant workers has shown increasing evidence of migrant workers' class consciousness largely associated with their economic interests (Chan 2012; 2013). And the younger generation of migrant workers presents a higher degree of consciousness as workers with much less of a 'peasant component' (Chan and Pun 2010; Pun and Lu 2010; Qiu and

Wang 2012). But compared to those who are urban laid-off public-sector workers, they exhibit less working-class consciousness accompanied by any political agenda (Lee 2007). The main concerns of migrant workers have been economic issues and extended citizenship rights (Lee 2009). In response to those concerns, the 'New Citizen' scheme launched by the Party-state brings further ambiguity in identifying urban workers, migrant workers, and peasants.

Land ownership has been a concentrated area of the farmers' economic interests. So far, collective actions in the countryside have largely been driven by land development during the urbanization process which has produced a large number of landless farmers. Some of them have been granted urban household registration and relocated to new urban housing development. Some of them have lost their farmland but stayed on in their village house sites despite their urban household registration status. And some of them have developed corporatist villages to manage unexpropriated land and the remainder of the village assets. The village shareholder corporation works closely together – in some cases with overlapping personnel – with the village government and village Party committee, to make profits which are largely used for the villagers' welfare (Chung and Unger 2013; Tang 2015). Since the exclusive membership of the village shareholding corporation determines the welfare of those landless farmers, for them, the identity has been contested through a stronger identity of shareholders than peasants or urban residents.

On the other hand, the changes in residence, employment, welfare coverage, and governance arrangements have produced an increasing urban identity for the landless farmers. Especially those moved to relocation neighbourhoods, the transformation of their daily activities and community life plays a particularly significant role in shaping their 'new citizen' identity. The relocated farmers find themselves experiencing different modes of social interactions and community life when dealing with new groups and organizations in their neighbourhoods. The collective recreational activities that are commonly observed in urban neighbourhoods help the relocated villagers to adapt to new living environment, to expand their social networks, as well as to form a new community identity. Fieldwork suggests that for those who participate in neighbourhood recreational activities regularly, they are more likely to address themselves with 'we are from Neighbourhood X' than 'I am from former Village X' (Tang 2021).

The middle class also presents a rather ambiguous collective identity. Both the origins and mechanisms of development of the middle class are more complex and complicated than their counterparts in capitalist industrial societies. As Chapter 2 pointed out, the major sources for the rise of the Chinese middle class include the transfer of previously held political power, market exchange, and personal social networking. Since the mid-1990s, a majority of Chinese have reported themselves as middle class (Wang and Davis 2010). A survey in 2013 showed that more than 59% of the population consider themselves as middle class (Boehler 2013). The heterogeneous family backgrounds and diverse occupations, as well as different upward mobility patterns – which some scholars consider as an 'inconsistency between social status and economic status' (Li Chunling 2010a) – have all contributed to a lack of a collective class identity and unified class consciousness for the Chinese middle class at large, and even internal divisions (Tsang 2014; Tang 2018). Home ownership is almost universally a shared characteristic for the Chinese middle class. A national survey showed that in 2007, China's home ownership rate reached 82% (Man 2010). However, this 'housing effect' (Tomba 2010: 193) also varies with locality, divisions within the homeowner group, and various forms of new hierarchy that have been created during this process (Tang 2013). Despite their shared interests in private property rights, Chinese middle-class homeowners have not developed a unified collective agency for political change, and their homeowner activism has largely been restricted to within single neighbourhoods (Rocca 2013; Tang 2018).

In addition, the rise of entrepreneurs as an economic force has also shown no sign of a capitalist class identity or class consciousness that desires political system change. Instead, entrepreneurs are observed to have varied identities due to their different access to resources and opportunities in the Party-state system (Tsai 2007; Chen and Dickson 2010). Since a sizeable proportion of private entrepreneurs were former public-sector employees and CCP members, their connections to the Party-state have played an important role in their successful business operations (Li 2019). Instead of developing and advocating a political agenda against the Party-state, they have developed a close working relationship with it, as 'allies' (Chen and Dickson 2010) through 'socialist corporatism' (Pearson 1994). Entrepreneurs are in general supportive of the status quo through the Party-state's support to their interests. In addition to entrepreneurs, intellectuals such as university academics (Wright 2010; Tang and Unger 2013), and professionals such as lawyers (Michelson and Liu 2010) have also become supporters of the Party-state, despite their sometimes criticisms of its specific political operations.

The lack of desire for radical political change towards liberal democracy among the Chinese middle classes, results from their increasing wealth and home ownership which has fostered a sense of security (Zhang 2010); a situation where upward mobility paths are dependent on the Party-state (Tang 2018); and the Party-state's active accommodation and incorporation of them in political participation. According to CGSS 2006, 46.4% of respondents considered 'There is no need to worry about democracy if the economy continues to show stable development' (Hsiao 2010: 273). Jie Chen's (2013) study shows that the Chinese middle class as a collective is not interested in promoting democratic changes such as introducing competitive elections, although they do favour individual rights and political freedom. And studies to date have shown that the Chinese new middle class is unable to form a distinct middle-class political culture in China. The Party-state has shown its reach and control of the society in the forms of state corporatism (Unger ed. 2008), while entrepreneurs, and by and large the new middle class, tend to prefer to maintain the status quo (Chen and Dickson 2008).

Political participation

The perceptions of social inequality as well as ambiguous class identity and consciousness are to a large extent intertwined with the political behaviour of different classes and their political interaction with the CCP. Both institutional links and operational connections have been strengthened between the Party-state and different classes with respect to political activities. In particular, the Party-state has adopted a co-optation strategy for private entrepreneurs especially those in the non-public sector. According to a 2006 survey, for those who registered as private business owners after 2002, more than 32% were CCP members (Li 2019: 94). Private entrepreneurs have also become members of Chambers of Commerce and business associations organized by and through local government (Chen and Dickson 2010: 45). And more and more entrepreneurs have occupied position as deputies to the National People's Congress (NPC) and Chinese People's Political Consultative Conference (CPPCC), as well as lower order People's Congresses and People's Political Consultative Conference. In 2013, around 300 entrepreneurs (among whom more than 80 were billionaires) were elected representatives to the NPC and CPPCC (Anderlini 2013). The private entrepreneurs' participation in formal institutions has become an instrumental tool for business operations, such as obtaining bank loans and financial subsidies from the government (Zhou 2009).

At the local level, citizens' political participation is organized and channelled through the so-called social management innovation scheme in recent years. This scheme lays a special emphasis on introducing new local governance mechanisms and considers this as a shift from a government-dominated administration mode to a co-governance mode that involves diverse actors and non-state organizations. This includes introducing market groups and citizen groups to decision-making in local governance affairs, as well as the introduction of unprecedented public service delivery models through contracting service delivery to private firms and non-profit organizations (Teets 2012). From the government's perspective, innovation rests on residents' 'self-governance' through which citizens are empowered to make decisions regarding neighbourhood affairs; operation through 'co-governance' in which multiple actors (including both state and non-state actors) participate; and eventually the achievement of 'good governance' in society (Wei 2014). For local officials, this governance technique prompts them to seek ways to promote their work and improve their performance, through demonstrable, practical problem-solving policy (Heberer and Göbel 2011). In recent years, local governments have gradually accommodated more citizens from different class backgrounds as well as experts into decision-making for local policies to address various kinds of issues, including participatory budgeting (Wu and Wang 2012), public consultations for the selection of local leaders (He and Thøgersen 2010), price adjustments at the local level (Ergenc 2014), and local environmental projects (Han 2014).

At the grassroots level, political participation has evolved from political interaction determined by family class labels under Mao to involvement in governance activities and affairs associated with the specific living environment of the neighbourhood attached to the socio-economic status of the residents. Two related aspects are of particular importance: participation in resident self-organized representative groups and participation in state-led resident groups. The most common and vivid example of the resident self-organized representative groups is the homeowner association in middle-class neighbourhoods. Since the early 2000s, nationwide a rising homeowner activism has been observed in the form of increasing frequency and severity of conflicts between middle-class homeowners and property management companies and associated real estate developers, with protests led by self-organized homeowner associations among the middle-class residents. Different from the longstanding government-run neighbourhood organizations, homeowner associations can be highly autonomous neighbourhood organizations that negotiate with market actors and the state, so that: 'They constitute a new model for private association in the PRC as well as an attractive laboratory for activists who have ambitions for far-reaching political change' (Read 2007: 150–151). The rising number of effective homeowner associations and growing conflicts associated with homeowner activism in the country has become an important constraint on local governments, although in most cases the homeowner activism has restricted its mission and activities to neighbourhood affairs only and has rarely gone beyond the neighbourhood.

Those 'governance innovations' are accompanied by consistent Party-building activities at all levels of government. CCP membership has increased from less than 4% of the population in 1978, to 5.2% in 2002, nearly 5.5% in 2008, and 6.5% in 2019 with over 90 million. By June 2020, there were about 4.68 million grassroots-level Party organizations (Xinhua 2020). And nearly 50% of CCP members had tertiary education. Around 24% were under the age of 35, and over 28% were above the age of 60. Under the CCP's 'comprehensive cover' and 'big Party' strategies, its member recruitment has been extended to non-state sectors and new social organizations which have emerged during China's market reform (Dickson 2007; Shambaugh 2008; Thornton 2012; Han 2015). Since the 1990s, the CCP has deemed Party organization building in urban residential communities to be a key grassroots-level strategy (Organization Department of the Central Committee of the CCP 1996). In all neighbourhoods, there is a strong state-led political participation through the agents of the Party-state such as Residents' Committees and the CCP-led resident groups. The Organization Department of the Central Committee of the CCP (Xinhua 2018) reports that nationwide 99% of the residential communities have established community Party organizations. For the 300,000 social organizations across the country, 61.7% of them have established CCP organizations. The statistics from the Ministry of Civil Affairs (2018) suggest that by 2016, over 54% of Residents' Committee staff were CCP members. The Party members, especially in neighbourhood governance, play a significant role in directing the political participation of the citizens. From homeowner activism in middle-class neighbourhoods to local public hearing meetings to political representation at the national level, all gradually growing class identity has been heavily shadowed by the Party leadership. Party-building activities, especially at local level, foster a stronger CCP identity than class identity.

Performance and political leadership

Despite the significant involvement of the market in (re)producing classes in China, the Party-state continuous to play an essential role in shaping the performance of class through its interventions in the market economy and its dominance in the construction of social discourses. Although there are varieties in the consumption patterns and lifestyles of different classes, they tend to exhibit a consistency when it comes to social and political behaviour, accompanied by their support for the Party-state and the CCP's leadership. Consumption and lifestyle are significant to the identification of class in China today, especially private home ownership and car ownership, which are considered significant in the identification of the middle class. Chinese society presents class-oriented, status-oriented, within-the-system-oriented consumer culture and lifestyles. The inequality of opportunity plays an essential role in explaining how and why the CCP has managed to maintain social stability alongside dramatically rising incomes since the introduction of economic reform. Across different classes in China today, there is little evidence for well-established class identity and clear class consciousness leading to class antagonism. The criticism of inequality and social injustice associated with class differentiation is more driven by the desire to become part of the dominant class, rather than class antagonism. Along with the involvement of diverse governance actors from different class backgrounds in governance practices and political participation, the CCP's leadership has been consistently enhanced and accepted.

4
THE PEASANTRY UNDER THE IMPACT OF INDUSTRIALIZATION, URBANIZATION AND HOUSEHOLD REGISTRATION

Yingjie Guo

The formation and decline of the peasant class in the PRC have received scant academic attention in China scholarship, even though peasants are the subject of a burgeoning body of scholarship attracting more academic attention than any other social group in the country. This is not surprising as the extant literature on rural China concentrates on internal migration, demography, industrialization, urbanization, social inequality and other problems accompanying major processes of social change without probing into the ideological implications of the processes for class mobility. This chapter bridges the gap by spotlighting the changing roles and status of peasants in the PRC since 1949 as an elemental class, its transformation as a result of household registration and under the impact of socialist industrialization and capitalist urbanization, and the ramifications for the class, the CCP and the PRC. The evolution of the class is noteworthy not least because it is a clear indicator of the Party's ideological shifts and transformation, an essential part of the PRC's transition towards socialism with notable ramifications on its economic base and ideological superstructure, and a key aspect of social change in the country.

The chapter does not simply dwell on specific push and pull factors affecting population movement in the PRC, as is the case with a large number of internal migration studies, but takes an approach that relates micro-level to macro-level factors, most especially the CCP's class discourse and meta-discourse of the Chinese Revolution. Though migration both ways are in some cases related to natural advantages and disadvantages, by far the most critical factors stem from the Party-state's developmental strategies and political ideologies, which are, in turn, shaped by hegemonic discourses of industrialization and urbanization, where Chinese peasants and the countryside are viewed as a problem to be tackled before China can become a people's or proletarian 'dictatorship' with a socialist economic base and superstructure and a modern, industrialized, and urbanized nation-state.

DOI: 10.4324/9781003255017-5

The role and status of Chinese peasants have changed significantly over time in the CCP's meta-discourse of the Chinese Revolution as the latter has been re-articulated again and again. The class became the principal subject of the Chinese Revolution between 1927 and 1949, and its members were further elevated in the PRC's status order and represented as 'masters of the country', together with the industrial workers, in official Party-state discourses from 1949 to 1978, when the CCP continued to uphold the Revolution. Yet they were at the same time subjected to the imperatives of the PRC's socialist industrial development and treated as a reserve labour force which could be conveniently drawn into urban areas when necessary or sent back to the villages as the need for cheap labour decreased. They have been continuing to play that role since 1978, but unlike in the past, they are turned into an object of capitalist urbanization. Rural migrant workers, in particular, are becoming a new proletariat in the cities despite their comparative advantage over city dwellers in terms of land use rights in the countryside and the prospect of equal citizenship rights in the cities. Moreover, their socio-political status has declined now that they are no longer a major part of the subject of the Revolution, which the CCP has abandoned except in rhetoric, re-orienting the PRC from socialism and communism towards economic development, combining socialist and capitalist modes of production, especially through incomplete marketization and limited privatization.

The most important direct source of impact on the peasantry in the past seven decades has been household registration, the PRC government's primary gate-keeping mechanism for controlling internal migration. The system has been used during the greater part of the PRC for a couple of purposes. One is to ensure that access to comparative advantages in the cities and countryside is not freely available to all PRC citizens but regulated by state agencies in accordance with its varying developmental goals. The other is to ensure the provision of food, housing, education, medical care, and social welfare, especially in the cities. As such, it defines and perpetuates a bundle of economic, civil, and political rights and duties, creates sizeable packages of advantages and disadvantages, and is therefore a major determinant of social–political status and life chances in the PRC. Though in theory it prevents both rural and urban residents from migrating freely between the countryside and the cities, its impact has been disproportionally confined to the peasants, given rural-to-urban migration has been the norm in the PRC.

More pertinent to the peasant class is the decisive role that household registration (*hukou* 户口) has played, together with political and occupational criteria, in making and unmaking classes by maintaining and removing the boundaries between rural and urban categories. Over the last seven decades, it is *hukou* which defines the peasants' official class identity, while occupation and residence are of no more than secondary importance, as the class membership of the peasants who do not obtain urban *hukou* remains unchanged even if they move into other occupations or live in the cities for extended periods of time. The classes were identified and re-identified during the Land Reform (1946–1952) and the 'socialist education campaign' (1963–1966) on the basis of the ownership of land and other property and according to political criteria. These and other class labels were used in official files till 2002, including public security records as well as personnel dossiers and archives, as noted in Chapter 1, while class membership was a major determinant of PRC citizens' socio-political status and life chances from 1949 to 1979.

Admittedly, the function, utility, and administration of *hukou* have undergone notable changes since 1949, especially between the late 1950s and the late 1960s and during the past four decades. Government control over internal migration has fluctuated too in response to its development priorities and the changing imperatives of industrialization and urbanization. In the meantime, the status and role of the peasantry in the PRC's polity and economy have varied as well. That notwithstanding, a couple of persisting patterns are detectable in the way the government uses *hukou* to regulate migration in accordance with the needs of industrialization and urbanization and to make and unmake classes by maintaining and removing class boundaries. One is the lasting contrast between the peasants' nominal political distinction and their obvious economic disadvantage throughout the PRC. Politically, they were represented as the 'masters of the country' and constituted 'the regime's only, or surely, most legitimate, political actors' (Solinger 2004: 54–55), together with the industrial proletariat and other privileged classes, or the subject and owners of the PRC's 'people's democratic dictatorship'. But economically, they were treated as a reserve labour force for industry, while agriculture was subjected to the imperatives of industrialization and urbanization. The other pattern is the steady decline of the peasantry in the reform era both as an occupational category and as a class amid the rapid development of industrial and service sectors. The decline of the class can be easily seen from the dramatic contraction of rural population, particularly the number of peasants actively engaged in farming. The percentage of the PRC's agricultural labour force in the national total dropped from 70.5% in 1978 to 42.90 in 2019, while that of the rural population went down from 82.08% to 39.40 in the same period. Of more significance to the CCP and the PRC are the peasant class' political decline and the loss of its meaning as represented in Party discourses from the mid-1920s to 1978.

The peasants' role and status in the Chinese Revolution

Historically, peasants enjoyed high social status in China's agrarian civilization, ranking above artisans and merchants among the 'four estates' that made up the mainstream traditional society. But this group was relegated to the periphery and treated as an object of social engineering in the modern era as the country's intellectual and political elites, with rare exceptions, hankered after modernization and became indifferent to and even contemptuous of peasants and the rural way of life. Among other things, modernization in China's discursive field since the mid-nineteenth century has come to mean industrialization and urbanization, or more precisely, the subordination of the rural periphery to the industrial, urban centre (Xu and Xu 1999: 1). The CCP has continued to look upon the peasants and the countryside through the same lens since 1949 while portraying both positively during its decades-long armed struggle and the Mao era not least because rural support was indispensable to the Party and its struggle.

The negative perception of the peasantry among early Chinese communist leaders was strikingly consistent with the views of pioneers of communism. Marx and Engels spoke of 'the idiocy of rural life' and compared the French peasants to a sack of potatoes on the grounds that their field of production permitted no division of labour in its cultivation, no application of science, no multifariousness of development, no diversity of talent, and no wealth of social relationships (Marx and Engels 1848): 14; Marx 1978 [1852]: 14). They also described the peasantry as isolated, unsophisticated, primitive, ignorant of the larger forces around them, conservative, reactionary, and unable to constitute a unified and purposive political force (Marx and Engels 1848): 17–18). Chen Duxiu (1984 [1923], 1995 [1921]) saw Chinese peasants in the same light, asserting that they were too uneducated, conservative and ignorant to fight for communism. Mao Zedong (1991 [1943]: 931), despite his involvement in peasant movements in the 1920s and 1930s, observed in 1943 that peasants' family-based farming formed the economic foundation of China's feudal rule. The CCP's central committee reminded the Party in 1953 that peasants were naturally predisposed towards capitalism even though they were prepared to embrace socialism (Central Committee of CCP 1989 [1953]: 213).

Nevertheless, the CCP gave poor and middle-class peasants an indispensable role to play in the Chinese Revolution from 1927 to 1949, most especially during the Party's Agrarian Revolution, the Land Reform, resistance against Japanese invasion, and military campaigns against the Guomindang. Party leaders had come to agree by 1927 that the Chinese Revolution could not succeed without the peasants' support and participation. As Mao Zedong stressed repeatedly, 'only by forming a firm alliance with the poor and middle peasants can the proletariat lead the revolution to victory' (Mao 1939: 324). Starting from the 1940s, Mao Zedong began to refer to the peasant class, together with the proletariat, petit bourgeoisie, and the national bourgeoisie, as 'the people'. He spoke on numerous occasions before 1949 about the critical importance of the peasantry to the CCP and the Chinese Revolution, acknowledging, in particular, the decisive role of the class during the anti-Japanese war and the War of Liberation. He characterized the former as essentially a peasant war (Mao 1940: 366–367) and regarded rural support as indispensable to the CCP's victory because it was mainly by relying on the 16 million peasants in the areas which had completed the Land Reform that the Party won the War of Liberation (Mao Zedong 1987 [1950b]: 397).

In 'On New Democracy', Mao thus summarized his views about the Chinese peasants which were scattered in his writings and speeches (Mao 1940: 350, 366–367):

- China's national question was essentially a peasant question.
- The Chinese Revolution was essentially 'a peasant revolution'.
- The peasant problem was 'the basic problem of the Chinese revolution'.
- The strength of the peasants was the main strength of the Chinese Revolution.

- The Three People's Principles were essentially 'the principles of a peasant revolution'.
- The politics of 'new democratic revolution' was to give peasants their rights.
- Mass culture meant raising the cultural levels of the peasants.
- The peasants were among the 'basic forces determining China's fate', together with the proletariat and the petit bourgeoisie, and the 'basic components of the state and governmental structure' in the future people's republic.

The CCP was no doubt obliged to adhere to Mao's views after 1949, keep its promises, and reward the peasants for their irreplaceable contribution to its victory over the Nationalist Party. Most important to the CCP were the nature and objectives of the Chinese Revolution, which Mao regarded as a 'peasant revolution' where the liberation of the peasant class was both a means and an end. The Revolution was not likely to succeed unless it liberated the peasants and incentivized them as part of their mobilization, while its success must be manifested by their liberation, which entailed material and symbolic rewards, most notably land ownership and political power and status. It was therefore logical for Mao to include the peasants in 'the people' who were to 'unite to form their own state' and to enjoy the right to vote and the freedom of speech, assembly, association, and so on in New China, and who were to enforce the 'people's democratic dictatorship' over bad elements and the enemy classes, suppressing them and forcing them to behave themselves (Mao 1961 [1949]: 417–418). Indisputably, it was as a class, not as an occupational category, that the peasantry was included in 'the people'.

The political status of the peasantry was upgraded in internal CCP documents circulated in 1951, which elevated the class, now widely known as 'the semi-proletariat', into the 'leading class' alongside the industrial proletariat. But the elevation was short-lived and came to an end when Mao Zedong rejected it (1999 [1951]). The Party officially designated 'the people' as the political subject of the PRC in the first state constitution, adopted at the first meeting of the First National People's Congress on 20 September 1954, and represented the constituent classes on the national flag and state insignia in the form of four small stars. Its status was somewhat downgraded in the constitution of 1975, or 'the constitution of the Cultural Revolution', which revised the PRC from 'people's democratic dictatorship' to 'proletarian dictatorship', although the class remained part of 'the people', which now included the workers, peasants, and soldiers. The constitution of 1982 reverted to the definition of the PRC as 'people's democratic dictatorship' without spelling out the composition of 'the people'. The latter definition has been retained in all the subsequent versions of the PRC constitution. The peasantry has thus remained one of the classes who are constitutionally entitled to own and implement the PRC's dictatorship.

However, CCP leaders were not so sure about what role to assign to the peasant class at each stage of the PRC's economy during its unmapped-out transition from the 'new democratic revolution' to the socialist stage of the Chinese Revolution. Their answer to that question depended upon their view of what sort of economic base should be constructed and what qualitative and quantitative criteria must be met before the transition could be completed. There were Party leaders who were not even sure that the new republic was ready to start transitioning into socialism given the backward productive forces and underdevelopment of capitalism in China before 1949. There was little in Marx's and Engels' works for the Party to draw on as the objective class condition of the peasants at the beginning of the PRC was not something that Marx and Engels could have predicted. Marx and Engels (1848: 17–18, 31) made it reasonably clear that

1) a socialist system would achieve the abolition of property in land and application of all rents of land to public purposes;
2) it would achieve the combination of agriculture with manufacturing industries and the abolition of the distinction between town and country;
3) the proletariat would centralize all instruments of production in the hands of the state;
4) the peasantry as a whole would have sunk into the proletariat in advanced capitalist societies (before socialism began), together with other lower strata of the middle class, including small tradespeople, shopkeepers and handicraftsmen, partly because their limited capital did not suffice for the scale on which modern industry was carried on and partly because their specialized skill was rendered worthless by new methods of production.

However, what the CCP took over in 1949 was not an advanced capitalist society where the peasant class had sunk into the proletariat, and in the first decade of the PRC, the CCP considered it to be unrealistic to abolish private property, centralize all instruments of production, or eliminate the rural–urban distinction. For a long time before the Cultural Revolution, the Party leadership did not reach clear consensus on when to begin the transition towards socialism, how to proceed, when to complete the transition, and what role to assign to the peasant class.

Mao's own thinking about the desirability of capitalist elements in the 'new democratic revolution' and under socialism shifted time and over again till the early 1960s. He stated repeatedly as early as the 1940s that the main target of the 'new democratic revolution' was imperialism and feudalism, not capitalism. Given the CCP's conception of feudalism, the primary domestic contradiction to be resolved during the PRC's transition was the exploitation of the peasant class by landlords and rich peasants. The Land Reform was thus the Party's top priority after the War of Resistance against Japan; it was designed to eradicate feudal modes of rural production and to 'liberate' the peasant class economically and politically. Mao reiterated consistently from the 1940s to 1950 that capitalism should be allowed and encouraged to develop further, sufficiently or freely in New China. Private land ownership was explicable and justifiable in this context.

Most pertinent to the CCP's thinking about capitalism in the early days of the PRC were the comments Mao made at the third session of the CCP's seventh national congress in June 1950. He warned Party leaders who advocated immediate action against capitalism, stating emphatically that 'The notion among some that we can eliminate capitalism and start socialism early is wrong and does not agree with the actual condition of our country' (Mao Zedong 1977 [1950a]: 81–82). But he changed his mind in June 1952, when he inserted a sentence in a document to be issued by the CCP's United Front Department to stress that 'Now that the landlord class and the bureaucratic bourgeoisie have been brought down, the principal contradiction in China is the contradiction between the proletariat and the national bourgeoisie' (Mao, cited in Pang Song and Lin Yunhui 1993: 296). He went further between then and late 1955. In 1953, he referred to the CCP's current struggle as 'a profound revolution' which would 'bury the capitalist system and all other systems of exploitation once and for all' (1977 [1953]: 94). He reminded the Party in 1955 that its aim was to obliterate capitalism from the PRC and the face of the earth, and that '[t]he purpose of our socialist transformation of agriculture is to cut off the source of capitalism in the vast countryside' and to establish a new alliance between the peasant class and the industrial proletariat (Mao 1977 [1953]: 212). He back-peddled in December 1956, presumably to appease prominent figures not affiliated to the CCP, assuring them that privately owned enterprises, including large factories, would be allowed to exist for another twenty years, while those owned by overseas Chinese would not be confiscated within a hundred years (Mao Zedong 1999 [1956b]: 170). Mao did not keep that promise but, during the Anti-Rightist Campaign in 1957, settled on a radical leftism that was determined to eliminate capitalism and to strive for socialism and communism.

Theoretically, the role and status of the peasantry would vary considerably in different scenarios where socialist and capitalist elements were variously combined in the PRC's modes of production. The existence of private land ownership in the countryside from 1949 and 1956 was consistent with the CCP's policy of allowing and encouraging capitalism to develop. Left to their own devices, it was possible for peasants to experience upward or downward mobility or maintain the status quo. Those who fared well could scale up to become middle peasants, rich peasants or landlords. Those who suffered increasing poverty would sink to the pre-1949 class condition of poor peasants or agricultural proletarians. For ideological reasons, the Party could not legitimately allow either scenario to happen. Its response to such scenarios was the collectivization of agriculture, as its leaders made clear, although it can be contended that collectivization was more geared towards industrialization than socialism. While collective land ownership and other means of production were presented by CCP as a step forward in the PRC's socialist transition, it fell far short of the socialist benchmark set by Marx and Engels and precluded the possibility of the class assuming roles and statuses as it would in a fully fledged socialist system or advanced capitalist societies. Moreover, the imperatives of the CCP's 'socialist industrialization' project between the 1950s and the 1970s, combined with historical contingencies, prevented its members from leaving the class *en masse*, as will be discussed in detail later. Still more importantly, tighter state control over rural-to-urban migration using *hukou* since the mid-1950s hardened the boundary between the rural and urban classes.

The peasants who moved into the cities between 1949 and 1956 could become temporary or permanent proletarians. It is worth noting, however, that there were two different proletarian classes in the cities during this period due to the PRC's hybrid economy with both socialist and capitalist elements. One comprised those who were employed in privately owned enterprises, and the other included the workers of state-owned enterprises. The former inhabited a class condition that differed little from that of proletarian classes in capitalist societies, although the condition was mediated to some extent by CCP ideologies and policies. The class identity of those employed in state-owned enterprises was essentially the same as that of the whole industrial workers across the country between 1956 and 1978, when the private ownership of productive property was abolished. The CCP backtracked in the reform era to the 'elementary stage of socialism' by introducing the 'household responsibility system' while maintaining collective land ownership and continuing, until recently, to segregate the PRC's rural and urban classes by the means of *hukou*. The latter remains the ultimate determinant of the peasants' class identity, and the responsibility system and land ownership combine to forestall the emergence of class conditions which can be found in capitalist systems where land is owned privately and treated as an exchangeable commodity.

At the same time, the cities have witnessed once again the bifurcation of the industrial proletariat into two classes which are usually lumped together in official CCP communications and the academic literature but which can be easily differentiated on the basis of their contrasting class conditions, particularly in terms of their relations to the means of production: one in the state- and collectively owned economy and the other in the private sector. Consequently, the PRC's current urban class map is similar to what existed between 1949 and 1956, although not the same class labels are used to identify the existing social groups. The 'national bourgeoisie', for instance, has disappeared from the CCP's reform-era terminology; private entrepreneurs are now referred to as 'new social groups', which do not belong to any of the officially designated classes. At any rate, the present and future roles and statuses of these classes differ and will continue to follow different trajectories depending on whether the CCP decides to transform the PRC's economic base in the direction of socialism or capitalism. The peasants who join different classes then have different futures in store.

Unlike in the pre-reform era, however, the government has relaxed political control over rural-to-urban migration in the past four decades in response to the demand of the PRC's partial market economy. Ironically, market economy and capitalist industrialization in the reform era have done what the planned economy and socialist industrialization during Mao era failed to do, that is, absorbing a large part of the surplus rural labour into industry and creating a 'new class of industrial workers'. Nevertheless, for a long time its members were unable to opt out of the peasant class and join the urban proletariat unless they obtained urban *hukou*. Class boundary in this case was a political product in so far as it was produced and maintained politically, whereas economic class conditions were at best of secondary importance. It was only a decade or so ago that the government began to gradually reduce the ambit of *hukou* so that peasants could settle in urban areas permanently. This time, the government is not motivated by socialist industrialization or socialist transition but by capitalist urbanization in response to the demand of market capitalism for cheap labour and increasing consumption and in accordance with received blueprints of 'modern' societies where the overwhelming majority of the populace live in urban areas.

Auxiliaries to socialist industrialization

The role that CCP assigned to the peasants in the PRC's transformation from 1949 to 1978 contrasts sharply with their task in the CCP's decades-long armed struggle, when the class played an indispensable part and constituted the principal subject of the Chinese Revolution. Most striking about the class during the period 1949–1978 was its divergent status in the polity and the economy. Politically, they were elevated to the top of the PRC's status order, ranked second only to the industrial workers; yet, their economic condition fell far short of their political prestige. They were treated as food providers not only for themselves but also for the urban residents, and as a convenient labour force which could be readily mobilized as the need arose and sent back to the countryside when the need decreased. Their dual role and contrasting status were dictated by the PRC's socialist transition and 'socialist industrialization'. *Hukou*, which initially served the purposes of household registration for law and order purposes, gradually became a migration-control mechanism by which the state segregated the countryside and the cities and maintained the boundary between the peasant class and the proletariat.

The PRC's socialist transition began in earnest in 1952. The process would be completed in ten to fifteen years, as Mao Zedong (cited in Bo Yibo 1996: 221) announced in the same year. Whether the task could be accomplished between 1962 and 1967 was another question; the economic base and ideological superstructure to emerge in the wake of the transition were bound to differ vastly from the socialist utopia that Marx and Engels had in mind. Consequently, the socialist system which eventually came into being would only be partially socialist at best by Marx and Engels' standards. The point of this observation is not to hold the CCP to vision of the communist pioneers, which may not be realizable in the PRC, or anywhere else, in the foreseeable future; rather, it highlights the Party's enormous difficulties in adapting Marxist theory to Chinese practice and in squaring its ideology with its shifting and pragmatic economic policies, which are easily discernible in the dynamics, trajectory and outcome of the PRC's socialist transition.

Though the timeframe of the transition was rather ambitious considering the underdeveloped productive forces in the PRC, which was widely acknowledged by CCP leaders, the latter were too impatient to stick to it. At its eighth national congress in 1956, the CCP declared that the transition from the 'new democratic revolution' to the 'socialist revolution' had been basically completed, and a socialist system had been basically established as a result of the Land Reform and the Socialist Transformation (1953–1956). It must be stressed though that the socialist transition was not meant to transform the PRC's entire economic base but concentrated on 'the gradual realization of socialist industrialization and the gradual socialist transformation of agriculture, handicraft industry, and capitalist industry and commerce' (The Constitution of the People's Republic of China 1954). As such, it did not and could not bring about Marx and Engels' socialist utopia, which was not simply characterized by state and collective ownership of productive property but by a range of other defining features as well. These include, as previously noted, the disappearance of the rural–urban distinction and the emergence of a new ruling class in the proletariat, which represented the productive forces in social production and assumed dominance in the polity.

The rural–urban distinction in the PRC in 1949 was too apparent to be denied. It had not diminished but had been expanded and intensified by the time the CCP announced the completion of the PRC's socialist transition. It has remained prominent ever since. That was not a natural development or an objective reality ensuing from existing modes of production, but in large part a result of ideological-political subjectivity, or state policies and decisions. The government deliberately maintained and hardened the distinction during the greater part of the first three decades of the republic, starting from 1952. Even if the CCP had been committed to eliminating the distinction, it would not likely achieve that goal during the socialist transition, as Marx and Engels anticipated to happen inevitably during all societies' metamorphosis from capitalism to socialism. Nor would the combination of agriculture with manufacturing industries take place. And nor would the peasantry sink into the proletariat. As a matter of fact, these defining features of Marx and Engels's version of socialism are still absent in the PRC today.

The first reason for that was the size of the Chinese proletariat. The class was merely the reputed ruling class in the polity but not the dominant class in the economy in terms of its total numbers or the proportion of industrial output in the country's GDP. As many as 89.4% of the populace lived in the countryside in 1949, whereas only 10.6% of China's total population (about 540 million) were urban residents (Hu Angang 2014: 61). There were only 21.28 million industrial workers in the PRC in 1952 (Nan Liangjin and Xue Jinjun 2002: 15). The country's industrial output in the same year amounted to no more than 10% of its total GDP (Zhang Zhongfa 2008: 40). It can therefore be argued that Marx and Engels set the bar too high for the PRC to reach, or that the objective economic conditions for the negation of capitalism by socialism had not taken shape in the country before the socialist transition began. It can be argued too that the CCP was not headed in the direction that the communist pioneers pointed to, that its economic development plan and the socialist transformation, particularly in the 1950s and 1960s, were not geared towards these goals despite official slogans which appear consistent with the latter.

In the countryside, land ownership after the Land Reform, together with rural *hukou*, had the effect of pinning the peasants down to the land and locking them into their officially designated class. Land Reform was not designed to abolish private ownership but to transfer ownership from landlords and rich peasants to poor and lower-middle class peasants. Though the campaign ostensibly sought to eliminate exploitation and feudalism, it was also aimed at rewarding the good rural classes for their contribution to the Chinese Revolution, securing their support for it instead of speeding up the transition towards socialism, and transforming the power structure and status order in rural society in line with the stated objectives of the Revolution. The Agricultural Cooperative Movement (1949–1956), combined with state control of migration by the means of *hukou* and state monopoly of purchase and sales of agricultural produce and products, did even more to constrain the peasant's mobility than private land ownership (Wu Li 2007: 24).

Of still more impact on the role and status of the peasant class was the government's development policy from the 1950s to the 1970s, which prioritized industry, particularly heavy industry, to the point of constraining the development of agriculture and subjecting the latter to its needs. The peasants were expected to contribute to the PRC's socialist industrialization and make sacrifices for the sake of the project instead of advancing productive forces in agriculture or whittling down the rural–urban distinction in a bid to speed up the socialist transition. As Chen Yun (cited in Li Debin 1989 [1950]: 20) put it candidly, in an agrarian economy like China's, industrialization depended on agriculture, and the government could not find the financial resources needed for industrial development unless it turned to the countryside. Mao Zedong (1999 [1955]: 431) confirmed in 1955 that a large part of the financial input into the PRC's industrialization must be accumulated in agriculture. As a matter of fact, agriculture contributed about 0.45 trillion *yuan* to industry between 1954 and 1978, or 155 hundred million *yuan* every year on average (Zhang Zhongfa 2007: 40). That was not the only contribution the peasants made to the PRC's socialist industrialization. On top of it, they served as additional labour to the industrial sector when it was needed and provided food and other essential agricultural produce to the urban residents.

Twenty-two million peasants migrated to urban areas in 1954 in response to growing demands for additional labour as a result of accelerated industrialization, and that number rose to 25 million in 1956 and 30 million in 1956 (Guojia tongjiju 1956: 409). Between 1958 and 1960, an average of 10 million peasants moved into the cities every year; as many as 32 million went to the cities in 1958 (Yang Yunyan 2003: 105). The number of industrial workers in state-owned enterprises jumped from 20.81 million in 1957 to 45.32 million in 1958 (Xu Dixin 1988: 287). It must be pointed out, however, that the PRC's socialist industrialization strategy from the 1950s to the 1970s actually constrained the capacity of industry to absorb rural labour and enable more peasants to join the proletariat, and that the peasants who entered the cities were not all able to stay there permanently or join the urban proletariat. Not that there was no rural surplus labour force or push and pull factors to drive rural-to-urban migration. A major push factor in the countryside was the stagnation of income starting from 1952 which poor and lower-middle class peasants experienced as the villages had run out of land for redistribution (Wang Haiguang 2011: 8). Much of the surplus labour force was keen to work in the cities due to widening rural–urban disparity in income and life chances. The urban industrial workers' wages rose by 60%–120% between 1949 and 1952, whereas the average annual household income in the countryside increased by around 30% (Xu Haoran 2017: 39). The emergence of rural surplus labour and growing rural–urban disparity combined with new opportunities in the cities to drive rural-to-urban migration in the 1950s.

Yet, industry's capacity to absorb the rural surplus labour and enable more peasants to join the proletariat was constrained as a result of the prioritization of capital-intensive heavy industry over labour-intensive light industry. Only 37.23 million new jobs were created in the industrial sector from 1952 to 1978; at the same time, the available workforce in the country increased by 191.72 million (Xu Jingyong 2001: 7). In all, around 20 million rural residents, including unemployed spouses and children, ended up staying in the cities and left the peasant class between 1955 and 1964 (Yang Yunyan 2003: 105), while the proportion of the urban population rose marginally from 12.5% in 1952 to 17.9% in 1978 (Guojia tongjiju 1984: 23). During the following decade, opportunities for peasants to join the proletariat remained limited due to employment and food-provision pressures in the cities under the impact of the Cultural Revolution. Large numbers of urban youths were sent down to the countryside to be 're-educated' by the peasant class and to reduce urban unemployment and the pressure on state-provided resources.

Coupled with the limited opportunities for employment arising from the PRC's socialist industrialization were dramatic fluctuations in economic development, which had even more devastating effects on the peasants' class mobility and the rural–urban distinction. The fluctuations had little to do with objective productive forces but resulted from unexpected events and sporadic political campaigns which led to substantial contraction of the industrial sector and notable decreases in the urban workforce. One study reveals the dramatic fluctuation with a simple indicator – the proportion of the rural labour force in the national total: 85% in 1952, when Land Reform was completed; 81% in 1957 as a result of accelerated industrialization; 58% during the Great Leap Forward in 1958; and 82% in 1962, when the government was forced to abandon its ambitious plans for accelerated, large-scale industrialization owning to the combined, catastrophic consequences of the campaign, natural disasters across the country, and the Sino-Soviet split (Hu Jingbei 2019: 6). Another study estimates that the PRC's total number of state-owned enterprises decreased by over 18,000 in 1962, while around 24.46 million industrial workers were laid off across the country, of which 16.41 million returned to the countryside (Dangdai Zhongguo bianjibu 1990: 132).

Also significant was the impact of the peasants' officially assigned role as food providers on their class mobility and the PRC's rural–urban distinction. Their role was determined by the government's urgent need to ensure agricultural production and keep its cost low so that food provision to urban residents, as well as peasants themselves, could be guaranteed. The challenge for the government was daunting despite noticeable increases in agricultural output following the Land Reform, as food shortage across the country had grown acute due to the devastating impact of protracted wars on agriculture and worsened after the new PRC government decided to stop importing grain in the early 1950s. China imported 1.26 million tonnes of wheat on average every year from 1922 to 1930, and the import increased significantly in the 1930s and 1940s (JDY 1954). But 'China's 50-year history of relying on imported rice and wheat had come to an end' by 1954, as Zhang Naiqi, head of the Ministry of Food, announced at the NPC (cited in Yang Jisheng 2008 [1954]: 38). Food shortage deteriorated further as a result of increasing urban population in the early 1950s, which rose from 57.65 million in 1949 to 82.49 in 1954 (Guojia tongjiju 1984: 81). The government was short of 2 million tonnes of grain between 1 July 1952 and 30 June 1953 alone (Zhang Naiqi in Yang Jisheng 2008 [1954]: 38). In 1957, the food for China's urban population of 99.49 million was supplied by the state (Guojia tongjiju 1984: 114). It was obviously necessary for the government to keep up and increase agricultural production and to limit food consumption by maintaining a large enough workforce in farming and by controlling rural-to-urban migration while allowing industry to recruit from among peasants. To this end, the government introduced the 'unified purchase and sale' of grain in 1953 – a policy that was implemented with varying rigour until 1992.

Admittedly, the government's new policy can be seen as part of the PRC's socialist transition in so far as it largely put an end to non-government purchase and sales of grain through the market and reduced the space for capitalist commodity exchange. However, the policy was, first and foremost, intended to facilitate industrialization while ensuring food provision and social stability in the country and particularly in the cities, as PRC analysts concur (Lu Feng 1989; Lin Yifu et al. 1994; Xu and Xu 1999; Liu Chuanjiang 2000; Wu Li 2001; Xu Jingyong 2001; Wang Haiguang 2011; Hu Angang 2014). It was certainly not designed to enable more peasants to join the proletariat or whittle down the rural–urban distinction. Actually, the opposite was true. On the one hand, the policy tied peasants to farming and to their designated class as never before; on the other, it made it more difficult than ever for them to enter the cities.

What specifically tied peasant to the land was the quotas on the amount of grain to be produced and sold to the state at low price, which varied to some extent from time to time and from place to place. The average amount of grain that eight townships in Hubei Province sold to the state in 1954 was 194.95 kilograms per head, or 45.6% of the per-capita yield, although a small part of it was resold and distributed to peasants within the townships who were exceptionally short of food (JZBW 1957: 36). In the same year, the proportion of grain sold to the state by ten townships in Jiangxi Province and taken out of the area by the state amounted to 35.9% of their total output (ZRGLB 1959: 3). Production and acquisition quotas were imposed on individual households before the collectivization of agriculture and on cooperatives, production teams, production brigades, and communes afterwards. In either case, production would be affected, making it harder for families and teams to fulfil their quotas, if able-bodied peasants left for the cities. Moreover, the new pressure on peasants to stay put in the countryside was combined with additional difficulties for living in the cities starting from August 1955, especially during the Cultural Revolution, when the rationing of food and essential goods, such as cooking oil, meat and cloth, was introduced in the cities and extended to an increasingly broader range of items. Though it was still possible for holders of rural *hukou* to buy a limited amount of food and essential goods on the 'black market' or through personal networks in urban areas, it was impossible for anyone without urban *hukou* to survive in the cities for long or settle there. Few peasants could transfer to urban *hukou* unless they were employed in an urban work unit on a permanent, not casual or temporary, basis.

In consequence, the function, utility and administration of *hukou* were transformed dramatically. Between 1949 and 1955, peasants had the opportunity to leave the countryside and the peasant class more freely, as local and departmental policies did not restrict the freedom of migration and were not concerned with residential or socio-economic benefits or entitlements, even though government control over rural-to-urban migration began to tighten in mid-1952. The first PRC constitution (1954) stated explicitly that Chinese citizens' freedom of migration would be protected. In June 1956, the State Council instructed relevant government departments and local authorities to establish a unified national *hukou* system. It made clear that rural and urban *hukou* were not to be differentiated. However, the government transformed the system drastically in late 1956 and 1957. For the first time, it began to treat rural and urban *hukou* as two categories and in effect put an end to the freedom of migration (NPC, Regulations on Household Registration of the People's Republic of China 1958). The freedom disappeared altogether from the PRC's 1975 constitution. Increasing control over migration in the 1950s was no doubt related to limited employment opportunities and mounting pressure for food provision in the cities. With the policy of 'unified purchase and sales', the government linked the *hukou* system to urban food and service provision and reinforced it as a control mechanism more rigorously than in the past, thus erecting a daunting barrier between the countryside and the cities and between rural and urban classes.

Historians, economists and social scientists have long lamented the peasants' loss of the freedom of migration, the economic and social segregation of rural and urban areas, and the creation of 'dual economies' and 'binary social structures' and 'one country, two systems', as well as negative effects of *hukou* on economic development, urbanization, and peasants' rights and life chances. What is rarely noted is the huge impact of the combination of *hukou* and 'unified purchase and sale' on the peasant's class mobility. In tying the majority of peasants to the land and in segregating the countryside and the cities, the PRC state also pinned the peasantry to their designated class, made it impossible for them to join the proletariat, solidified and enlarged the rural–urban distinction, and steered the PRC away from Marx and Engels's socialist utopia.

Objects of capitalist urbanization

The PRC's 'reform and opening-up' programme since 1978 is a systemic negation or disarticulation of the Chinese Revolution and of socialism as Marx, Engels, and

Mao Zedong envisioned it, despite the CCP's claims to the contrary. The Party's dramatic discursive shift was marked by its fundamental departures from Maoism and accepted notions of socialism in the PRC, which the Party's central committee articulated unequivocally at the third session of its eleventh national congress in December 1978. It reiterated that 'reform and opening-up' meant, above all, the repudiation of the 'erroneous theory and practice of taking class struggle as the key link', the rejection of 'continuous revolution under the people's dictatorship', and the 'historic' shift in the focus of its work onto economic development (Central Committee, 22 December 1978). What was not stated so explicitly was the top Party leaders' decision to allow marketization and privatization and to gradually switch to a predominantly capitalist mode of production. The role and status of the peasant class since 1978 have been transformed accordingly, while obvious differences exist between 1978 and 2011 and the past decade due to the 'new urbanization' programme and major *hukou* policy changes in the Xi Jinping era.

The most clearly articulated goal of economic development in the reform era is to enable and encourage Chinese citizens to get rich, instead of being geared towards achieving the abolition of private property or the centralization of all instruments of production in the hands of the state, as Marx and Engels anticipated to happen in all socialist societies. Thus, the PRC's economy is not intended to adhere to a socialist mode of production, as during the Mao era. Quite the contrary: the CCP's new mantra since 1978 is the liberation of productive forces which, ironically, are believed to be fettered by the socialist mode of production of the Mao era. As openly abandoning socialism is not an acceptable option for the Party, it can only re-define it or backtrack. Hence, the top leadership declared in October 1987 that the PRC was still at the 'elementary stage of socialism', which would last at least a century. The thrust of the discursive re-articulation of socialist development is essentially twofold. One, the PRC's transition from 1949 to 1978, including its socialist industrialization, proceeded from hot-headed, leftist assumptions about the productive forces, and the mistake must be corrected. Two, a more realistic and appropriate economic base would be less socialist and allow capitalist and other non-socialist elements.

The principal mistakes to be corrected in the countryside in the early days of the reform era were collectivization and tight state restriction on commodity exchange through market mechanisms. The new 'household responsibility system', which was a compromise between private and collective land ownership, granted land use rights to the peasants while retaining land in the hands of administrative villages. The goal of rural reform was to rid rural areas of poverty and backward socio-economic conditions, transform China from an agrarian society to a modern, industrial country, and develop a 'highly developed commercial economy' to supplant China's predominantly 'natural and semi-natural economy' (Central Committee, 22 December 1978). The combination of agriculture with manufacturing industries and the abolition of rural–urban distinction has rarely been mentioned since 1978 in CCP communications as goals of economic development or Chinese socialism.

Consequently, the peasant class, like the proletariat, is entirely detached from the socialist transition and the Chinese Revolution, now that the CCP has put these ideological-political projects on hold for a century. The class's declining status was symbolized most expressively by the demotion of Chen Yonggui (1914–1986), who rose from Party Secretary of Dazhai Village to Vice-Premier of the State Council, from the top leadership in 1980. There has never been a single peasant representative on the CCP's Politburo or anywhere else in the top Party-state apparatus ever since. Since Jiang Zemin launched his theory of 'three represents' in the early 2000s, 'the people' has been re-defined and come to refer to the whole PRC citizenry and the ethnic-cultural Chinese nation more broadly. Though the peasants' nominal political role and status remain intact in the constitutions of the CCP and the PRC, there is now even less substance to it than during the Mao era. They are neither the principal subject of the Chinese Revolution nor collective owners of the 'people's democratic dictatorship'. In fact, the peasant class is little more than an occupational category with no political role to play in the PRC's polity other than as ordinary citizens and as the largest social group that the CCP claims to represent for the sake of its legitimacy.

The peasants' role in the economy of the reform era has changed as well. They are no longer auxiliaries to socialist industrialization not just because industrialization now takes place in a fledgling non-socialist market economy, irrespective of its official description as 'socialist market economy', and is driven by private as well as state capital, but also because agriculture is unable to financially support industrial development. They are not compelled to provide food to urban residents either thanks to new state policies, most notably the gradual phasing out of the 'unified purchase and sales' of grain and other agricultural produce, the abolition of agricultural tax, and increasing reliance on commercial incentives and market mechanisms to ensure food supply. Starting from 1983, the government began to allow peasants to sell part of what used to be delivered to the state as 'tax grain' and reduced the range of state collection. In 1980, the government collected 183 varieties of produce but this had reduced to 38 at the end of 1984. State monopoly on grain was officially terminated in 1992. Peasants in Shanghai stopped delivering tax grain to the state as early as 2000, following the abolition of the agricultural tax in the municipality. Twenty-eight provincial jurisdictions followed its example between March 2004 and the end of 2005. For the first time in China's long history, agricultural tax was abolished across the country in January 2006, lifting a huge burden on the peasants, reducing their pressure for grain production, and freeing large numbers of peasants from the land. As a result of government policy changes, the role of reform-era peasants is to create wealth for themselves and contribute to the PRC's economic development, most especially as an irreplaceable source of cheap labour for the urban industrial and service sectors.

Accelerated economic development through marketization and privatization has created unprecedented employment and business opportunities in urban areas throughout the reform era and led to increased relaxation of state control over internal migration, enabling large numbers of peasants to work in towns and cities.

TABLE 4.1 China's labour force in agricultural and non-agricultural sectors, 1978–2019

Year	Total Employed (million)	Agricultural (million)	Non-Agricultural (million)	Percentage of Agricultural (%)	Percentage of Non-Agricultural (%)
1978	401.52	283.13	118.39	70.5	29.5
1980	423.61	291.17	132.44	68.7	31.3
1985	498.73	311.05	187.68	62.4	37.6
1990	639.09	384.28	254.81	60.1	39.9
1995	679.47	354.68	324.79	52.2	47.8
2000	720.85	489.34	231.51	67.88	32.12
2005	746.47	462.58	283.89	61.97	38.03
2010	761.05	414.18	346.87	54.42	45.58
2015	774.51	370.41	404.10	47.82	52.18
2019	774.71	332.24	442.47	42.90	57.10

Source: *Zhongguo tongji nianjian* 2020 [China Statistical Yearbook 2020]

In the first four decades of the reform era, around 640 million peasants moved into the cities, pushing China's urbanization in terms of the number of long-term urban residents up from 17.9% to 58.5%. Of those peasants, about 116 million entered non-agricultural sectors, with the total number increasing 8.9% per annum on average, or by 5.55 million persons per year, as Table 4.1 indicates. By the end of 2019, China's urban population had reached 848.43 million, or 60.60% of the total, although urban *hukou* holders represent 44.38%, while the number of rural migrant workers had increased to 290.77 million by the end of 2019 (Guojia tongjiju 2020a and b). In consequence, the peasant class has become much smaller since 1978, while the percentage of the rural population in the nation has gone down by more than a half between 1949 and 2019, as can be seen from Table 4.2.

There is no denying that these reform measures and new employment opportunities enabled most peasants to become richer in the reform era than at any other time before 1978. Still, it was still rather difficult until recently for the majority of rural migrant workers to obtain urban *hukou*, so that most of them remained migrants and were formally locked into the peasant class. That is no longer the case in the Xi Jinping era, thanks to the government's 'new urbanization' programme, which has consciously ramped up China's urbanization to ensure it joins the ranks of modern nation-states not simply by setting quota for transferring rural population to urban areas but also by reforming the *hukou* system more drastically than ever before. Unlike the urbanization in capitalist societies, as Marx and Engels (1848: 14) described the process, it is the CCP more than the bourgeoisie which 'has subjected the country to the rule of the towns', 'created enormous cities', and 'greatly increased the urban population as compared with the rural'. It is safe to assert that China's urbanization, like its economic development in the reform era as a whole, is a result of the collaboration between the Party and capitalists. One of their common goals is greater consumption and increasing urbanization. From

TABLE 4.2 China's rural and urban population, 1949–2019

Year	Total Population (million)	Rural (million)	Urban (million)	Percentage of Rural (%)	Percentage of Urban (%)
1949	541.67	484.02	57.65	89.36	10.64
1978	962.59	790.14	172.45	82.08	17.92
1980	987.05	795.65	191.40	80.61	19.39
1985	1058.51	811.41	250.94	75.48	23.71
1990	1143.33	846.20	301.95	73.60	26.14
1995	1211.21	859.47	351.74	70.96	29.04
2000	1267.43	808.37	459.06	63.78	36.22
2005	1307.56	745.44	562.12	57.01	42.99
2010	1340.91	671.13	669.78	50.05	49.95
2015	1374.62	603.46	771.16	43.90	56.10
2019	1400.05	551.62	848.43	39.40	60.60

Source: *Zhongguo tongji nianjian* 2020 [China Statistical Yearbook 2020]

the Party-state's viewpoint, consumption is an overriding concern. As Premier Li Keqiang (*Zhongguo zhengfu wang* 2015) stated explicitly on 16 September 2014:

> Urbanization is the largest generator of domestic consumption. It creates enormous supply chains and consumption chains. The renovation of shanty areas in the cities and the purchase of furniture, white goods and other household items by peasants living in the urban areas are massive needs. Even the needs for security guards, domestic workers and restauranteurs create considerable employment.

The government's 'new urbanization' programme has gathered force in the past decade, drawing increasing numbers of peasants into the cities and allowing more rural migrant workers than ever to obtain urban *hukou*. It has been boosted further as the need for increasing domestic consumption, which has taken on additional urgency since the beginning of the China-US trade war and COVID-19. In what is generally considered to be the most consequential reform since 1949, the State Council revamped the *hukou* regulations drastically in 2014 and abolished the distinction between agricultural and non-agricultural *hukou* under a unified household registration system, as was the case in the early 1950s. The new system is named 'household registration of residents' and is meant to serve registration and administration purposes only. The holders of 'residential certificates' are now eligible to apply for 'household registration for long-term residents', which entitles them to the same rights as local *hukou* holders while retaining their land use rights in their villages, and every rural *hukou* holder who has lived in a city for six months or longer is eligible to apply for a certificate.

Specifically, the State Council removed existing restrictions completely to allow the family members (including their spouses, children under 18 years of age, and parents) of urban *hukou* holders in towns and small cities with a smaller population than half a million to obtain urban *hukou*. It opened up cities with populations between half a million and a million to rural *hukou* holders and enabled those with stable employment and stable accommodation there, as well as their families, to apply for local *hukou*. It allowed rural *hukou* holders who had had stable employment for an unspecified number of years and stable accommodation in cities with populations between 1 million and 3 million and their families to apply for local *hukou*. In addition, while stressing the importance of controlling the size of megacities with 5 million people or more, it left the door open to holders of rural *hukou* by allowing them and their families to apply for local *hukou* through a locally administered point-scoring system based on the length of employment, accommodation, and insurance policies.

The introduction of these reform measures was clearly intended to accelerate China's urbanization at a time when there was an urgent need for the government to boost domestic consumption; the specified target to be met by the end of 2020 was an increase of a hundred million holders of urban *hukou*. The target has been met already, as Li Keqiang confirmed in his work report to the deputies at the fourth session of the 13th National People's Congress on 5 March 2021, although he did not clarify whether the hundred million people were new, long-term urban residents, or urban *hukou* holders. The government has pledged to achieve 70% urbanization in terms of population composition by 2030 and to 'basically complete' the process of urbanization by 2035. It prmosed at the fourth session that all the rural population who had settled in the urban areas would be 'fully integrated' into the local communities. If so, *hukou* will lose its longstanding function of demarcating classes, as well as its role as an administrative mechanism for controlling rural-to-urban migration.

As things stand, *hukou* has both positive and negative effects on the peasants' social status, life chance and class mobility. On the one hand, it provides welcome housing and economic security to rural migrant workers and is seen as their own self-welfare fund too; they have the advantage over their counterparts in capitalist societies of being able to return to and make a living in the countryside as long as their land use rights remain available. On the other hand, though it does not prevent rural migrant workers from living in the towns and cities for extended periods of time, as was the case between the 1950s and 1978, it still does not mean that rural migrant workers are automatically granted local *hukou*. Most cities use point-scoring systems as protectionist, gate-keeping mechanisms for barring rural migrant workers and attracting applicants with educational qualifications, trade certificates, and special skills and occupations. Thus, *hukou* continues to constrain class mobility, even though it has ceased to restrict internal migration, until it is no longer used to demarcate rural and urban classes. It is already relaxed further under the government's 'new urbanization' programme to allow increasingly more peasants to obtain urban *hukou* more easily. Further relaxation of the system, whether land use rights are retained or not, is bound to enable many peasants to opt out of their officially designated class and lead to the increasing diminution of the class.

It is worth noting that the decline of the peasant class, like the proletariat, is of no concern to the CCP; in fact, the decline is taking place by design. Social classes and the Maoist notion of class have no place in the CCP's discourse of 'reform' and 'opening-up'; they are actually something to play down and forget. Thus, they have been rendered meaningless and redundant in the reform era, except in the CCP and PRC constitutions and occasional Party communications, in that class is no longer treated as a collective actor or a motor of history driving the PRC forward from feudalism and capitalism to socialism and communism. Differently restated, the Party's loss of interest in class is a logical and inevitable result of its abandonment of the Chinese Revolution and socialism as Marx, Engels and Mao conceived it. In the new milieu, peasants are treated as objects of urbanization and consumers whose purchasing power can be greatly enhanced if they are relocated to urban areas.

The roles and status of the peasantry in the PRC's reform-era polity and economy are results of three determinants. The first is unprecedented demand for cheap labour in China's industrial and service sectors, which have thrived on burgeoning public and private capital as well as creative capitalist entrepreneurship. The second is collective land ownership combined with private land use rights. The third is the government's changing *hukou* policies. The soaring demand for cheap rural labour in China's booming urban economy has compelled the government to relax control over rural-to-urban migration as never before. In this context, *hukou* is no longer a necessary or useful mechanism for controlling internal migration, but it continues to act as the ultimate determinant of rural classes and to maintain the boundary between rural and urban classes before the system reverts to its function in the early 1950s of household registration for rule and law and statistical purposes.

The future of the peasant class

It should not come as a surprise at all that the role and status of the Chinese peasantry in the Chinese Revolution have changed drastically given the dramatic shifts in the Revolution. The CCP treated the peasant class as the principal subject of its armed struggle from 1927 to 1949 and elevated its members between 1949 and 1978 to the status of owners of the 'people's democratic dictatorship' and 'masters of the country', while subjecting them to the imperatives of the PRC's socialist industrialization and treating them as objects of capitalist urbanization in the past four decades. Since the Party switched from the Chinese Revolution to economic development in 1978, the peasantry has gradually ceased to be a class understood as a collective actor that seeks to transform the economic base and ideological superstructure of the PRC and morphed into an occupational category which is best diminished in order that the rural population and the rural area will represent no more than a small minority in the national total of a modern, urbanized China. If it can still be thought of as a class, it is a different kind of class – one that is defined with exclusive reference to occupation, not to relations of economic production or roles to be played in the Chinese Revolution.

The transformation of the peasant class does not simply concern itself but is also a telling manifestation of the metamorphosis of the CCP and the PRC and of related social change in the country since 1949. Unlike in the Mao era, peasants have been by and large private producers in the past four decades, except that they do not own the land they till, consumers who are enabled and encouraged to consume even more for the sake of the country's GDP growth and economic prosperity, and an irreplaceable source of cheap labour for the urban industrial and service sectors. Despite notable differences, the class bears striking resemblance to the peasantry of the imperial past, which, together with scholar-officials, artisans and merchants, constituted mainstream society. Similarly, the Party-state plays more or less the same role in the reform era that benevolent monarchs in imperial China did, namely, to 'enrich the people' as an end in itself and as a means to a higher end. The latter is the CCP's moral and political legitimacy and the PRC's economic prosperity and military strength.

A major difference is that it is much harder in the PRC for peasants to opt out of the category due to *hukou* restrictions. Another major difference is their low ranking in the country's current status order, which is determined by power, wealth, occupation, and residential location, among other things. Amid China's fervour for wealth, modernization and urbanization, farming has become one of the least prestigious and profitable occupations in the PRC, and the countryside is commonly perceived to be a backwater and treated as a major source of problems to be tackled by the Party-state and a place to be civilized, modernized, and developed by local entrepreneurs and urban capital.

The class condition in the reform era is characterized, above all, by the combination of state-protected land use rights and collective ownership. The combination has created a peculiar pattern of class formation and class mobility in the PRC. It precludes the possibility of the peasant class in the country evolving in the same way as in Marx and Engels' ideal types of capitalist and social societies. The peasants who retain their land use rights and work on the land will constitute the mainstream of the social category, which will have dwindled after children, the elderly and others not engaged in farming are excluded from it. Those peasants are not likely to degenerate into a landless class of poor peasants and rural proletariat, as many did before 1949. At the same time, the combination has given rise to a class of rural migrant workers with distinct Chinese characteristics that is rarely found in capitalist societies or other socialist systems. This is a new social category with dual-class membership. On the one hand, it is commonly referred to as a 'new class of industrial workers' due to their employment and rural *hukou*. Except for the latter, it inhabits an economic class condition similar to that of the established urban proletariat in the PRC or that of the proletariat in capitalist societies in so far as they do not own the means of production but sell their labour power. On the other hand, the category is officially labelled until recently as a class almost exclusively on the basis of *hukou*. This class is not merely an occupational category but a collective actor and a subject with an ideological-political, albeit largely nominal, mission.

The combination of land use rights and collective land ownership also precludes the possibility of rich and poor peasants evolving into landlords. But it does not prevent the emergence of a new class of rich peasants or urban and rural capitalists who amass land use rights without owning the land they use, or develop large-scale farming or agri-businesses, although such a class has not appeared due to the lack of liberalization. However, recent government policies and further relaxation of government control are beginning to make it easier for peasants and collective owners to commercially capitalize on and gradually relinquish their rights and ownership. Though these policies are designed to boost the rural economy by increasing the value of rural land and making it available for commercial exploitation and to rejuvenate the countryside, they are also liable to have the effect of altering the rural class condition and lay the foundation upon which a new class map will take shape, one that may comprise new classes, including a rural bourgeoisie and a rural proletariat.

The peasants who move into urban areas and settle there following the reform of *hukou* are mostly like to join two classes to be found in capitalist societies as conceived of by Marx, Engels and Mao. One is the urban proletariat; the other is the petit bourgeoisie, most especially small business owners. It matters little whether the new proletarians are employed in state-owned enterprises or private companies and businesses; they would qualify as proletarians as Marx and Engels described the term so long as they do not own the means of production. Nominal ownership and symbolic ownership as small shareholders will not fundamentally alter their class conditions. The relationship between the proletariat and the Party-state does not differ much from that between the proletariat and the welfare state in capitalist societies. The major difference is that the CCP is ideologically obliged to make believe that it remains the vanguard of the class and safeguards the latter's interests. This claim will be put to the test in the event of labour–capital conflicts, where the Party-state needs to play the role of a third-party arbitrator and law enforcer rather than the representative of proletarian interests only. Indeed, siding with the proletariat in contravention of the law is not an option, while protecting the interest of capital at the cost of the proletariat, even for the sake of China's social order and economic prosperity, contradicts the self-claimed role of the Party as the vanguard and representative of the proletariat as well as the constitutional definition of the PRC, which, in theory, empowers the proletarian and peasant classes to suppress the enemy classes, including the bourgeoise.

There is no need to follow Marx, Engels and Mao and assume that the bourgeoisie exploits the proletariat and that the exploitation inevitably leads to class struggle. It is implausible for the CCP or anybody else to claim that there are no exploiting and exploited classes in the PRC today which meet the criteria of Marx, Engels and Mao. It is equally implausible to assert that the Party at the same time stands for the best interests of the proletariat and the bourgeoisie as well as other classes in the PRC. To that extent, the CCP cannot be said to unproblematically represent the working class and the whole Chinese nation, and the PRC is no longer a 'people's democratic dictatorship'. A CCP that is prepared to call a spade a spade will need to revise both definitions.

The contraction of the peasantry as a class and an occupational category is no doubt a good thing from the viewpoint of reform-era CCP leaders and advocates of industrialization, urbanization, free migration, labour mobility, rural–urban equality, and so on. But it poses an ideological-political challenge to the CCP and the PRC. The thorniest question for the Party concerns the political status and role of the class as defined in the PRC constitution and as represented on the national flag and in the state insignia, as well as the nature and identity of the Party and the state. Specifically, how does the socially engineered decline of the peasant class affect the composition of the class-based 'people' and the nature of the 'people's democratic dictatorship'? In what way can the remaining peasants and the proletariat continue to be considered 'masters of the country' and owners of the 'people's democratic dictatorship'? Is the PRC still a 'people's democratic dictatorship' based on the alliance of workers and peasants? Is the CCP still the vanguard of the industrial proletariat? How is the peasant class, as well as the Marxist and Maoist concept of class, still meaningful in the PRC's emergent milieu after the supersession of the Chinese Revolution by the 'moderately well-off society' and Chinese Dream? These questions cannot be raised in the PRC not least because the Party does not have convincing answers. Unless and until the questions are addressed honestly and satisfactorily, the CCP's credibility will remain stretched, and it will remain unable to enhance its members' and Chinese citizens' confidence in the PRC's socialist road, ideology and political system as its top leaders are keen to do but will instead continue to breed cynicism about these.

5
ECONOMIC GROWTH AND WORKING-CLASS DECLINE
Structural reform and social change after 1978

Marc Blecher

The structural reforms that began in 1979, and that in industry went into high gear in the early 1990s, have produced significant social change for the Chinese working class. Economically, many urban-resident workers, even rural migrants, have seen their incomes and standards of living rise, but many others – especially those who have become unemployed or have had to find new work due to industrial restructuring and the rise of the labour market – have not. Those who remain employed in state industry have lost the social welfare benefits that came with their jobs in state-owned firms. Socially, the working class expanded exponentially, diversified radically, became subject to capitalistic[1] wage labour, moved out of its tight-knit workplace-based residential communities, and lost both its high social status and any political influence it had achieved in enterprise operations. The working class's ideas about itself and its place in the world were transformed to reflect its new subordinations. The economic and social changes were brought about mainly by the Party-state and China's new capitalistic forces without much worker participation, and workers have not been able to resist them, though they have managed to reverse a few of the worst effects. Workers played a bigger role in forging their own ideational adaptations rather than adopting them from government propaganda.

This chapter examines the nature of economic, social, and ideational change for the working class. It then analyses the roles and interrelationships among the Party-state, the new capitalistic political economy, and the working class itself in bringing about and setting the limits on those changes.

The decline of the working class

The economic

Under structural reform, the overall economic position of China's working class improved absolutely, declined relatively, and became much more uneven. Both

DOI: 10.4324/9781003255017-6

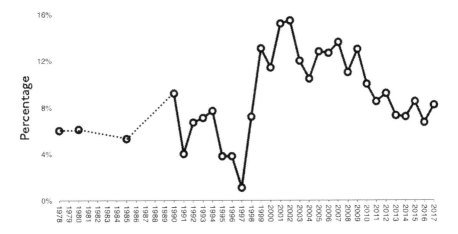

FIGURE 5.1 Average annual industrial real wage increases, 1978–2017

Source: Calculated from *China Statistical Yearbook 2007*, table 5–22, *China Statistical Yearbook 2014*, table 4–11, and *China Statistical Yearbook 2018*, table 4–11.

urban-resident workers and rural migrants have experienced considerable improvements in their incomes and standards of living. Average real wages rose at an average annual rate of around 8% between 1978 and 2017.[2] The increases have been distributed very unevenly over time and space. Real annual rises in the 4–8% range through 1999 (Figure 5.1) were very significant compared with the overall wage stagnation of the Maoist decades; those in the 10–15% range in the first decade of the new century were extraordinary. Yet the rate of increase has been slowing significantly since 2009. In spatial terms (Figure 5.2), average wages in 2017 in 22 of China's 31 provinces and provincial-level municipalities clustered in a relatively narrow band between ¥55,000 and ¥72,000 per year. But five out of eight of the highest average wages were found in the great industrial centres of Beijing, Tianjin, Shanghai, Zhejiang, Jiangsu, and Guangdong, as well as the two remote provinces of Tibet and Qinghai, where they are required to attract needed workers to so remote and, for Han people, culturally foreign an area.

In sweatshops, wages can run to as little as a few dollars a day. Often workers are not even told what the wage is at the time they are hired, and they are never sure what to expect in their pay packets (interview, November 2002). Pay has risen since the middle of the first decade of the new century due to a labour shortage produced by the confluence of ever-rising export demand and the long-term demographic effects of the one-child policy. Yet workers' incomes are also subject to various deductions for dormitory and hiring fees as well as all manner of fines for infractions of elaborate, draconian labour rules. Forced, unpaid overtime is endemic (Wong 2008: 103). Then there are the fees or deposits that are charged just to land a job, which can run as high as ¥6,000 (interview, November 2002). Pushing wages levels to their lowest limit of zero, wage arrears are endemic,[3] which discourages workers from quitting when

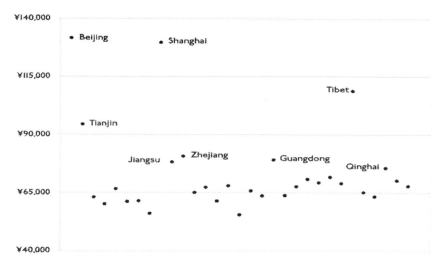

FIGURE 5.2 Average annual industrial wages by province, 2017

Source: *China Statistical Yearbook 2018*, table 4–11.

conditions become unbearable; still worse, even slavery has returned under some circumstances (Blecher 2021).

Even according to official statistics, which do not count workers who are 'laid off' for under 3 years, unemployment nearly doubled from 1990 to 2015.[4] This was due heavily to the 1997 decision to privatize or close many state-owned enterprises. Around the turn of the century, the number of laid-off urban-resident workers increased over tenfold to 21 million (at a time when official unemployment statistics were around 7 million) (Li 2004). At least they could draw meagre subsidies and remain in their squalid housing. By contrast, the 20 million rural migrant workers fired in the 2008 depression could not even get that (N.a. 2009). So desperate are workers in troubled firms that in some cases they have paid more than a year's wages to employers in bribes and 'fees' to keep their jobs[5] – effectively, yet another form of working for free. But in 2017, when 2 million steelworkers and coal miners were fired when the government closed their enterprises, they received generous severance packages to help preserve political 'stability' (LeVine 2017).

State-owned firms no longer offer urban-resident workers the welfare benefits they once did, and private and hybrid[6] employers certainly do not. Health care and education are now provided on a fee basis, and the charges can be significant. Even urban-resident workers in state enterprises no longer receive housing benefits. Many migrant workers live in crowded factory dormitories and eat in canteens run by their employers *cum* landlords, who are, as Lenin put it in a different context, 'skinning the ox twice' as these costs can consume most of workers' wages (Lenin 1917).

In short, Chinese workers' compensation and material life under structural reform offer a mixed picture. While urban-resident workers who have held on to factory employment have seen significant increases in real wages since the onset of the structural reforms, many among them have lost their jobs altogether and been unable to find re-employment. And even employed urban-resident workers have lost the economic and employment security and benefits to which they had become accustomed in Maoist days. Meanwhile, rural migrants have added significantly to their incomes, even as they hold very low-paid and insecure jobs.

The social

Structural reform radically upended working-class social life quantitatively and qualitatively. The working class ballooned, incorporating huge phalanxes of rural migrants; moreover, they became proletarianized in the formal sense – employed as capitalist wage labourers rather than as state socialist workers who enjoyed significant guarantees and protections. Meanwhile, the urban-resident stratum that had been the mainstay of the working class in the Maoist period shrunk to a shadow of its former self and eventually became proletarianized as well. The working class also became even more deeply cleaved than before into widely different strata: not just rural migrant and urban, but employed and unemployed, male and female, older and younger, skilled and unskilled, native and adventive. Old communities are grounded in the congruence of workplace and home fractured. Social hierarchies and workplace power relations were turned upside down – or, from the vantage point of the newly capitalistic mode of production, right-side up.

Since 1978 but especially 1992, when urban industrial development took off, China has produced the biggest, most rapid spurt of proletarianization in world history. Accurate numbers do not exist, but the scale is well into hundreds of millions. In 1985, there were 381 million workers; three decades later, there were 623 million (State Statistical Bureau 1986: 192; Thibaud 2016). They emanated overwhelmingly from rural migration – 291 million in 2019 – rather than urban population growth. The new recruits were employed in the rapidly growing private and hybrid sector, which also took on vast numbers of former state and collective industry workers who were discharged in the massive 1998 wave of layoffs that resulted from the restructuring of the state sector (Walker and Buck 2007: 43). By 2018, only 81 million urban-resident workers were employed in mining, manufacturing, construction, and logistics, the vast majority of which were private and hybrid firms. Only 4.7 million remained in the state sector, which at its peak in 1995 employed 110 million (State Statistical Bureau 2001: Table 5–8, 2020: Table 4–4). In addition, tens of millions were or had been unemployed. In short, this was proletarianization on a vast scale and in a double sense: hundreds of millions of farmers became wage labourers, and so did tens of millions of state workers who had previously worked on state socialist rather than capitalist terms.

From the outset of the rapid industrialization starting in 1992, the new Chinese proletariat underwent significant feminization, as younger age cohorts were far more female than older ones (ACFTU 1999: 1272; ACFTU 2006: 853). In 2010, women comprised almost one-third of industrial employment, far more than

Brazil, Mexico, the UK, or the US. Women tend to be concentrated in less-skilled industrial occupations, less technologically sophisticated sectors, and less modern plants (ACFTU 1999: 1269; ACFTU 2006: 850). They are also more concentrated among rural migrants than urban-resident workers (N.a. 2013: 3). Generally, they experience less employment security than men; they bore the brunt of the wave of layoffs in 1998, for example (Mo 2001).

The age profile of the working class has traced a U-shaped pattern since the early 1990s. Despite the stereotype of callow youth working assembly lines in Chinese sweatshops, the country's working class has actually been ageing. Early on, the influx of young migrants – who averaged 29 years of age in 2003, compared with 41 for the working class overall – made the working class younger (World Bank 2009: 101: ACFTU 2006: 924). And the massive 1998 layoffs mainly affected workers over 35 (N.a. 2000; Zhao 2001: 12–13; Mo 2001). But since then, most migrant workers have stayed on as they aged, averaging 41 in 2020 (CEIC Data n.d.).

The Chinese working class has become well educated.[7] As early as 1984, one Tianjin electrical pump factory required all new hires to have finished high school. In 1997, 43% of industrial workers had high school or vocational high school educations (ACFTU 1999: 1272; ACFTU 2006: 853). And the majority of workers laid off in the late 1990s had junior high school educations at best (N.a. 2000; Zhao 2001; Mo 2001). In 2019, 72% of migrant workers had junior or senior high school educations (CEIC Data n.d.).

The strong congruence of workplace and residence in the Maoist period has been weakened considerably. In some flagship state-owned enterprises, the factory-based welfare state lived on into the early years of structural reform. For example, in 1995, Yunnan Steel was still providing its workers with not just housing but the likes of discounted phone service, free bus transportation, and free supper for the night shift.[8] And even where work has disappeared, many workers still live in or around their factories alongside their fellow unemployed co-workers. Here, the old sense of workplace community can remain strong, as already noted, the former workers share pride in their past accomplishments and sacrifices as well as shared anger and disillusionment about their mistreatment under structural reform (Cho 2013). Yet most workers in state firms that once provided housing have now moved on to new or at least different dwellings that are no longer occupied only by other workers in their enterprise.

Small- and medium-sized private and hybrid firms have generally not provided housing in the first place, so their workers do not live together as neighbours. But many of the larger ones house their young migrant workers in sweatshop dormitories. Of course, these places are not what we normally think of as residential communities – historically rooted places where continuous social relationships can develop – but, rather, as temporary accommodation for the teenagers and 20-somethings who stay a only few years. Nonetheless, intense (if transient) social relationships are formed there. Workers inhabiting them share gossip, news, and often their deepest feelings (Pun 2005: 17). They also act spontaneously to strengthen bonds of community. 'Workers frequently changed beds to form kin and ethnic clusters because they found it easier to cope with each other' (Pun 2005: 105). Yet such bonds are also easily and summarily dissolved by workers' frequent job changes (Lee 2007: 196). Moreover, management undermines the breadth of community by providing several levels of housing accommodation, with the best to educated specialists, slightly less good but still better than average rooms to shop floor line leaders, and eight-to-a-room steerage to the line workers (Pun 2005: 124, 126). These situations proliferate well beyond the southeastern export platforms with which they are commonly associated.[9] But homogenizing the ordinary workers may actually strengthen their sub-community, which of course is a large majority in any factory anyway.

The working class's social status has plummeted. The not atypical decision made by one bright Maoist era high school graduate to take a factory job rather than a university seat, because workers were so exalted while being an intellectual caused too much trouble (Interview, 1974), is unimaginable today. Already in 2002, only .7% of workers hoped their children too would follow suit (Chen 2002: 15); 46.3% of workers said that over the previous 5 years their position as 'masters of the enterprise' – a common Maoist era trope – had declined a great deal (19.8%) or at least somewhat (26.5%) (ACFTU 2006: 1239–1241, 1260). One older worker reported that 'Workers today are having more trouble getting married, which is an indicator of their declining social status' (Interview, 29 June 1996). The collapse in urban workers' social status is greatest among the hard-core unemployed. And many of them compensate by condescending to rural migrants.

As enterprises have expanded, their workforces have often grown more heterogeneous, and social relations among their workers concomitantly more complex and often strained. In two Wenzhou private firms, '[T]he personal charisma and commitment of firm founders and the informal norms of trust and reciprocity enhanced accountability and a sense of common purpose, which . . . in turn stabilized shop floor dynamics' (Chen 2008: 26). But as they upgraded, they hired more technical experts and other non-Wenzhounese. This brought into play the pointed regional animosities that have plagued China for millennia. These new employees did not speak the local dialect, which transformed the very basis of day-to-day communication in the plant as the locals had to switch from their beloved Wenzhounese to Modern Standard Mandarin. Moreover, the newcomers had to be paid a great deal more than the locals and offered all manner of other emoluments. All that created a new status hierarchy that demoralized the original local staff and undermined their commitment to the firm (Chen 2008: 116–123; Pun 2005: 126–131). In Nawon Textiles – a South Korean firm outside Qingdao – a different but equally complex pattern of social stratification also developed, here around nationality and gender. At the top of the heap were the ethnically Korean-Chinese white-collar office workers and shop floor deputy leaders. The workers were primarily Han Chinese women, who were condescended to, insulted, mistreated, and segregated residentially, in inferior quarters, from the Korean-Chinese. Below them, at the very bottom of the social hierarchy, were Han Chinese men working unskilled, menial jobs as packers, and porters. Confused and angry at their social subordination to women, they developed aggressive and even pathological, self-harming behaviours in a vain attempt to prove their masculinity. A strike by the Han Chinese women actually excluded the men (Kim 2013).

The gains that the Chinese working class achieved during the Maoist period in power relations on the shop floor and in employment terms are broadly gone. In state-owned enterprises, the situation ranges widely from despotic to relatively relaxed. Yet even the latter amounts to a setback for workers. Towards the end of the century, relations between management and labour in many state-owned enterprises still had affinities with the better situations of the Maoist period. In 1996, a worker in a state-owned accordion plant in Tianjin reported:

> There is no big social gap between workshop heads and workers. The workers don't fear them. Moreover, each workshop has several teams. The team heads are pretty much engaged in production full time – say, around 97% of the time. There is not much of a gap between them and the workers. The team heads get the same wages as the workers, though they also get and a slightly higher bonus. Direct supervision of each worker's work is done by themselves.
> *(Interview, June 30, 1996)*

> We complain to our factory manager all the time. Naturally we don't make a special visit go to their office for this; we just say something while joking with them in the plant. For example, some workers will be chatting in the factory, and if the boss comes over, we would just say that things should be done this way and not that way. We can speak very frankly. . . . For example, our factory has two labs, both of which have lots of administrators and experimentation personnel; but they have nothing to do. . . . We feel that the bosses should . . . close one lab.
> *(Interview, May 26, 1999)*

But such free and easy relationships did not, of course, amount to worker democracy or even influence. In this last case:

> But the boss said he won't do it. He likes to have two laboratories around . . . We workers shouldn't have to pay for this. But the manager runs the factory like a patriarch. Our leaders are numbskulls; they don't think flexibly.
> *(Interview, May 25, 1999)*

Over time, and especially with the rise of private and hybrid ownership, worker-management relations have generally become more commodified, alienated, and despotic (Hung and Chiu 2009: 108; Interviews, July 9, 1996, June 8, 1999, June 10, 1999).

> In the past people really listened to the factory leadership. We were together in shared responsibility for meeting the quota sent down from the higher

levels. We all took seriously our responsibility for meeting the quota; indeed, we wanted to meet it. At that time, people really listened to Mao and to the leadership. Now it's different. If the leadership wants workers to do more, it has to pay them more.

(Interview, June 10, 1999)

Taylorist labour processes, piece rates, draconian management, and mutual surveillance have returned with a vengeance (Zhao and Nichols 1996).

In enterprises with large numbers of young migrant women, patriarchy permeates and intensifies factory power relations. In such plants, management and especially skilled technical and staff positions are heavily male, while line workers are predominantly female. In one electronics factory, even the most capable female workers chosen as deputy line leaders were no match for the rest of the (male) management. One admitted: 'It is difficult to find the right people for leaders among the line girls. Girls are so talkative when they crowd together. But at work, they are so timid and afraid to criticize others' (Pun 2005: 149). And the fact that the gender-based division of labour produces significant functional and pay differentials (Pun 2005: 149) only reinforces the patriarchal nature of power relationships in the factory.

In short, since 1949 the working class has undergone a second sea change in its social life – who comprises it, the terms on which it is employed, how much social status it has, how and how much workers live together and relate to each other, how they are subjected to workplace authority, and how women experience patriarchy.

The ideational

All this has produced a corresponding second transformation in the ways Chinese workers have understood themselves, the forces acting on them, and the possibilities before them. Gone is the oppositional, workerist sensibility nurtured by Maoist politics among the urban-resident working class. It has been replaced by several distinct, complex ways of thinking, each of which is loosely associated with specific sets of material conditions that tend to prevail in particular regions of the country. In the rustbelts of the northeast and inland areas with 'third front'[10] factories, where unemployment is sky high and opportunities for re-employment minimal, the largely laid-off working class has developed a desperate, moralistic, nostalgic, and fatalistic focus on bare subsistence. Under better employment conditions, such as the central and eastern coast, both employed and unemployed workers have by and large accepted the hegemony of the market and the state. Rural migrant workers, who proliferate across the country but are most concentrated in the southeast, still focus intensely on sweatshop conditions. The assertive outrage that they evinced in the Cultural Revolution at their inferior economic and social status *vis-à-vis* their urban-resident co-workers has been transformed into a fatalistic, and by turns depressed and self-sacrificing sensibility that is now focused on abusive factory managers rather than, as in the Maoist period, state and factory political power and the structural gap between rural and urban institutions the former had established. Overall, then, the working class's consciousness has become much more variegated, divided, complex, introverted, and apolitical.

Rustbelt Atavism Where the great heavy industries that were the pride of China's import-substitution industrialization in the 1950s and 1960s have been shuttered with little or nothing to replace them, unemployed and even some still employed workers' sensibilities begin with a wistful look back to those better days, which they compare favourably to the situation after structural reform. Workers remember themselves as honest, conscientious, assiduous, and earnest (Hung and Chiu 2009: 96; Interviews, 29 June 1996 and 8 June 1999). Incomes were low, and life was simple, but workers enjoyed security of employment and social provision. 'Society was stable and the masses had a sense of purpose' (Lee 2007: 144).

> Our old factory director was very concerned about workers' welfare. For women workers in particular we had a clinic – they distributed sanitary napkins to women – a nursery, a mess hall, a factory bus, a barber shop, a workers' culture palace.
>
> *(Lee 2007: 142)*

Education and skill enabled workers to develop *esprit de corps*, to feel part of something larger than themselves, to be willing to sacrifice, to upgrade and take pride in their work and their contribution to the country, and to feel confident and fulfilled as human beings.

> I felt particularly excited and content because I could learn new technologies. I was very hard-working . . . At that time, production was for our country, for building socialism. I had a very advanced mentality.
>
> Q: Was it only a slogan?
> A: It's what the slogan said, but it's also my genuine feeling. (Lee 2007: 146)

Many former state industry workers hold a strong and distinctly though only implicitly Marxian sense that the industrial achievements of the Maoist period were products of their own labour. This produced feelings of pride, but also both possession of their factories and identification with the state, which formally owns them. What Ching Kwan Lee terms '[t]his extraordinarily deep and unique "class feeling"' has helped fuel outrage when state firms have been put into bankruptcy; the assets being liquidated are, many workers feel, *theirs*, and their losses are nothing less than exploitation in the strict (and sometimes articulated) sense of appropriation of the product of their labour. And when workers have protested, they have felt they are protecting both their own economic class interests but also those of the state, which for them really was, in important senses, a workers' state (Lee 2007: 91).

No longer, though.

> Nowadays people's thinking is more chaotic. They are not clear who they work for: the country, the factory, their children, the factory leadership, themselves. If workers only consider themselves, there's no way for the enterprise to do well.
>
> *(Interview, June 29, 1996)*

To workers' minds, the shop floor changes and expropriations wrought by structural reform have not just happened unintentionally or resulted from inexorable structural forces. On the contrary, they represent a betrayal. During the 2002 strike at the Daqing Oilfield – a Maoist era model – laid-off workers complained bitterly.

> [When we were persuaded to apply for our layoff buyout, we] were completely cheated. No wonder everyone is so angry now.
>
> *(Interview, March 2002)*

> Workers in the Daqing Oilfield have made a great contribution to the country, earning it tens of billions [of *yuan*] every year. But they simply sold out the senior workers. I mean, we were cheated.
>
> *(Interview, March 2002)*

The theme of officials being bad parents – a particularly profound and damning accusation – is common.

> Everyone needs someone to back them up. We bring up children hoping they will look after us when we are old. If we didn't need to be backed up, we wouldn't have to bother having children. . . . It's a socialist country, so there should be somebody to take care of us.
>
> *(Interview, March 2002)*

> We simply became lambs to be slaughtered. We are like the children deprived of mothers.
>
> *(Wong 2008: 102)*

Moreover, the betrayal involved trickery.

> The workers are brainwashed, blindfolded and fooled. Officials use their authority selfishly to obtain benefits for themselves.
>
> *(Interview, March 2002)*

Yet some also blame themselves for being gullible or naïve, feeling they should have known.

> The sly and cunning would have left the enterprise long ago, or they would have profited, like the managers, by taking advantage of the enterprise. It was the workers, the honest and simple-minded, who thought of nothing but their loyal service to the enterprise, who were met with the fate of [being laid off].
>
> *(Hung and Chiu 2009: 105)*

Their palpable anger is mixed with heavy doses of depression.

> I felt very depressed after being laid-off two years ago. I just stay at home. I had worked more than twenty years, after all. After I was laid off, I felt completely aimless.
>
> *(Interview, June 18, 2002)*

The word 'pitiful' recurs in workers' self-descriptions (Lee 2007: 115, 142, 150).

> It costs me three hundred *yuan* for an injection and some medicine! If we were Shenzhen locals or state-owned enterprise workers, we would not have to pay that outrageous amount. We are a pitiful lot in the city. We get no welfare from the government even though we contribute our labor.
>
> *(Lee 2007: 199)*

> Now I understand what *exploitation* means. We are really pitiful. In the old days, if you needed housing, the factory would give you housing. Now, no single apartment has been built. Mine is a three-person household and we still cannot buy our own apartment unit.
>
> *(Lee 2007: 142)*

All this adds up to feelings of powerlessness. Workers had *power*, but no longer. 'Gradually, all kinds of power the masses had under Mao have been taken away bit by bit' (Lee 2007: 142).

> The most important thing is that today's workers have no power, the power that Mao gave workers, the power to criticize the director and write big-character posters.
>
> *(Lee 2007: 144)*

> Everyone here says this: our lives would be so much better if there were still struggle meetings and political campaigns . . . Back then [in Mao's time], we masses had a weapon against corrupt cadres. Many people miss mass campaigns. People always say these cadres [of today] would have been criticized and executed many times over now for the amount of their graft.
>
> *(Lee, 119)*

> 'The working class takes leadership in everything' was a popular slogan under Mao and now workers bitterly and self-mockingly describe their situation by turning the claim into 'Everything leads the working class.'
>
> *(Lee 2007: 114)*

This toxic combination of depression and feelings of powerlessness leaves most rustbelt workers not just pessimistic, but hopeless.

> Now we're all just donkeys, harnessed, and day and day pushing to grind the mill. You want to get out of the harness, but it's completely impossible.
>
> *(Wong 2008: 103)*

Market and state hegemony In many areas outside China's rustbelts, many workers, including the unemployed and those in economic straits, broadly accept the basic values of the state and the structural reforms it has fostered (Blecher 2002).

> Enterprises' development should not all proceed the same way. I support reform. It is necessary. Competition is right.
>
> *(Interview, May 28, 1999)*

This sentiment was surprising coming from a 47-year-old worker whose building materials factory was economically endangered, who was not readily reemployable, and who also had serious complaints:

> Competition is right. But what should we do about the workers in bankrupt enterprises? There are lots of things about which I am dissatisfied. My wages are so low. We barely have enough to eat, and can't save anything. Our life is pretty tight.
>
> *(Interview, May 28, 1999)*

One sea change for workers brought about by marketization occurred when, starting in the middle to late 1980s, their wages and livelihoods became dependent on the economic health of their particular enterprise rather than on the state more broadly – a matter of the luck of the draw. Yet the following responses were typical.

> Yes, I guess it's unfair that some people lose out simply because their enterprises are doing badly. I felt this. But I didn't express it. Partly this is because I saw that enterprises all over Tianjin were suffering. Mine wasn't the worst.
>
> *(Interview, June 10, 1999)*

Underlying these responses is a strong sense of fatalism.

> Many workers just feel that they have a bad fate, that they went through the wrong door – *i.e.*, if they had joined another industry when they first started work, things would be all right.
>
> *(Interview, May 25, 1999)*

These workers' penchant for hegemonic thinking in terms of the inevitability and implacability of the market rather than any underlying political causes is reflected too in their behavioural responses.

> Yes, of course it's unfair that some workers lose out just because their factories are doing badly. But most workers think that the way to deal with the inequality is to try to make more money for themselves.
>
> *(Interview, June 7, 1999)*

Quantitative, questionnaire-based research on Tianjin workers' underlying patterns of thought at the turn of the century turned up the following main components of working-class thinking: broad acceptance of the market, including the labour market, even by those who have suffered layoffs; disinclination to blame the government for workers' problems; fatalism; political passivity; and a demonstrable sense that the solution for workers in need is to get a job (Blecher 2008).

Rural migrants: attraction and repulsion Rural migrants evince a definite sense of being profoundly different from urban-resident workers. Ordinary language makes this clear to both. Urban workers, including even the rustbelt unemployed, are known as *gongren* 工人 – workers. But migrants are *dagong* 打工 or *nongmingong* 农民工 – literally, 'those who work' or 'farmers who [do urban] work' – but whose identity is not 'worker'. They feel deeply the burden of their rural origins; it is an albatross they believe, rightly, they can never throw off. 'As a peasant, I just feel naturally inferior. I cannot explain why' (Lee 2007: 217). They refer to themselves as 'low level' (Florence 2008: 274). Bosses regularly berate female migrants as 'rural girls' with 'coarse hands and feet' (Pun 2005: 116–117). This leads to feelings of confusion and disorientation.

> I missed my home while I was out to *dagong*. When I returned home, I thought of going out again.
>
> *(Pun and Lu 2010)*

> There's nowhere I could find myself happy. No matter where I go, I'm not calm and balanced.
>
> *(Pun and Lu 2010)*

Still worse, migrants can develop feelings of worthlessness and even self-hatred.

> I felt that the value of my labor was really insignificant. . . . We workers didn't consider ourselves to be worth much . . . I really didn't have any status.
>
> *(Interview, September 2002)*

> People with money look down on poor people. I am a peasant, but I myself despise peasants because we are so poor.
>
> *(Lee 2007: 217)*

Thus, they feel alone, with no one to rely on but themselves. They express this alienation in all the forms discussed by Marx, sometimes using his very words without knowing it (Marx 1844). Materially, they are alienated from their labour and the product they produce. Migrants refer to *dagong* employment as selling 'selling one's body', a term also used for sex work. Continuing this trope, they are also alienated from the process of production.

> In the factory, your entire body is under [the employer's] control. You lose control over yourself. You have to do whatever he wants you to do. It's like you're sold to him.
>
> *(Lee 2007: 197)*

Rural migrant workers are also alienated socially.

> Workers in dormitories are alienated from their hometown and their parents, working within factories dominated by unfamiliar others, languages, food, production methods and products. Yet these objects and subjects confront the new worker virtually 24 hours per day, seven days a week and often throughout the year.
>
> *(Pun and Smith, 32–33)*

And in existential terms, migrants are alienated from what Marx called their species-being.

> It's like in the old society, I give you my money and you become my slave, a lesser human being. In the countryside, even if you are poor, people look down on you but still as a human being.
>
> *(Lee 2007: 197)*

They see themselves as being treated like 'cattle and horses', the common feeling before 1949.

> We are second-class citizens, and not even that sometimes, just beasts.
>
> *(Lee 2007: 198)*

> How can we go on with such inhuman treatment?
>
> *(Thireau and Hua 2003: 98)*

> We are not considered human beings.
>
> *(Thireau and Hua 2003: 99)*

Yet they cling to a glimmer of hopeful agency. Their decision to migrate in the first place is generally driven both by an implacable necessity to escape rural poverty in the only way possible and by the wish to make a success of themselves by earning money and acquiring skills, not to mention the lure of the city's bright lights.

> My sister and I wanted to come out to the city to learn new skills and experience the city way of life . . . I thought coming to Shenzhen would give me a feel of the real world and society.
>
> *(Interview, September 2002)*

> I started working at the factory when I was fifteen. . . . I had very little education or skill and my family wasn't financially well off. There was no point for me to stay home . . . Farming wouldn't lead me to a bright future. I would just end up spending my entire life in the pit and not learn anything new.
>
> > Q: [After experiencing sweatshop conditions] did you feel like going back home?
> >
> > A: Not really. What would I do back home? At least here I had the opportunity to learn new things and better myself.
>
> *(Interview, September 2002)*

> > Q: Why did you choose to come here?
> >
> > A: That's hard to say. I guess I just wanted to see the world outside my village.
>
> *(Interview, September 2002)*

What emerges from migrants' experience of material compulsion, draconian oppression, exploitation, social exclusion, and multifaceted alienation is a sensibility that somehow combines fatalism and agency, hopelessness and hope. Pun found that '[s]ome workers consoled themselves with the thought that "fate takes turns, so fate will turn one day"' (Pun 2005: 183). As a worker who lost a hand in a factory 'accident' put it:

Q: So was it a good move to come here to Shenzhen?

A: I guess if the accident didn't occur it wouldn't be that bad. But I can't even blame it on the accident. I cannot regret my decision. The accident was inevitable. (Interview, September 2002)

Rural migrants' world view, then, is profoundly contradictory. They are pushed but also pulled into a world in which they are regarded and treated as alien, inferior, and not fully human. They suffer terribly, but somehow manage to keep some small hope alive. They not only are fatalistic but also believe that they can triumph over fate. They are willing, or at least able, to take extraordinary risks for the most meagre rewards.

The working class's social decline and disaggregation have produced a new, sharply differentiated, and deeply contradictory panoply of ways workers think about their world (or, better, worlds). What they all share, though, is that none harken back to the radicalism of the Maoist era working class. As such, they are all consistent with the hegemony of the market and the state, and they reinforce the power of both.

The politics of working-class decline

In the Republican era, the working class did not experience significant broad-scale social change. In the Maoist period, it did, as a result of both its own efforts and those of the Party-state. Under structural reform, workers' economic lives experienced gains and losses, socially their status deteriorated and their lives became more complex, and their ideas also became more complicated, contradictory, and defeatist. These profound changes were wrought much less by working-class agency than by the new capitalistic relations and by the state which promoted them. Workers continued to advocate for themselves, but in a much more defensive and reactive manner, and a less radical one, than in the Maoist decades.

From 1978 to the early 1990s, average wages began to increase after decades of stagnation, as the Party-state sought to curry favour with the working class for the structural reforms. With the rise of private and hybrid ownership from the early 1990s onward, wages were set increasingly by the new labour market rather than government ministries. This produced unprecedented volatility, due in part to capitalistic forces but also to the Party-state's decision to lay off tens of millions of workers in 1998. After some initial recovery that saw wage increases rise to unprecedented levels through 2002 for those workers who kept their jobs, wage increases have remained healthy but in secular decline year-on-year – changes in which the Party-state had little hand. This resulted, rather, from the high-powered economic growth of the Chinese industrial economy on the demand side and, on the supply side, contradictory forces such as the influx of rural migrants alongside the squeeze due to the effects of the one-child policy. Burgeoning working-class collective action starting at the end of 1990s did little to shape overall wage levels, directed as it was at economic depredations in particular factories – such as wage arrears, corrupt closures, and abusive management – rather than collective bargaining.

Likewise, the disappearance of benefits originated from both the Party-state and the market. The government decided to end work unit benefits – 'to smash the iron rice bowl'. It commodified and under-invested in health care and housing. The millions of newly impoverished unemployed received impossibly low subsistence payments. The private and hybrid sector which increasingly replaced state enterprise did not provide such benefits in the first place (except for woefully inadequate dormitory housing and first-aid clinics in sweatshops).

Equally momentous has been the abolition of ironclad employment security for the urban-resident working class in the Maoist decades, first by the Party-state and then by the labour market it conjured up. 1986 regulations stipulated that newly hired workers would receive only limited-term contracts and that workers could be fired (Ngok 2008: 47). 1988 legislation provided for shuttering state enterprises. The 1994 Labor Law put all state employment on a contract basis, and ended state allocation of labour to its own enterprises. The rapid rise of the capitalistic economy extended employment precarity to all workers. By the turn of the century, then, lifetime employment was dead.

Working-class political agency has played a limited role in countering egregious economic abuses in selected enterprises. Not long after the transition to capitalistic ownership and workplace relations began in earnest in the early and mid-'90s, wildcat strikes, often including local protests beyond enterprises' confines, began to become endemic over time, place, and sector. That said, in the context of China's vast industrial economy, they are not particularly frequent. In 2019, reports of only 1,385 strikes and protests emerged across China's 378,000 factories[11] (China Labour Bulletin; State Statistical Bureau 2020: Table 13–1). The vast majority have focused on material issues such as wage arrears, excessive and/or unpaid overtime, asset stripping amidst closures, or employers reneging on insurance contributions. They have not been connected with collective bargaining over generalized wage setting, which does not occur in China.

Likewise, workers have exercised almost no political agency in reshaping their social lives. To be sure, they exercised tremendous agency by migrating in vast numbers from the countryside to seek better economic and social lives. But this is not political agency: they did not have to fight to be allowed to make this move. Instead, it was the Party-state which lifted the Maoist era restrictions on urban migration, and the newly capitalistic forces in the private and hybrid and even the state sectors which provided the employment. And workers haven't fought the terms on which they have been allowed into urban industrial employment: there have been almost no protests against the household registration system and the gap it maintains between migrant and urban-resident workers.

The fact that the working class has not just expanded enormously but also become proletarianized resulted from political agency by global capital and the Party-state. At first, this transformation took place in joint ventures between state firms and foreign capitalists who demanded it. But quickly domestic state employers adopted it as well (Gallagher 2005). It may seem fatuous to point out that workers played no political role in advocating for the transition to wage labour; but in fact many Soviet workers did just that at the moment of régime change, thinking that it would prove fairer than their own state socialist payment system (Crowley 1997).

Some of the diversification of the working class – into rural migrant and urban-resident strata and increasing numbers of women and youths – resulted in part both from capital's ever-increasing demand for labour and from the Party-state's decision to relax restrictions on rural migration. Other new forms of variegation had more to do with the Party-state alone. Its decision to shutter large numbers of plants, and to lay off tens of millions of state sector workers, created for the first time since 1949 a huge reserve army of unemployed. And by upgrading the educational system, increasingly segmenting it into vocational and academic tracks, and pursuing an aggressive programme of technology transfer from its global joint-venture partners, it was primarily responsible for the rise of a highly skilled stratum of workers alongside the burgeoning ranks of the semi-skilled. In all these major social changes, workers were passive objects rather than active subjects.

Working-class agency was similarly absent from the obliteration of the work unit community, a social change with enormous effects on workers' daily lives. Workers did not militate for it – there is no evidence that they were 'yearning to be free' from life organized so completely around their workplaces. To be sure, the work unit social community was no socialist nirvana: housing was often overcrowded, and allocations involved a good deal of favouritism, unfairness, and bickering. But all of that did not provoke working-class demands to dismantle the work unit in favour of a market-based system. The work unit social community was abolished, rather, at the behest of the Party-state, in the interests of advancing labour market flexibility and reducing state industry costs.

The political initiative to abolish Maoist participatory modalities in management and factory authority – triple combination teams, cadre participation in labour, staff and workers' congresses, flattened pay scales, collective and politically inflected incentive schemes, workplace competitions, and political movements that afforded opportunities to criticize management – resulted from both the Party-state's new growth-oriented industrial policy and the rise of the private and hybrid sector. To be sure, many workers had grown weary at best, and disgusted and disillusioned at worst, of the Maoist era political innovations in their factories. Many hated the endless meetings and sharp conflict. But they also miss the definite reciprocity of authority relations with management and resent the lack of accountability by their bosses. Here again, despite the drawbacks of participatory management, workers did not militate for its abolition; rather, they acquiesced, nostalgically, and dolefully, in its demise.

By contrast, the various ideational formations that have emerged in the working class under structural reform have emerged from the workers themselves as they responded differently to the different material circumstances in which they have found themselves. In the Maoist period, this was also broadly true: both the 'workerism' and the 'economism' evinced, respectively, by urban-resident and rural migrant workers often conflicted even with the official messaging of the Party-state that had nonetheless created the conditions for their emergence (as Ch. 6 in vol. 1 discussed). But both strata of workers also took definite advantage of the Party-state's messaging by either adopting its language or holding it to its own standard and finding it wanting. Under structural reform, the role of Party-state messaging – which mainly emphasizes economic modernization and social stabilization – in shaping ideational change has become more attenuated and diminished. Partly this is due to the overall diminution of the sheer volume and intensity of such messaging. But the relationship is more complex than that.

For rustbelt atavism, the modernization is palpably absent at best or is responsible for the decline of their local economies at worst. And social stability only exists as stagnant immiseration. So both of the Party-state's messages are irrelevant and fall on deaf ears. The only official political discourse that figures in these workers' thinking is that of the bygone Maoist days. Yet somehow those values still transfer in these workers' minds to the present Party-state even though it has now renounced them, producing passivity or abject hope around the idea that the Party-state's institutional continuity remains worth something despite the radical change in what it stands for and what it is doing (Cho 2013).

One might expect market and state hegemony to result from the effects of the government's discourses, and in a diffuse way it surely does. But the workers who evince it do so without reference to Party-state vocabularies, and in ways that appear to spring genuinely from their own lived experience. One laid-off Tianjin worker who was depressed about having been cast aside after decades of 'contributing to the revolution and socialism' – clearly invoking Maoist tropes – explained why she wasn't also angry. She said obliquely that there are just too many unemployed workers for the government to support. But she also felt she could not be angry because structural reforms had also created opportunities for her children and had produced visible prosperity in her city, in which she took pride (interview, June 10, 1999). Her responses were fully consistent with official Party-state messages, but they didn't originate from them in any direct way; rather, they came straight out of her own experience and understanding.

Similarly, migrant workers' attraction and repulsion arises from their own complex experiences and equally ambiguous feelings about them. The Party-state's own messaging does not address rural migrants in any significant way. It has not had to encourage them to migrate, and it does not try to justify its efforts to regulate or reverse their movements. Even when they have pushed back against the depredations they experience in their factories – by striking and protesting, or by suing for compensation for injuries – they generally do so apolitically, targeting their employer far more than the Party-state (which they distinguish from their often complicit local governments).

In short, then, the vast changes in working-class ideation, all of which were functional for the Party-state's structural reforms, did not originate from it in any direct way. Rather, they were all products of ways that workers grasped the new worlds into which structural reform has plunged them.

Structural reform and the working class

Structural reform brought massive social change overall for the Chinese working class. Wages have risen significantly though unevenly, while urban-resident workers' benefits and employment security have collapsed. In social terms, the working class ballooned, proletarianized, stratified, declined in status, saw its tight workplace communities and enterprise political influence abolished, and experienced more patriarchy. Its thinking deradicalized.

The working class played a much smaller and more passive role in bringing about these profound social changes than it did during the Maoist period, when it shaped radical social change more actively. Rather, the economic and social changes were produced mainly by a complex set of relationships between capital and the Party-state. Ideational change generally emerged spontaneously from the working class itself as it experienced and struggled to process those economic and social developments.

Structural reform represents a profound historical discontinuity for the Chinese working class. In the Republican era, it actively sought radical change but could not achieve it. In the Maoist period, it also actively sought radically new forms of social change, and it did achieve them for a time. Structural reform brought new economic and social changes that unwound the Maoist ones, but here the working class was much more object than subject. That is, the process was driven mainly by the Party-state and capital. Ideational change did emanate far more from the working class itself but was broadly adaptive and acquiescent to the new economic and social realities. Profound social change, then, has been visited on the working class rather than developing with its active participation.

Notes

1 The Chinese economy that has developed under structural reform does not conform to even the most flexible or nuanced conceptualizations of political economy (such as "varieties of capitalism" or "market socialism"), involving a mix of novel ownership forms (see footnote 7) and allocative mechanisms (market but also state fiat, especially in finance). While not "capitalist" in any of the standard senses, it is nonetheless characterized broadly by wage labor and the attendant features of employment relations. "Market" seems too narrow, referring as it does mainly to relations of distribution and allocation rather than production. To capture all this, "capitalistic" seems appropriate.
2 Calculated from *China Statistical Yearbook 2007*, table 5–22 and *China Statistical Yearbook 2018*, table 4–12, which yielded a figure of 8.9%. These figures include some professionals and low-level managers, so those for actual blue-collar workers were probably a bit less; but since workers comprised the vast majority of employees, the actual levels are probably not significantly lower.
3 Interview, November 2002. In January 2015, two protests against wage arrears running as high as ¥900,000 resulted in two deaths. 'Contractor's teenage daughter falls to her death in wage arrears protest', *China Labour Bulletin* January 21, 2015 (www.clb.org.hk/en/content/contractor%E2%80%99s-teenage-daughter-falls-her-death-wage-arrears-protest). In September 2020, the State Council ordered the Dafang County government to pay its teachers ¥470 million yuan in wage arrears. '关于贵州省毕节市大方县拖欠教师工资补贴挤占挪用教育经费等问题的督查情况通报' (www.gov.cn/hudong/ducha/2020-09/04/content_5540680.htm). In November wage arrears in the delivery sector provoked strikes in Suzhou. Zhao Yiwei, 'Amid Price War and Unpaid Wages, Couriers Strike and Strive,' *Sixth Tone* November 7, 2020 (www.sixthtone.com/news/1006403/amid-price-war-and-unpaid-wages%2C-couriers-strike-and-strive).
4 Calculated from *China Statistical Yearbook*, 2016, table 4–17. The data are aggregated by province and exclude Chongqing and Tibet, for which there were no 1990 data.

5 Personal communication from Prof. William Hurst.
6 In addition to state-owned and domestic and foreign-owned private firms is a vast sector of mixed ownership forms, such as joint ventures between Chinese and foreign owners, and "private" firms owned by state enterprises or government entities.
7 Interview, June 29, 1996.
8 Interview, December 5, 1995.
9 For example, see (especially chapter 2 of) Kim (2013), a study of a factory in the rural environs of Qingdao, Shandong.
10 A program of heavy industrialization in China's hinterlands, constructed in the early 1960s for defensive purposes.
11 Surely there were many more. But even if this number amounts to only one-tenth of the actual number of strikes, only 3.7% of industrial enterprises would have experienced them.

6
THE MIDDLE CLASS IN REFORMING CHINA

The dream of a classless society

Jean-Louis Rocca

After the beginning of the twenty-first century, the issue of the middle class permeated China's academic journals, the media, official speeches, and even discussions between friends to a considerable extent. China has become passionate about the topic. An increasing number of Chinese and Western scholars have attempted to grasp the substance of this new social group, each researcher giving their own definition. From the start, it was obvious to everyone that the 'middle class' existed in modern societies and that the Chinese case would not escape the phenomenon (Goodman 1999, 2014a; Rocca 2016). For some scholars, the determining factor was income, the structure of consumption, or even occupation. For others, the level of education was the only necessary qualification, with entry to university appearing as the required threshold.

With the passage of time, the criteria have multiplied and been refined, the middle class imagined with its specific lifestyles, values, and political attitudes. Members of the middle class have been alleged to be very interested in politics and the country's major challenges, to be active in NGOs, to participate in social movements, and, in short, to be ready to defend their rights but without giving in to violent and radical practices. The variety of criteria led to a diversity of descriptions: the 'authentic', 'real', or 'core', 'upper', 'middle', 'lower', 'within the system', 'outside the system' middle class (Zhou Xiaohong 2008; Li and Zhang 2008; Liu Xin 2010; Qi Xingfa 2010; Li Chunling 2017).

Many debates emerged about the percentage of the population corresponding to these various requirements. Given the diversity of definitions, the responses varied to a great extent. According to some perspectives and some data, from 20% to 30% of the Chinese and half of the urban Chinese have already entered the middle class (Rocca 2016: Ch.2). If the simple fact of benefiting from an average salary and of owning an apartment and a car ensures membership of the middle class – as is often said to be the case within China – the size of the group is impressive.

DOI: 10.4324/9781003255017-7

But those who might qualify by having a substantial income, affluent consumption, the right job, the right level of education, the right lifestyle, the right values, and the right political attitudes – those widely regarded as the 'genuine' middle class – can barely amount to no more than a few percent of the entire population (Li and Zhang 2008; Zhou Xiaohong 2002, 2008).

Nonetheless, this variety and range of meanings do not mean that there is no real 'Chinese middle class'. On the contrary, the discourse on the middle class in Chinese society has become omnipresent in Chinese society with increasing numbers emulating middle-class behaviour. Good taste has become 'middle class' (neither 'redneck' nor 'parvenu'), as have new public gathering places and new media (Xiong Yihan 2019; He Jin 2012; Song and Lee 2010). Moreover, prominent scholars and the government itself are convinced that the middle class is now the most important social group and that public policies must contribute to increase its number. In essence, the middle class has become the ideal class to solve the main flaws of the modernization process and, to a certain extent, to replace the proletariat as the univerzaliing class constituting the core of the society. The performative effect of a public discussion along those lines gives substance to a new approach to social as well as economic development. Dealing with the middle class then means not only analysing the real and objective changes constituting social stratification but also taking into account the subjective and political nature of any attempt to define the middle class as a social group and evaluating the impact of these attempts on peoples' behaviour and self-representation (Goodman 1999; Rocca 2016; Li and Wang 2017). This approach which sees concepts as socially constructed is close to the one used by Luc Boltanski at the beginning of the 1980s when he dealt with *Les cadres* (management executives in private and public institutions) the emblematic group of the French new middle class which emerged in the 1960s.

> One may speak of cadres as if they constituted a unified group, indeed, a collective subject with a will of their own and an ability to act . . . or else one may argue that cadres are so varied, so different from one another, that it is wrong to speak of them collectively as a social group at all. . . . But in that case how does one explain that real flesh-and-blood individuals claim to be cadres and to belong to this allegedly nonexistent group? And how does one account for the attitudes and behavior of such people when these appear to be determined not by the market, with his aggressive logic, not by some sort of mechanical interactions of individual strategies and utilitarian calculations, but rather by belief in the existence of a concrete social group.
>
> *(Boltanski 1987: 27–28)*

As the academic and public debate about the Chinese middle class revolves around a comparison between the assumed characteristics of the middle class in developed countries and in China, the appeal to an approach elaborated decades ago in a European country seems appropriate (Li Chunling 2012; Goodman 2016; Rocca 2016). Moreover, the various definitions of the middle class used by researchers, whether Chinese or foreign, are borrowed from Western research. They insist on related concepts such as consumer society, distinction, status, identification, class in itself/class for itself, new social movements, and liberalism found in the works of Marx, Weber, Mills, Wright, Giddens, and Bourdieu (Zhang Xing 2003; Lu Xueyi 2002, 2004, 2005; Li and Kong 2017; Li Hongyan 2017). Mostly, modernization theorists are the main source of inspiration for Chinese scholars. They see an objective definition of the middle class as the norm, and the issue is to measure the gap between 'the' definition and Chinese reality. Is there a real Chinese middle class with the same characteristics, behaviour, and potential for action as exists in the Western middle class? Interestingly, the debate about the Chinese working class during the early twentieth century took exactly the same form: a comparison with both the Marxist model and the European working class on the one hand and what was going on and supposed to going on in China on the other hand. Was the Chinese proletariat a real proletariat? Is the Chinese middle class a real middle class?

This chapter tries to go further by making comparisons about the development of the middle class more precisely in France and China. In the French case (1946–1976) as well in the Chinese case (since the end of the 1990s), the emergence of a 'new middle class' was triggered by dramatic changes in society. Society was completely reshaped. In both countries, decades of growth have resulted in the emergence of new ways of life and consumption, new outlooks on the world, and new behaviours. These phenomena concern a particular group of individuals who can be called 'intermediary', in the sense that they are situated between the 'poor and dominated' and the 'rich and dominant'. No phenomenon exists without representation, or any representation without facts. Interpretations create new facts by causing people to act in a certain way, and facts force representations to evolve. This objectification of discourse, this construction of phenomena is carried out at multiple levels, which leads to a necessary diversification of sources. First of all, there is the academic discourse which is displayed in scholarly literature but also during interactions between power holders and scholars. Second, there are media production and official speeches which partially take up scholarly discourse by adapting it to the popular readership and bureaucratic practice. Finally, individual appropriation translates these discourses into actions. The feeling to belong to a group is important. But more importantly, it is only because a group of people acts according to a certain number of objectives, values, and norms that the class as structure becomes a class in action and then a class with a certain level of consciousness. In short, it is a question of comparing both the objective phenomena – the facts that took place at different times and in different contexts – and the imaginaries that give them meanings. This separation between reality and imaginary is only used for clarification and, so to speak, for pedagogic purpose.

In China in the 1990s and 2000s as in France some decades earlier, social stratification dramatically changed. New intermediary classes emerged, and then the intermediary classes changed in composition and size. This event went hand in hand with different interpretations of what a middle class is, its characteristics, and above all its function in the process of modernization. Like the proletariat in the past, the middle class is given different kinds of duty and in particular a political duty.

The idea is not at all to use the European case as a standard metre against which the 'progress' of the Chinese case could be measured but to highlight the commonalities and the differences without assuming that there are intangible norms. In other words, the emergence of the middle class should not be seen as a pure Chinese phenomenon, neither can it be seen as a simple repetition of a universal phenomenon. In that matter, the differences between historical contexts can explain why the use of the same concepts or expressions can give birth to very different contents and phenomena. In the case of China, the 'exit from socialism' is a particularly determinant event. Three key differences are to be found in the emergence of a new middle class in France and China: social stratification was at odds; the composition of the middle class was dissimilar; and its historical missions were defined differently.

At the origin of the new middle classes

France during the 30 glorious years (1946–1976) (Fourastié 1979; Lejeune 2015) and China (Naughton 1995, 2007) during the reform period starting at the end of the 1970s experienced a process of modernization and intense economic growth. The lagged sectors of the French economy such as agriculture or trade were undergoing rapid transformation. The number of peasants declined rapidly, and many workers took up stable, full-time, and skilled jobs in administration and big firms. From the mid-1990s on, a series of reforms led China to enter the era of capitalist practices: a type of society in which, labour, money, and land are transformed into commodities, thus creating the basis for the extension of market regulation to the whole of society (Polanyi 1944). The public employment system was abolished, economic planning withdrawn, migration allowed, land use rights sold, the financial system liberalized, and markets introduced determining the price of land and labour. In both countries, economic growth has led to the development of large enterprises.

The philosophies of these approaches to change were at odds. In France, the role of the state increased in the economy; in China liberal reforms co-existed with the continued role of the CCP as the key actor. But in the two societies, these changes opened a phase of prosperity which in turn contributed to a considerable increase in the standard of living of the population. Urbanization soared causing a decrease in the number of rural dwellers; the service economy developed; demand for skilled workers and professionals exploded producing new intermediate social strata, neither poor nor rich, and educated, whose relative prosperity induced a radical transformation of lifestyles, that is a set of practices and representations specific to a social group. Due to the exponential and continuous productivity growth, there was now a greater need for consumers than producers, leading to the emergence of a consumer society. Home ownership became the rule among urban dwellers, the car industry grew exponentially, and the leisure economy became the centre of consumer concerns.

Linked to the development of brainwork, the 'massification' of secondary and tertiary education system constitutes another element which profoundly transformed the social structures in France (Merle 2009) and China. In China, the gross higher education enrolment ratio was 1.56% in 1978 and 30% in 2013. The rise was particularly dramatic between 1999 and 2003, during which the number of places in higher education institutions increased by 20% every year (Wang Fenghuang 2013). The entire population saw its levels of education and qualification increased considerably. Higher education which had been limited to a small proportion of the population in the two societies became a major asset to successful life outcomes (Li Chunling 2010b; Merle 2009). The number of professionals (engineers, designers, marketing and packaging specialists, advertisers, traders, medical doctors, lawyers) has exploded (Zhang and Wu 2016). Soaring urbanization has reshaped social relationships, making them more fluid, broader, less linked to family and neighbourhood. Cities have been redesigned to respond to and facilitate the dramatic increase in business and consumption. Large and high buildings were erected everywhere; means of transportation (public transport and private cars) were modernized (Fulong 2015).

All these changes produced mythologies of modernity which gradually infused all social categories including peasants and workers (Ross 1996 for France; Gerth 2010 for China). For a large proportion of urban residents, consumption has become an end in itself. To be middle class, an individual must own at least an apartment in a new residence as well as a car (Zhang Li 2010; Zhang Jun 2019). They must also have been able to furnish and fit out their own house, travel, and own a dog. New values (speed, hygiene, comfort, personal development, property ownership) and new practices (sport, leisure, psychology, vacations, American-style management) emerged. The body (including health and sexuality) has become the major concern of individuals (Boltanski and Chiapello 2005 for France; Anagnost 1997 for China). The great theologico-political systems (Catholicism and socialism in France, Marxism-Leninism in China) have had to leave room for more diversified philosophies. New ages in life, such as adolescence and youth, appeared. Finally, new products were consumed. 'Modern' drinks conquer the market – Coca Cola, for example, and related refreshments – but also tea and whiskey in France; coffee, wine, and cognac in China. Access to the real estate market (and everything that goes with it, furniture, decoration, household appliances) and private cars alone symbolize this shift in the relationship with the material culture (Zhang Li 2010). In brief, a relatively large proportion of the society took advantage of these mutations to change their lives, and many of those who were not successful in changing comprehensively wished they had.

Social stratification

During the 1980s, China underwent reforms but without changing its social system. Special economic zones were opened to attract foreign companies but were limited in size; migration was allowed even if many restrictions were still imposed; enterprises gained some room for manoeuvre in terms of investment; work, production management, and land use rights were provided to peasants (but not private ownership); small private businesses were introduced in the cities, and private and collective enterprises in the countryside. But the economic and social control systems remained in the hands of the state (Naughton 1995). Most urban workers were still members of work units and could not find another job in the absence of a labour market (Lü and Perry 1997). The access to university was slightly easier but still narrow, limiting the number of professionals (Pepper 1996). Most peasants were forced to remain in the countryside (Solinger 1999). Although cadres, professionals, workers, and peasants experienced wage increases, inflation started to consume most of this increase. Goods were easier to obtain as a result of the development of free markets and light industry, but Chinese society remained substantially a shortage economy. The few opportunities to change lifestyles and status, as well as the limited improvement in living standards led to a degree of frustration among the population. In urban China, these circumstances and feelings contributed to popular demonstrations in many places at the end of the 1980s of which the most famous was that which gathered in Tiananmen Square (Walder and Gong 1993).

Social stratification did not change significantly until the mid-1990s, and certainly until then there was no mention of a middle class (or middle classes) in the Chinese media or among academics, outside let alone inside China (Rocca 2016; Lu Xueyi 2002). The external debate focused on whether the few but dynamic private businessmen might overthrow the system and take precedence over the cadres in terms of economic and political power. Could a new bourgeoisie (even if the word was never used) replace the CCP's cadres as a dominant class? (Nee and Lian 1994; Nee 1996; Nee and Yang 1999).

Everything began to change in the 1990s. China introduced capitalist practices (Naughton 2007). At the same time, the contrast with France in terms of social stratification was striking. In France, before the 1960s, the lower classes were made up of peasants without land and most of the workers (the unskilled). The middle classes were the petite bourgeoisie, professionals, and financially comfortable (without being rich) landowning farmers (Castel 2002). In China, social stratification largely followed the lines of the divisions between urban and rural dwellers. Professionals, ordinary and middle-rank cadres, and most urban workers were members of the middle classes. The lower classes included the peasants, a small number of urban workers, and the alleged enemies of the regime. The socialist middle classes represented the core of the urban areas where socio-political, economic, and cultural assets were concentrated. In terms of access to consumption, personal networks, and education, living in a city was a huge advantage. Even if the social categories of professionals and intellectuals were present in both China and France, the other significant part of the French middle class – the petite bourgeoisie – was absent in China. This social group including small merchants, petty capitalists, and artisans existed before 1949 but was eliminated by the CCP during the 1950s. Their means of production were collectivized along with their economic capital, the source of their social status. Depending on individual circumstances, they became workers, were classified as enemies of the regime, or became employees of collective enterprises. In some cases, they even became Party and government officials.

A very different middle class

The comparison with France indicates the specific characteristics of the Chinese new middle classes. In France, the new middle class was formed through the social integration of the working class (including domestic peasant migrants) and their relative embourgeoisement: it was a vertical upward mobility. The 1950s, 1960s, 1970s, and 1980s saw the lives of many workers and peasants (through rural exodus) radically transformed (Castel 2002). Many of the former left their status as precarious workers, often poorly housed, for stable work; this turning point was often followed by the purchase of an apartment and of the goods necessary for accessing the 'comfortable life'. Their children had access to secondary and university education, unthinkable in previous generations. Precariousness as well as degraded living and working conditions became the fate of immigrant workers. Admittedly, the new middle classes also included a number of 'petty-bourgeois layers' (traders, artisans, rentiers, small businessmen) who had been disadvantaged by capitalist development and concentration; as well as some downwardly mobile children of the former who had been the victims of the concentration of business in the hands of transnational firms (Boltanski 1987). China was dramatically different.

Reproduction of the middle class

In China, the middle class has different origins, not least because in large measure the socialist-era middle classes succeeded in maintaining their prominent position and became the new middle class, for a number of reasons.

The new middle classes are mainly urban residents (and their descendants) living in the big cities of the east coast (Lu Xueyi 2004 and 2012; Li and Xu 2017). The best schools, the best jobs, and the best career opportunities are to be found in the very largest megalopolises, and even living in a small city is clearly a disadvantage (Li Chunling 2010a; Wang Mengqi 2017; Lin and Sun 2010; Carrillo 2011). From 2005 to 2013, the proportion of people having a middle-class income living in the eastern regions increased from 53.3% to 66.65%; the proportion of people having a middle-class education (university graduates) increased from 39.21% to 55.91%; and the percentage of professionals in the workforce increased from 40.92% to 56.17% (Li Qiang 2016).

Many young people are reluctant to work in small cities after graduating from college because they know the best opportunities are in the biggest cities (Li Qiang 2016). The administrative status of individuals also plays a major role in this calculus. Every Chinese has a residence permit which determines their civic entitlement in terms of their place of residence (as between urban and rural areas) and as between agricultural and non-agricultural employment. In the big cities, migration has created two different populations. There are permanent residents with the right to live locally, generally employed in non-agricultural activities; and there are migrant workers from the countryside, who may live more or less permanently in the cities (Solinger 1999; Chan and Buckingham 2008). In Beijing, the permanent resident population in 2020 is only 12 million, and the permanent migrant population is more than 10 million (Li Qiang 2016). The opportunities for peasants to become middle class are few and far between. Among the 260 million to 270 million peasant migrant workers in cities, few have the money and the distinction to put their children in good schools. Most retain their agricultural status and have a non-skilled job, with extremely limited access to education and professional training (Zhan Shaohua 2011). The urban middle class from the big eastern seaboard cities were able to take advantage of the period of growth in order to maintain its privileges. This situation can be explained by 'opportunity hoarding' (Tilly 1998) that allows powerful groups to exclude others from access to resources or benefits.

Since the 1980s, access to higher education has become one of the paths to social success. A good education results in high qualification, prestige, self-confidence, and large relationship networks. The increase in returns to education in terms of income reveals the focus on education in the labour market (Zhao et al. 2005; Liu Zhiqiang 2007; Liu and Shu 2013). Education also provides prestige and social capital. In China, graduating from college or university is a mark of personal accomplishment and is perceived as a guarantee of intelligence, quality, skills, and even good manners (Hanser 2008; Rocca 2016, Chapter 4). Although determined by a system of meritocratic exams, university entry de facto favours urban residents. The best secondary schools are in big cities. Locals need less points than non-locals for accessing a university in the city where they live; and the level of their income allows them to pay extra-school tuition (Wang Xin 2020). The most prestigious universities like Peking University or Tsinghua University select students even before the state university entrance examination to be sure to get the best students. They sign agreements with two or three secondary schools in each province, the best ones, all in the province's biggest city (Li Chunling 2010b; Rocca 2016 Ch.2). In terms of cultural capital, the children of urban residents comply with the evaluative standards of schooling. Compared to rural residents, parental involvement and parental choice in schooling operate to reproduce educational privileges. For example, urban parents buy apartments in neighbourhoods where they are sure there are good schools (Wang Mengqi 2018). The sense of superiority and self-confidence possessed by families in the urban middle classes gives them an enormous privilege in matters of school selection over the 'rural bumpkins' (Hannum and Adams 2009) and explains why the massification of higher education in the 2000s was not a democratization and resulted in an over-representation of urbanites in higher education institutions (Li Chunling 2010b). The new jobs are in the city and especially in the big cities. Social networks of mutual knowledge play a central role in access to good jobs, and local urbanites are most endowed with them. They are the ones who have the closest relations with the Party and the government.

In terms of social stratification, the only serious attempts to draw a clear picture of the Chinese society take occupation as basic criterion. From this point of view, Chinese scholars are in line with Western sociologists (Wright 1997; Erikson and Goldthorpe 1992) and largely quote them. The most famous of these attempts, the ten-group typology of the Chinese social stratification developed by Lu Xueyi in 2002, clearly refers to neo-Marxist and neo-Weberian approach of class (Lu Xueyi 2002: 1–32). He refers also to the three-class model most sociologists rely on from the 1960s (Bourdieu 1984; Wright 1997). Lu Xueyi built up socio-professional groups according to three capitals – economic capital, social capital, and education. He considers that these three assets increase with place on the social hierarchy. In other words, those at the top possess a disproportionately large amount of money as well as similar amounts of social and cultural capital. This classification has many common points with the Goldthorpe's Neo-Weberian class model also based on occupations and used by many researchers in Asia to describe class distribution (Erikson and Goldthorpe 1992; Hsiao 1999).

In defining the middle class, Lu Xueyi identifies three urban groups who in the Chinese context constitute the greatest proportion of urban residents:

1 Professional and technical staff: the persons who are devoted to specialized, skilled and scientific tasks, irrespective of the sector in which they work (state, public, party-related organizations, collective and non-public enterprises). Most received middle or higher education and technical specialized professional training. They have the kind of specialized skills and specific knowledge that fit with the demand of large-scale production modernizing society. They do not possess means of production but have the characteristics of high and middle white collars in terms of autonomy.
2 'Administrative staff' is defined as 'full-time office workers who are responsible for daily administrative affairs in departments and assistance units. This group is mainly composed of low and middle ranks officials in state and party organizations and non-specialized civil servants and basic managers in social institutions and enterprises of all types of ownership. They are low-rank white collars who do not possess means of production, inside or outside the system.'
3 'Industry and trade individual entrepreneurs': refer to people who make a living by running productive, circulating service activities and other business activities or activities in the finance and security markets and using low quantity of capital. For example, small business owners and small employers (people who have enough capital to employ a small number of workers but who directly participate to work and to production management), self-employers (people who have enough capital to start their own business but not enough to hire workers), small shareholders, house-owners renting a small number of houses, etc. They are self-employed, low-level blue and white collars.

(Lu Xueyi 2004: 150–159)

The first two groups correspond to ordinary and middle-rank cadres and professionals. They have it in common that they work in the state administration or the new sector of the economy, are educated, and essentially brain workers. As for cadres, far from having been replaced by private entrepreneurs in the control of economic capital, they have largely benefitted from the reforms. They are called the 'within system' middle class by Chinese scholars, meaning both that they are in the Party-state apparatus and that they take advantage of it. They are in charge of developing business and wealth from local business. They and their children are in good position to cope with new requirements in and of education (Wank 1999; Guo Xuezhi 2001; Goodman 2008; Tsai 2007; Dickson 2010).

Chinese scholars often suggest that professionals and cadres are in opposition: the juxtaposition of those within the system and those outside the system (Li Chunling 2017). The reasons for this suggestion are fairly apparent. The growing role played by the market and the meritocratic system of education might have provided people 'outside the system' with personal opportunities to enter the ranks of the middle class. In addition, it is assumed that those people outside the system would have a different mentality, less wedded to the political attitudes and behaviours found within the system. In practice, the difference between professionals and cadres is not so huge. The emphasis on technical skills and bureaucratic procedures in both public administration and the management of big private companies leads to combined political power and technocracy. Professional and technical personnel account for the highest proportion of the new 'within the system' middle class (Li Chunling 2017). There is clearly difficulty in determining whether a young engineer working for a public building company or a law graduate appointed as a party secretary of a small county is a professional or a cadre. In any case, in generational terms, in Mao's China there were few people 'outside the system' and certainly no independent professionals. Therefore, in the new generations the only difference between 'in' and 'out' is probably limited to the kind of employer they are working for. Working for a foreign company or a Chinese public company or for the state certainly contributes to differences in terms of lifestyles and political attitudes, but research into these provides few if any significant differences, and certainly not in terms of political attitudes and actions, as will become apparent shortly. In addition, social reproduction contributes to homogenization: it seems that children of cadres become professionals and vice versa. They can work for foreign companies or for Chinese public firms quite indifferently.

It may seem paradoxical to include workers in state companies as part of the middle class. Many had lost their jobs or retired early at the end of 1990s or the beginning of the 2000s in a rare and probably unique phenomenon where an entire social group all but disappeared so quickly. At that time, most state-owned enterprises were closed or merged. Workers lost not only their jobs but also their benefits. The dismantling of the work unit system opened the road to an increasing commodification of life. No more collective consumption such as free or nearly free meals taken in canteens; no more provision of housing and health protection; no more provision of durable goods in times of scarcity; and no more free delivery of cabbage (in wintertime) or watermelons (in summertime) (Rocca 2003; Lee Ching Kwan 2007; Hurst 2009).

Nonetheless, most families of workers preserved their status as members of the middle class. This was achieved because they took advantage of their position in the formal class system and were able to convince national and local governments that their decline could be the end of the regime. During Mao's era, a new category of 'employees and workers' was created and constituted a sort of social base for the socialist regime. Workers enjoyed many privileges in terms of income and living and working conditions that provided them with prestige and a specific relationship with the power holders. In work units, cadres and workers lived together, and at that time there were rare but real opportunities for the latter to enter the ranks of the cadres. In terms of symbolic capital, they were situated just below the elite. Conversely, unrest among workers influenced Party policies to a great extent, and working-class behaviours were determinant in political conflicts within the Party apparatus. After the introduction of reform, the regime had no reason to radically change the balance of power. The regime gave urban dwellers opportunities to improve their living conditions through inflation and the still limited scope of opportunities did not provide them with large benefits. Many workers expressed their discontent during the demonstrations in Tiananmen Square in 1989 (Walder and Gong 1993). The new reforms adopted after the middle of the 1990s were aimed precisely at increasing life-chance opportunities. At the same time, the dismantling of the public sector led to redundancies for dozens of millions of middle-aged urban workers, which contributed to endangering social order in most cities. Thousands of incidents, some violent, broke out all over industrial cities (Cai Yongshun 2002; Rocca 2003; Chen Feng 2006; Hurst 2009). Local governments immediately adopted social policies in order to limit the impact of workers' anger and to allow fired workers to survive the crisis. Most were allowed to become the owners of their homes, and most of them received modest subsidies for 2 to 3 years. They enjoyed preferential programmes for re-employment, particularly in the small trade and petty jobs sector (Kernen and Rocca 2000; Rocca 2000). Thereafter, during the period of Hu Jintao's leadership (2002–2012), urban workers continued to enjoy subsidies because 'any further reductions in their social benefits could drive them over the edge of tolerance and turn to protest' (Gao et al. 2019: 102).

The government's concern for workers in trouble was not only linked to the maintenance of public order. The habitus that the local cadres had embodied in the 1950s made them sensitive to the fate of urban workers. The two groups were still linked, often by kinship ties, but also by the existence of superior-subaltern or patron-client relations (Walder 1986). Finally, the importance of local governments in the Chinese political structure obliges them to take care of locals. Local government is not just the representative of central government at grassroots level. Rather, it is responsible for the local population, and particularly for adapting global policies to local contexts. Most ordinary and middle-rank cadres spend their professional career in a small territory. For all these reasons, the distance between local cadres and workers was small (Kernen and Rocca 2000; Rocca 2000). China is still a socialist country in its own self-view where cadres must 'serve the people' (Blecher 2004, 2006) and with the growing importance of public opinion, the support of locals is an important guarantee of an official's career (Tang Wenfang 2005; Chen Dan 2017). Workers were therefore in a position to hold local governments to account and to demand help (Rocca 2006b). In this context, it is easy to understand why the government did not call into question urban privileges to access higher education. While education capital has become one of the main assets on the road to success, there has been no reason to eliminate urban dwellers' control of the education system, which provides them with an enormous advantage.

In a sense, like a chrysalis becoming a butterfly, the class of urban employees and workers died to transform themselves into a 'new middle stratum'. They have maintained and even improved their condition. Some of them never got new jobs and had a hard time surviving but most found a new way of making a living, sometimes accumulating both small jobs and even a pension (Rocca 2006a). Moreover, the apartments that many urban dwellers were allotted at the end of 1990s have gained in value due to the increase in real estate prices, even when their property was often modest and dilapidated. Local urbanites have thus gained access to home ownership and property. Urban middle- and lower-class children have taken advantage of the opening up of the access to higher education which most of their parents had not enjoyed in the past. And it has not been rare to see the children of those who had lost their jobs taking charge of their parents when the latter encountered difficulties: a clear advantage of the children's access to higher education (Rocca 2006a and 2006b).

Socialist workers (and their descendants) were also turned into members of the new middle class because of the emergence of a new working class composed of migrant workers (Chan and Pun 2009). Certainly, the emergence of urban poverty at the end of the 1990s is well documented but the urban poor are few, the vast majority of urban residents belonging to the new middle class. The once socialist working class came to occupy positions as professionals and white-collar workers. The new working class is based on the migrant workers from the countryside whose living and working conditions are equivalent to those of the proletariat in capitalist societies. More precisely, these conditions are identical in all respects to foreign migrant workers who came to Europe after the 1950s. They are the exploited class of the Chinese miracle and are segregated in all areas: legally, culturally, and economically. They even experience a double phenomenon of segregation, as both unskilled workers and non-locals. They do not enjoy the status of urban residents and meet great difficulties in access to public services and welfare systems. They usually cannot afford to rent a house on the local rent market and have to find a dilapidated space on the informal real estate market. Their children have problems going to school in town and especially getting to a good school. They are discriminated against by urban society which regards them as inherently inferior (Sun Wanning 2014).

Two middle classes: the new middle class and the petty bourgeoisie

A final difference in comparison with the French new social stratification is the simultaneous development of a petty bourgeoisie and a new middle stratum. In France, one replaced the other – without making it completely disappear. The petite bourgeoisie appeared to be 'old-fashioned', condemned by history and attracting very little interest from sociologists and the media. In China, on the other hand, there is no substitution but complementarity of the one and the other: the commodification of society after more than 30 years of a totally planned economy has led to the revival of a small capitalism – crafts, small businesses, and individual businesses (Anderson et al. 2003). These activities concern certain niches that the big companies cannot satisfy: local consumption, small-scale production, subcontracting activities, and exports to low-income countries.

This petite bourgeoisie, whose status depends on the ownership of the means of production, is partly made up of city dwellers. They are either graduates who prefer to do business and create an enterprise rather than become cadres or professionals, or urban non-graduates who find (often thanks to their social capital) a way forward through these activities. Some though are rural migrant workers who succeeded in developing a business and have become a kind of urban–rural middle class, typically in small cities. Unfortunately, this latter phenomenon is poorly documented and its existence only appears epiphenomenally.[1] Due to the importance of social and political capital in business, the number of migrants probably does not make up a significant proportion of this petite bourgeoisie. At the same time, there is undoubtedly a petty bourgeoisie in the Chinese countryside, drawn mainly from trade, small-scale industry, and agricultural production activities. Unfortunately, according to Chinese scholars themselves, this phenomenon is also poorly documented in academic research (Yuan et al. 2012).

The very limited social change in the composition of the post-1978 middle class despite the profound transformations of the society epitomizes the conservatism of social stratification and the importance of social reproduction in China (Li Lulu 2003). Unlike the experience of France and Western Europe, the lower classes did not experience significant upward mobility. This is not to say that such a phenomenon may not occur in future, but for the time being the membership of the middle class remains broadly the same as before. This resilience is due to both the previous social stratification and some reproduction mechanisms. In order to preserve social stability and to have an available and exploitable workforce replacing the privileged former working class, positions in social space have been frozen. If, contrary to some expectations, state workers who lost their jobs and status did not attempt to overthrow the regime, it is precisely because of this very limited scope of change. The capitals needed to seize opportunities (education and money) stayed in the hands of the cadres, professionals, and state workers, that is, urban residents of the eastern big cities. These assets were transferred to their children who have taken advantage of their cumulative circulation. Social and political capitals (the simple fact of being an urban resident) provide cultural capital which guarantee a good job and then economic capital and prestige. Having money facilitates the acquisition of cultural capital, social capital, and even, though sometimes through corruption, political capital.

The middle class and politics

How the emergence of the new middle class is interpreted also marks the profound differences between France and China. The political context is radically different. The France of the 30 glorious years has been a democracy for a long time. Nothing like this in China, no elections apart from village elections, no institutionalization of the protest, and no right to organize. Certainly, social conflicts are numerous in China, and it is undeniable that there is a field of protest, but no possibility for protesters to create legal, representative stable, and independent organizations. In China, the absence of right of association and organization of social groups does not allow social categories 'to represent themselves'. It is through academic production, and in particular sociological, rapidly relayed by the media and the government and CCP discourses, that the new intermediate strata have become new middle classes. The promiscuity between the intelligentsia, the media, and the political circles facilitates the circulation of the 'middle class' imaginary. Chinese sociologists, even the most critical, are in a position to influence public policies and propaganda. Likewise, when intellectuals do not themselves spread their thoughts on the internet, the media are fond of their analysis. Despite these essential differences, it is striking to note that in both France and China, debates around the middle class have become debates about the link between middle class and modernization (Goodman 1999; Rocca 2016).

In France, two camps clashed. In the 1950s and the 1960s, France was regarded as archaic by the French media. Les cadres, that is to say, the legitimate middle class, were supposed to modernize the French society. However, there was another way of talking about les cadres and the middle class. In the 1960s, Marxism which was taking the lead in the intellectual circles was facing a major crisis. The working class was experiencing a process of embourgeoisement and appeared less and less able to fulfil Marx's prediction. Where to find a new revolutionary subject? The French Maoists would find it among workers who have not yet been embourgeoisé, that is to say, immigrant workers. But according to most intellectuals, the fact that cadres are henceforth the driving force of the economy could lead the middle class to be a revolutionary agent (Boltanski 1987). Moreover, the development of the 'new social movements' (NSM) contributed to make of the middle class the new 'universalizing class'. These conflicts were identified through the emergence of new social strata (white-collar workers, technicians, professionals, etc.) well educated, well integrated into society, possessing prestige and good income, having the capacity, and the desire to defend causes. Traditional demands linked to working conditions and levels of remuneration have been replaced by new demands focusing on the rights of women, sexual, or ethnic minorities and local communities. They oppose institutions of social control (mental institution, hospital, prison, school) and aim at protecting the environment (anti-nuclear or anti-pollution movements) and consumers. However, hopes that these movements would overthrow capitalism were quickly dashed (Cleveland 2003). Most of them do not really attack the state and do not question social stratification or power relations as a whole. In many of these movements, residents oppose new developments in the local area which were perceived as damaging neighbourhood interests and ways of life. A new acronym (NIMBY, 'not in my back yard') was created to express the fact that such residents would stop opposition if the developments were built in another place. Critics of the new middle class see these movements as a proof of the individualism of the middle class and its incapacity to defend collective and global interests (Lake 1986 and 1993).

Building an ideal class for modernizing China

In China, the debate on how to conceptualize and define the middle class emanates from several points within society (sociologists, politicians, journalists, trade unionists, various personalities) and was rapidly led and articulated by the CCP itself. After the mid-1990s, when the reforms started to profoundly transform social structures, Party leaders began to be worried about their impact on Chinese society. Research was financed to analyse social stratification in modernized countries in order to foresee changes and the possible future transformation of Chinese society. By the end of 1990s, that research turned to consider the Chinese middle class. In the process, the correlation between middle class and modernization has been created as an absolute dogma (Lu Xueyi 2002, 2004; Rocca 2016). The influence of modernization theory on academic circles is easy to explain. The revival of Chinese social sciences in the early 1980s owed much to the American research system. In the field of sociology, American scholars, particularly of Chinese descent, came very early to form cohorts of young students who would later become eminent professors in China or in the United States. Also, American universities and foundations, in particular, the Ford Foundation, quickly flooded the academic world with funding to study the development of civil society, gender, and the empowerment of vulnerable groups (Rocca 2016). Adopting the modernization theory framework, Chinese researchers (Yingjie 2009; Rocca 2016) and many Western scholars (Chen Jie 2013) established the middle class as the main driver of change in modernizing societies.

The experience of Western countries was vaguely evoked, and diverse schools of thought were mentioned. However, it was the recent history of some Asian countries that was commonly taken as the example to justify that point of view. Scholars considered that the Taiwanese, Korean, and Thai experiences show that it is the emergence of a new middle class which contributed the most to social changes and in particular to political change. Generated by economic growth, the middle class was supposed to spontaneously trigger the democratization process. This commonplace interpretation, which is called into question by numerous works (Koo 1991; Jones 1995), nevertheless had a considerable influence on the imaginary construction of the Chinese middle class (Chen Jie and Lu Chunlong 2006).

The discourse on the middle class therefore leads to the creation of a sort of ideal class which is supposed to solve the problems facing China in its 'modernization process'. The definition of this middle class and its social 'missions' then becomes key to the identification of the 'right' middle class. In that process, questions of scope and scale, as well as current and future social development have become central issues.

Income appeared to be the most obvious criterion that might be used to determine membership of the middle class (Shen Liren 2004; Li Chunling 2016a; Zhou and Hu 2020). Very quickly the problems turned out to be more complex. What is the threshold for leaving poverty and which for entry to the ranks of the wealthy? The question is all the more important since many people in China, and particularly leaders within the Party-state, equate belonging to the middle class to 'small prosperity'. This notion which is largely used in official documents is difficult to define. Below this level, people are 'warmly dressed and fed to satiety'; above this level, people are rich. How to calculate the income corresponding to 'small prosperity'? By taking into account household income or individual income? The standard of living is extremely variable across China, so should there be a global threshold or should it be assessed by locality? In any case, the very possibility of being able to calculate the income of the Chinese population is problematic. Many have informal jobs, and the rest receive bonuses, allowances, or benefits that appear nowhere. Some have two employment contracts, one with low remuneration to avoid paying too much tax, the other internal to the company, the difference being paid in cash. The extreme case is that of civil servants who have modest salaries but who enjoy many in-kind benefits, are provided with low-cost housing, and profit from successful arrangements with businessmen, not to mention bribes (Li and Niu 2003; Rocca 2016).

Social stratification may also be marked by the level of education. Researchers have come to the conclusion that obtaining a university degree puts everyone in the middle class. The very difficult entrance examination in higher education is in fact supposed not only to ensure an educational level but also to be a pledge of culture and good manners. For some, it is the occupation that is highly discriminating. Being a professional (professors, lawyers, engineers, designers, and doctors, for example) and having a job in the modern sector might define membership of the middle class. Equally common is the equation of the middle class with white-collar workers (Lin et al. 2010; Tang and Unger 2013; Wang Xin 2020). This definition though omits the possibility of small entrepreneurs, individual workers, and others who have an average standard of living from being considered middle class.

These attempts to define the middle class rely on a notion of class defined by the position of people in social structures. People are classified according to objective criteria. The middle-income group provides a large number of people having in common a clear – but difficult to operationalize – characteristic (Li Qiang 2016).

The middle class by education and the middle class by occupation are easy to conceptualize but exclude an important percentage of middle incomers, the petty bourgeoisie.

Some Chinese and Western scholars question the relevance of a social structure-based approach. According to them, the notion of class supposes to take into account other dimensions like the identification process itself, lifestyles, political attitudes, and modes of action. In this approach, in terms of lifestyle, the member of the middle class will be modern, open, constantly ready to 'progress' and 'develop'. They rely only on their talents, skills, and work to be successful. They go out with friends, travel, and know foreign countries. They are also interested in cultural activities; always behave 'correctly in society'; and are of 'good quality' (Rocca 2016 Ch.4).

From this viewpoint to be middle class, the individual will be interested in politics, be a member of associations or NGOs, or even participate in social movements. In any case, the individual member of the middle class is expected to defend their rights but be moderate in politics, ready to be involved in political conflicts but without using radical and violent means (Chen and Lu 2006). Gradually, the picture becomes more precise. The members of the new middle class have the necessary resources to represent public opinion. They are educated, they follow political news, and they can rely on a large social network in case of problems. They are not very interested in democratic reforms (that is elections) but advocate for more political transparency and improvement of the legal system. They can see the problems from an international and broader point of view but they are fierce nationalists. They are though not completely westernized (Xiong Yihan 2019). Middle-class people are aware of the importance of individual rights and play a determinant role when public scandals occur (Li Hongyan 2017). During social conflicts, they avoid making a mountain out of a molehill by creating problems. They advocate for equal opportunities for every citizen, upward mobility, and competition between individuals (Xiong Yihan 2020). They prefer to negotiate and use legal means (Wang and Han 2020). Comparison between peasants' protests and Chinese social movements of other kinds reveal huge dissimilarities. The repertoires of contention are more diversified, depoliticized, and innovative among middle-class protesters. They can build different discourses for the media and maintain the media attention, making their protests more successful. These characteristics are due to an ambiguous boundary between the middle class and the state. Many local leaders belong to the middle class and are then willing to support collective action (Xie and Lin 2016).

Despite the vast amount of research devoted to the topic, the precise definition and identification of the 'authentic' middle class with all these attributes remain unanswered. Most Chinese researchers are now convinced that the notion of the middle class is not a 'scientific and rigorous' concept (Li and Kong 2017) but many continue to search for the 'chosen people'. For starters, the translation of the term 'middle class' in Chinese varies according to the political use that people want to make of it. The use of the statistical concepts of 'middle incomers' or of 'small prosperity' is found in official documents. But researchers prefer to use more politically marked terms such as 'middle class' or 'intermediate class' or the relatively neutral expression of 'middle stratum' without giving more precise definition or explanation. The expression 'middle class' is the most problematic. In Chinese, this is rendered as a stratum: *zhongchan jieceng* 中产阶层 literally 'the middle propertied stratum'. In the Marxist vocabulary, 'class' evokes revolution, while the character *chan* 产 signifies heritage, property, and capital. Hence, the difficulties encountered when Chinese people are asked whether they belong to the middle class. Many answer negatively because they refuse to be assimilated to the class of the 'haves', that is to say, a social stratum whose wealth is seen to result from its political connections and possible corruption. Even entrepreneurs who have made a fortune by developing services on the internet are reluctant to consider themselves as anything other than 'belonging to the people' because they do not have an official political position (Rocca 2016: Ch.3). In Chinese too, of course the singular also acts for the plural in many ways and on many occasions so it is not possible, as in Western languages, to play on the plural to hide the diversity of categories by placing them under a collective name: middle classes. Yet, despite this particular context, the great majority of the population acknowledges the intellectual existence of the 'middle class' which began at the end of 1990s with the publication of more and more massive academic works. The norm is to belong to the middle class or to dream of belonging to it. When urbanites are asked if they are part of the poor, the middle class, or the rich, the vast majority answer 'middle' (Rocca 2016: Ch.2; Goodman 2014a). In addition, everything that defines an attractive lifestyle in the media refers to the characteristics of the alleged middle-class model (Hanser 2008; Zhang Li 2010; Tang Beibei 2013; Xiong Yihan 2019).

None of these attempts to objectify the middle class is really convincing, and they do not converge at all to give a precise picture. For example, according to the World Bank's standard of 10–100 US dollars per person per day for middle-income groups, the proportion of middle-income groups in China rose from 0 to 44% during 1989–2015. On the other hand, according to the PRC's National Bureau of Statistics, the proportion of middle incomers in China has only risen from 0 to 20% during the same period (Li Peilin 2017). Li Chunling used the East Asian Middle Classes Project sponsored by Academia Sinica (Hsiao 1999) and grounded on Goldthorpe's Neo-Weberian class model to estimate that the middle class at large, including the new middle class, the old middle class (small-scale employers, small-scale business owners, and self-employed people) and the marginal middle class – that is the lower-middle class – represent about 55% of the urban population and 27% of the total population (Li Chunling 2017). Here, the middle class is equivalent to middle incomers. But according to the same researcher the 'core middle class' (i.e. the new middle class) accounts only for 15–18% of the urban population and 8–9% of the Chinese population. The core middle class is composed of professionals, managers, and government's officials: a social group whose members are middle class from all points of view (education, profession, politics). She finally considers that the middle class must be actually divided into three groups: the old middle class accounted for 42%, the new middle class 'within the system' (31.6% of the total in 2015), and 'outside the system' (26.4%). It is only this last group that really constitutes the core of the middle class (Li Chunling 2017).

Actually, in the Chinese context, these definitions aim less at grasping the middle-class reality than defining different social groups corresponding to the alleged missions of the middle class: driving economic growth by consuming; civilizing the Chinese population; and imposing political reform without destabilizing the regime.

Socio-economic modernization through consumption

In recent years, the government has announced a change in the Chinese economic model. The economy would need to rely increasingly on consumption and domestic demand to sustain growth to the detriment of foreign investment and exports. For this, it is necessary to considerably increase the standard of living of the population and thus increase the size of the middle class whose members are consumers of high added-value products. It is no surprise that it is among those who regard income and consumption as essential that we find the most optimistic estimates of the proportion of the middle class in the population as if they try to convince themselves. They are large business consulting firms like McKinsey or Merrill Lynch or banks like Credit Suisse and the Chinese government itself. According to them, the middle class will not only drive Chinese growth but also save Western economies. For that purpose, the notion of middle incomers is perfect. For McKinsey, the middle class would be made up of 630 million Chinese in 2022 or 76% of urban families against 68% in 2012. As for the upper middle class – families with incomes between 106,000 yuan and 229,000 yuan per year – it will account for 54% of urban households in 2022 against 14% in 2011. This rise of the middle class presupposes galloping urbanization. For McKinsey, the urban population will increase from 52% of the total population in 2012 to 63% in 2022 (Orr 2014).

According to the Party, this urban growth must trigger a phenomenon quite comparable to what happened during the 30 glorious years in France – the upward mobility of part of the working classes. The need to constantly increase consumption in order to drive growth therefore implies a continuous integration of rural migrants into the 'small prosperity' urban population. On 1 July 2001, for the anniversary of the foundation of the Party, Jiang Zemin declared that

> Leading officials should care for and trust people of talent and do their best to create good working conditions for these people. It is necessary to expedite the establishment of an income distribution mechanism which is designed to keep the talented and bring out the best in them so as to put in place a system which guarantees that their rewards are commensurate with their endeavours and contributions.
>
> *(Jiang Zemin 2001)*

At the 16th Party Congress (2002), Jiang Zemin's report introduced the neutral notion of the middle-income group, stating that 'we should try to raise the proportion of the middle-income group and increase the income of the low-income group' (Jiang Zemin 2002). The same expression was used during the 17th Congress (Hu Jintao 2007) and the 18th Congress (Hu Jintao 2012). The 13th Five-Year Plan (2016–2020) considers the increase in the proportion of the middle-income group of the population as a major objective (Li Hongyan 2017; Li Chunling 2016a). On 16 May 2016, during the 13th meeting of the Central Leading Group on Financial and Economic Affairs, the highest body of decision-making on issues related to the economy, Xi Jinping emphasized that

> Enlarging the middle-income group is instrumental to realizing the goal of building a moderately prosperous society, attaining structural reforms, maintaining social peace, harmony and stability, and is necessary for the country's lasting well-being. Vital to the transition toward an olive-shaped social structure is a high quality, inclusive new type of urbanization, which will generate economic opportunities for all – an inclusive growth will prevent a class 'solidification' and allow a virtuous circle of efficiency and justice about China's middle class population.
>
> *(Zhou and Hu 2020: 84)*

Behind these statements is a well-targeted population, that is, rural migrant workers. Advocating 'high quality, inclusive new type of urbanization' means allowing a growing number of rural migrant workers to experience upward mobility by lifting legal and social discrimination. The CCP is then committed to provide migrant workers (and their children) with opportunities to climb the social ladder in order to make China shift from a pyramid-shaped to an 'olive-shaped social structure'.

Civilizing China

At the same time, for most Chinese researchers, the modernization of Chinese society cannot be limited to a continuous increase in income and consumption. The core middle class as an ideal class must take charge of the upgrading of the other social groups (Huang 2003; Fang 2007; Rocca 2016). Because of their skills, attitudes, good manner, and level of education, they have the 'distinction' (in Bourdieu's term) to be a model and to civilize the rest of the population (Liu Xin 2010). 'Education' is not limited to academic skills. Being a university professor means not only having a prestigious profession and being educated but also behaving correctly. The notion of 'civilization' is very broad, from university graduation to lifestyles and good manners: not to spit, respecting the rules, standing in line, protecting historical monuments, speaking in a low voice and in a calm and discreet manner, having impeccable hygiene, and being well dressed. This portrait looks like those who draw it: the professionals and cadres. The core of the middle class claims even more social and cultural legitimacy than the current elites (Sigley 2004, 2009; Tomba 2004). It is about waging a moral war against those cliques (the elite) who rely on string-pulling and corruption to succeed (Rocca 2016). In contrast to France where those who considered themselves to be the true managers of the economy and of the society were harshly criticizing the talentless capitalists whose only title is to be heirs, here the moral attack targets the CCP leaders and their sons and grandsons who take advantage of their positions of power acquired by their forbears. For those who scorn the red elite, only the core of the middle class holds the appropriate standards of the good life because unlike the rich and the powerful, they do not consider that money replaces the culture of good taste and refined consumption (Xue Yong 2009; Rocca 2017; Rocca interviews 2019[2]).

At the other end of the social spectrum, this insistence on standards, values, education, and skills excludes the new working classes. Peasants and migrants must also be civilized, but for reasons other than those which disqualify the rich. Of course, they are the counter-example not to be followed. They speak Chinese with a horrible accent, eat vulgar food noisily, speak loudly, and lack hygiene. They are naive and prisoners of their primitive instincts. Yet they are less actors than victims of natural bad taste. Although until the end of 1990s, the tone of the press and popular speeches vis-à-vis rural migrants was marked mainly by contempt, it has since been mastered by compassion. Their courage has been praised, and if they are still seen as the bottom of the social pyramid it is not because of their lack of talent but rather because of the opportunities to study and learn how to behave. It is therefore a question of transforming them into true modern citizens. In other words, contempt and compassion are two different manners of discriminating and dominating rural migrant workers. Compassion aims at changing the customs of the latter so that they follow the good example of the core middle class and for their own benefit (Rocca 2016: Ch.4). The language used is particularly brutal not far from the symbolic violence practiced in France by the holders of legitimate culture towards the popular classes (Bourdieu 1984).

Solving political dilemmas

The discourse on the middle class finally serves to circumvent the question of political reform, that is to say, democratization and ultimately elections. For the Party as well as for researchers, Chinese journalists, and the protesters themselves, it is only the growth of the middle class which could change politics without destabilizing the country. In this view, elections presuppose the existence of a large majority of well-educated, civilized, financially comfortable people who as owners of property and rational people have the legitimacy to give their opinion, improve the legal system, choose power holders, and influence policies. Taking representative democracy too seriously, they believe that the Chinese must first become citizens before becoming voters. Despite the lessons of history which show the opposite – it is the practice of voting that makes the citizen – this elitist vision of democracy remains dominant in China. As the people – made up of peasants and rural migrants – are perceived as incapable of governing themselves and then behaving as rational citizens, Chinese society cannot abandon the one-party system. For most intellectuals (Rocca Interviews 2005–2018; Frenkiel 2014), and even dissidents (Liu Xiaobo 2011), the people are not a real political 'subject' yet because they are victims of their passions and their basic instincts. Power must remain in the hands of an elite, an intellectual elite not a political or economic elite. This contempt for people who are not a legitimate electoral body leads to a strong concern about the instability that might result from the creation of a representative democracy (Rocca 2016: Ch.5; Rocca interviews 2019).

The memory of political difficulties such as the Cultural Revolution or the Tiananmen Square event in 1989 is still alive. 'Political problems are dangerous' is the general leitmotif. This concern leads many to wonder whether risking the current 'small prosperity' for the sake of a possible better future is a good idea. After all, most of the large 'developing' countries where democracy reigns (Brazil, India, South Africa) are less prosperous, more unequal, and more unstable than China. In addition, the doubts that many Western observers express today about the decision-making process in democratic regimes do little to encourage China to change its institutions. It is not difficult to understand the attraction of a government that is certainly authoritarian, but strong, efficient, and pragmatic, as opposed to elected officials chosen by people who are not educated enough (Rocca 2016: Ch.5; Frenkiel 2014).

Nobody questions the idea that power must come from the people and serve the interests of the people. The problem is to determine how to ensure the expression and the defence of this general interest. Are the people able to know what is good for them? Is it good that democratization becomes a political problem, that is to say, a source of conflict? The solution could be to wait until the moment the middle class would represent the majority (Rocca interviews 2005–2018).

However, in the meantime, there is the question of how to reform the political system. According to Chinese researchers and the Chinese media, although middle-class people are few, their influence on public opinion and their political attitudes makes them able to effect change in politics without first changing the system (Li and Kong 2017; Xiong Yihan 2019; Pan and Xu 2018). They advocate the further development of the legal system and for more transparency without promoting the immediate introduction of fair and regular elections. They are ready to participate in protest movements when their material interests and property ownership and maintenance are challenged. So, for example, there are new homeowners who protest against the quality of construction and the way residences are managed, or residents who demonstrate against factories that pollute or factory construction projects that damage the local environment. Recent food scandals provoked the outcry of netizens worried about their health and that of their children. According to some sociologists, as in the case of the European middle class, new social movements are supposed to usher in a new era in power relations (Wang and Han 2020).

On the one hand, the middle class is viewed as representing a danger to social stability, and the government has to cope with new forms of social movements

(Li Hongyan 2017). On the other hand, middle-class people are considered conservative and favour negotiated and peaceful solutions to solve conflicts. They do not support immediate democratization because of the risk that their privileges might be lost. Despite the supposed ways in which they have been influenced by individualism and Western values, they are reluctant to adopt any kind of class discipline (Li Hongyan 2017). Middle-class protest movements might force the government to adopt new laws and regulations but never lead to violent or revolutionary actions. In brief, their modes of action demonstrate that by having acquired property and self-confidence they have become citizens. By imposing a new relationship between the state and the citizens, they could lead the whole population towards political reforms. Some go further and claim that it is through these protests, in which middle incomers defend a certain 'lifestyle', and a certain 'environment' in the broad meaning of the word, that China could begin a process of democratization (Chen Yingfang 2006; Guo et al. 2014). Researchers and intellectuals advise the government to support this category of the population and, in particular, to improve their material conditions in order to avoid revolution (Chen Yingfang 2006).

Return to reality

There can be no doubt that China is now a consumer society (Gerth 2010) and that whatever its definition, the middle class is a driving force in the Chinese economy. Nevertheless, there is a gap between the representation of the missions of the middle class and the reality. Middle incomers are meeting difficulties in being happy middle incomers, and the integration of rural migrant workers is far from being completed. As for the political domain, middle-class attitudes seem to satisfy many people except those who would welcome the collapse of the regime.

The middle class got the blues

Middle-class people often express their fatigue and anxiety. According to the 2015 national sample survey data of the Institute of Sociology of the Chinese Academy of Social Sciences, 'about 40% (39.4%) of the middle class claimed that the burden of living is very heavy and stressful' (Li Chunling 2016b: 36). The middle class has no problem to solve basic needs in terms of housing, children's education, medical care, and elderly care, but they are not satisfied. As they are apparently required to play a major role in the development of Chinese prosperity, the middle class feel society should respect them. They work a lot, and they are always under pressure, trying to constantly improve their situation. Their young generation is borrowing more and more and is now living under the pressure of loan repayments as 'loan slaves' (Li Chunling 2016b; Rocca 2016).

In order to match what they consider to be the status of the middle class, they need to live in spacious and comfortable houses situated in the best neighbourhood, their children must go to the best schools and receive the best education, and they deserve to have the best medical treatment. The middle class complains that prices in real estate market are too high and that the new generation cannot afford it (Li Chunling 2017; Xiong 2020). According to the 2015 national sample survey data, 94.4% of the middle class own private real estate, and 34.4% own two or more properties. However, due to the constant rise in prices in the real estate market, the number of middle-class people who are not homeowners is increasing. They are mainly concentrated in large cities, especially megacities, and the vast majority of them are young and middle class. The proportion of middle-class young people under the age of 30 who have no private real estate is 8.2%, but in megacities, this proportion has risen to 16.6%. Middle-class members who own real estate also have problems. Nearly, one-quarter of them (24.2%) claim that their housing conditions are substandard but that they are too poor to buy a better house (Li Chunling 2016b). On the other hand, middle-class households save a lot, and while many people have lost money on the stock market in the recent years they invest in real estate.

The education expenditure of most middle-class families accounts for less than 20% of their income and medical expenditure for less than 10% of their income. But due to problems in the welfare system, 58.8% of the middle-class state that they 'save as much as possible' to ensure that they would not experience a decline in life quality when they retire (Li Chunling 2016b). The paradox is that any drop on the real estate market would ease the purchase of a better house but would also lead to a significant decrease in the savings of the middle classes. The pension system clearly has problems, and most urban dwellers have no guarantee of receiving something in the future (Frazier 2004). The prices of medical treatments are constantly increasing. 62.9% of the middle-class believe that 'the level of social security is too low to provide protection'. In many middle-class families, the income of one spouse is sufficient to maintain the family's daily expenses, while the other spouse's income is used for savings, real estate investment, children's education, and other investments (Li Chunling 2016b).

The middle class does not feel safe. According to the 2013 national sample survey data from the Institute of Sociology of the Chinese Academy of Social Sciences, 72.8% of the middle class considers that 'food safety' is not guaranteed, 54.6% that there is a lack of 'personal information, privacy and security', and 48.3% that there is a lack of a suitable 'ecological environment' (Li Chunling 2016b).

This anxiety is reminiscent of that described for the French (Bourdieu 1984) or American (Mills 1951) middle class. People situated between the lower classes and the elite aspire to be part of the upper classes but above all fear a downward decline. They have been the beneficiary of rapid economic growth in the past 30 years. Their income has increased almost every year, and their material living standards have improved step by step. This increases their expectations for the future: they want to earn more money, buy a bigger house, and change to a better car (Song and Lee 2010; Zhang Jun 2019).

The Chinese middle class is also worried because they have to choose. The lower class has no choice in terms of consumption and saving. The middle incomers must buy in the right place not only for prestige purposes as part of gentrification (Non 2018) but also to find a neighbourhood with good schools. Big cities are experiencing a phenomenon of gentrification where middle-class people replace previous residents because of the high-quality education in the neighbourhood. They must choose the right school, purchase the right car, and invest the right way. Is it better to go to an elite Chinese University or an average foreign college (Chen Shuhong 2008; Liu Jingming 2006; Wang Xin 2020; Rocca interviews 2018–2019)? They constantly live in uncertainty about making the right decision. They are worries not only for themselves but also for their children. They are doing their best to provide their child with life-chance opportunities but they fear they will not be able to transmit their status to their child (Wang Mengqi 2018; Xiong Yihan 2020). From this point of view, the situation is particularly worrying. Graduates and postgraduates are increasingly more numerous yet unable to find suitable employment. The labour market for students with a higher education already seems crowded (Bai Limin 2006).

The integration of rural migrants

Becoming middle class was the dream of many college graduates, but it is now the dream of many rural migrant workers. It may even be the dream of Chinese and foreign businessmen and of the CCP itself to achieve the same. Yet this dream is very difficult to realize and for the moment a minority of rural migrants have managed to climb the social ladder. The biggest problem preventing them from experiencing such a process is no longer the household residence system but the access to education, housing, professional training, and the formal labour market (Zhan Shaohua 2011; Huang and Yi 2015). All these problems were supposed to be solved as for a long time the government and the Party have considered the 'upgrading' of migrants as a major objective (Yu Jianping 2003: 42–43; Zhang Xing 2003: 14–16). Many prominent researchers criticized public policy for not having addressed these problems adequately and changing the situation. They recalled the long litany of speeches, regulations, resolutions, documents, and policies which emphasized the enlargement of the middle-income group in order to create an olive-shaped society (Xiong Yihan 2019 and 2020; Li Hongyan 2017; Li Chunling 2016a; Li Qiang 2016; Li and Wang 2017; Zhou and Hu 2020). They also continued to give advice. The government should pay attention to industrial innovation and industrial upgrading, urbanization transformation, and the construction of a social security system. They should develop education and lower barriers to market entry (Li Qiang 2016). According to Li and Wang, it is necessary to reduce the gap between urban and rural areas; as well as between the eastern region on the one hand and the central and western regions on the other. In their view, as the development of the middle class in the primary sector (where migrant workers work) meets great obstacles, the government should strengthen the middle class, increase income, reorganize industry and the occupational structure, popularize education, develop the middle class in rural areas, the central and western regions, and help migrant workers move into the middle class through the improvement of their skills (Li and Wang 2017: 176).

Actually, the social position of migrant workers in urban society depends on the size of the city and on the policies adopted by city governments. It seems that in the smaller cities, the entry of migrants to the middle classes is easier. In those cases, even if locals keep some privileges the inequalities between migrants and locals in terms of education, income, or occupation are weak. The competition for entry to the best school is not so fierce, and the real estate market is affordable for migrants (Zhan Shaohua 2011).

At the opposite end of the spectrum, in Chinese megalopolises, migrant workers have contributed to a dramatic increase in the urban population. To limit the demographic pressure on infrastructure, city government usually aims to reduce the number of migrants. In these cities, the gap between urban residents and migrants is so important that migrants cannot escape their marginality. In terms of income, cultural capital, and social capital, the two groups live in separate worlds. Access to good schools and in particular to good universities, which are located in megalopolises, is still very difficult for them. Thirty-five million migrant children live in cities and nearly 14 million are between 6 and 14 years old. Many have to attend migrant children-only schools, private institutions in which learning and teaching conditions are very low (Yu and Crowley 2020; Friedman 2017).

Very few initiatives try to solve other problems related to housing, professional training, or access to social security schemes (Zhan Shaohua 2011; Li Qiang 2016). Even the formalization of contractual relations does little to reduce precariousness for the migrant agency workers who work for state companies (Feng 2019). Moreover, the limited transferability of acquired social rights regarding pension or health care constitutes an obstacle to labour migration and the possible assimilation of migrant workers into the middle class (Zhan Shaohua 2011: 243–285; Zhang and Li 2018).

Social movements: a disappointment

After two decades of new social movements, there is disappointment among those who believed that they could trigger radical political changes. On the other hand, those who were only requiring or expecting that more space might be made for the operation of laws and regulations could be satisfied. Middle-class protesters succeeded in persuading the CCP to adopt new regulations to protect the rights of homeowners, consumers, and residents. At the same time, the governments and the CCP are determining the rhythm and the content of change without letting protesters create a space for their organizations or having room for independent manoeuvre.

Since the 1990s, many ENGOs (environmental NGOs) have been set up but most and particularly the largest ones are managed by a handful of people who maintain good relationships with Party organizations. They may still criticize public policies and even participate in and organize protest movements. At the same time, they face a significant dilemma: their capacity to influence policymaking processes supposes a paradoxical proximity with the state. The biography of most founders of ENGOs reveals close relationships with the administration (Lu Yiyi 2009). As China has aspirations to be a leader in terms of environment protection, these conflicts are not a matter of radical disagreement between the national leadership and the middle class as long as a change in political regime is not at stake. For both, environment safety has become a major issue. However, protest movements create important tensions within the state apparatus, revealing the existence of divergent positions and interests. The goal of the central government being to protect the environment, the issue for the local governments is how to protect the environment while sustaining economic growth. Final decisions are made according to the balance of power, taking into account domestic and international elements, economic concerns, and demands for a better quality of life. ENGOs have become an important force in Chinese politics, not as challengers but as disturbing allies of the central government in its attempt to green public policies. Environmental activists are a force that participates in the modernization of the Chinese economy (Sun and Zhao 2008; Lu Yiyi 2009).

Participants in protest movements for environment protection are usually local residents whose first concern is to get rid of a specific problem: river pollution, polluting factories, for example. Once the problem is solved, they return to their usual occupations. Activists, or more often environmental protection 'professionals', can sustain and extend the conflict by aiming at more general objectives, but as social movements, environmental protection conflicts remain very limited in scope. Most of these protest movements can be considered 'not in my back yard' as participants have no intention to be involved in broader activities.

Since the beginning of the 2000s, an array of food scandals have resulted in panic and distrust of the state's capacity to protect consumers' health. Counterfeit infant formula killed 13 babies in 2003. In 2004, several persons died after consuming counterfeit alcoholic drinks. In 2008, baby milk contaminated with melamine killed six toddlers and poisoned several others. More recently, pesticide was found in *mantou* 馒头 (a type of steamed bread), and egg products were contaminated with melamine. Pork, lamb, beef, and chicken meat unfit for human consumption have been discovered in different locations. From 2013 to 2016, a series of vaccine scandals was attributed to the deaths of 21 infants. Local officials in eastern China investigated complaints that more than 100 children received expired polio vaccines after aggrieved parents protested violently, the latest in a string of such vaccine scandals that provoked nationwide anger. These scandals triggered fierce reactions on the internet but no nationwide or local large-scale movements. These reactions, viewed as coming from the middle class, have not challenged the regime or even the way the state apparatus deals with food trade. Very few netizens go beyond individual complaints. Such protesters are usually severely punished when they cross the red line of dissent. This is why middle-class consumers try to find alternative solutions: changing their purchase of trademarks, buying organic food, and putting pressure on the governments through social networks in order to induce them to adopt stricter controls of goods. Beijingers buy vegetables and fruit from farmers when they travel out to the countryside. The media relay the concerns of the middle class but consumerism is no longer a source of political conflict. Fundamentally, the interest of consumers and CCP leaders are the same: developing consumer society and then improving goods safety. Consumers aim for better legal protection and more transparency, not regime change (Lora-Wainwright 2013; Klein 2013; Yang Guobin 2013).

At the end of 1990s, the CCP established a real estate market from scratch. Almost no urban permanent resident owned their apartment before this reform. Today, most of the permanent non-migrant residents are homeowners (Hsing 2010; Zhang Li 2010; Wang Mengqi 2017, 2018). The residence style is standardized, based on the gated community model with high walls and guards. As a result, a new social group has emerged which coincides with the middle class in the social imaginary. Homeowner identity is only defined as a source of prestige. Owning an apartment is also a way to accumulate wealth. The regular and spectacular increase in prices on the real estate market has provided urban residents with a source of enrichment. Moreover, residences also have commercial activities. They own facilities, parking lots and basements, shops, and gyms which are rented to outsiders for the benefit (theoretically) of homeowners. In many places, homeowners were constrained in defending their property rights and value against the malpractices of developers, building enterprises, and companies managing housing estates, many of which were owned or controlled by local bureaucrats (Rocca 2016: Ch.5; Cai Yongshun 2005). Being homeowner is a 'way of life', the fact that middle-class family can live in a nice 'garden' (Zhang Li 2010), well protected from the outdoor dangers.

Here also, Chinese intellectuals who believed that homeowner identity could cause people to question the regime were disappointed. What most homeowners are worried about is the value of their property and the quality of their lifestyle, including security. The bad quality of building materials, the destruction of a garden to build another building, a feeling of insecurity, an increase in management fees, the inefficiency of the management company, and so forth all contribute to the depreciation of the value of the owners' properties. The scope of their protests and social movements is very limited. Action is centred on the *xiaoqu* 小区 (literally the 'small area'), the neighbourhood. Homeowners are obviously wary of being involved in 'mass' demonstrations. One of the leaders' main tasks is to mobilize a significant proportion of homeowners. The task has proven difficult because most people work long hours and have no time and energy for extra activities. Most actions are carried out 'within the system'. Activists negotiate with the developers and the management company, inform and put pressure on local institutions, circulate and present petitions, write documents, and collect laws and regulations. In order to reinforce their positions, they contact newspapers and important people. The objective is to get the support of public opinion and prominent people. In doing so, the participants try to increase the pressure on the developers and the management company. More aggressive means can be mobilized in case of failure but it is rare. A complaint is lodged against companies with the local court.

Sometimes, a small-scale demonstration is organized in the neighbourhood or in front of the local administration buildings or some people go on a hunger strike. The violence is used at the last resort, and usually as a reaction against the violence used by the other side. Whatever the means and the modes of action chosen by a movement, documents, slogans, articles, and petitions, all use the words of official discourse and very rarely question the Party rule. The lack of long-term involvement of participants gives leaders of protest movements a large room for manoeuvre. They develop close relationships with local officials and management companies. They sometimes become 'partners' of the local government in order to restore harmony and find rational solutions. For protesters, it is important to prove that the demands go hand in hand with the regime objectives and that everybody speaks the same language: rule of law, social harmony, defence of property, small prosperity, social mobility, social justice, social stability, civilized society, and raising the quality of the population (Rocca 2013; Rocca 2016: Ch.5).

Homeowners' movements have contributed to the improvement of the situation in Beijing. New regulations have been adopted, and it is now far more difficult than before for developers and management companies to take advantage of citizens. In each residence, homeowner associations are in charge of choosing, dismissing, and controlling management companies. In middle-class neighbourhoods, although disputes continue to erupt from time to time, relationships between the local administration, the residents, and the management companies are on the way to being normalized (Rocca 2013; Rocca 2016: Ch.5).

The Chinese middle class in wider context

The emergence of the Chinese middle class is not the cloning of a simple universal scientific concept – the middle class – in China. There are many commonalities between the development of the Chinese middle class and similar phenomena elsewhere, as in France, but there are also dissimilarities which are no less important. Middle strata seem to emerge whenever a country experiences a long period of growth. This would seem to be an inevitability of capitalist development. At some point, producers have to become consumers or fall into marginality. An important part of the society escapes poverty to enter the middle strata in terms of income, consumption, and education. Calling them 'middle class' is the outcome of processes in which representations, interpretations, imaginaries, and specific agendas play a major role. In China, hopes and expectations of the middle class do not seem fundamentally different from those of the European one: finding a good job, consuming, helping children. Moreover, since the 1980s, the party has embarked on a process of standardization of the population. Just as cities (Samara 2015) and means of transportation (Qian Junxi 2015) have to look like an international model, so the Chinese have to live up to a certain standard.

As elsewhere, the specificities of the Chinese middle class have not resulted from sort of 'everlasting cultural background' but from specific historical configurations, notably the exit from socialism. Unlike countries where the middle strata include a large part of the working class who climbed the social ladder, in China it is mainly the former middle strata – cadres, professionals, and state urban workers – who became the new middle strata with the reform era. The sizeable challenge provided by the upward mobility of the lower classes lies in China's future along with the proposed emergence of an olive-shaped society including migrant workers. This difference has important political implications. Even if a small part of rural labourers experienced upward mobility notably in small cities, most of the current middle class is composed of people who were and are attached to the state and CCP institutions, either directly ('within the system') or indirectly ('outside the system' but as the product of reform policy).

The Chinese middle class is a catch-all phrase that everyone – leaders, journalists, scholars, businessmen, and ordinary people, not to mention foreign observers – can identify in different ways. This represents a significant political change since the CCP is no longer able to solely determine the identification of people by class. The leadership of the Party-state must now take into account the opinions of scholars, the media, and social networks, as well as the behaviour of people in business circles. By claiming to want to transform a large part of the population into middle-incomers enjoying small prosperity, the Party is trying to ensure political control. In doing so, it is also trying to hide the fact that there is still a dominant class in China and that China is not at all a classless society.

One way of identifying the middle class is as those with middle-level incomes. Where middle incomers are accurately the focus, they are by definition a large group of people: consumers. The portrayal though that follows that equation is rather vague, not to say dull. It is the image of the 'little man' (Fallada 1933) of the contemporary society. According to Wright Mills, 'whatever history they [the new middle class members] have had is a history without events; whatever common interests they have do not lead to unity; whatever future they have will not be of their own making. The political problem posed by these people is not so much what the direction may be as whether they will take any political direction' (Mills 1951: xvii). 'Estranged from community and society in a context of distrust and manipulation; alienated from work and, on the personality market, and politically apathetic these are the new little people, the unwilling vanguard of modern society' (Mills 1951: xviii).

The second way of identifying the middle class focuses on people who are not only middle incomers but also university graduates. This social group is composed of ordinary and middle-rank cadres and professionals and is particularly keen on expressing their points of view on social networks which have become the main channels both of information and for criticism. The authorities are fully aware of this fact and they supervise social networks but also see it as the place where public opinion is formed. As and when the middle class is seen as being based on university graduates, then it is also regarded as having the mission to civilize the rural population. They have the right lifestyle; the good manners; they are westernized but not too much; and they are alleged to be able to improve the 'quality of the Chinese population' (Anagnost 2004; Kipnis 2006).

Bourdieu states that the political position and behaviour of the French new middle class is determined by its inability to oppose the bourgeois set of values because of its material and cultural dependence. Unable to produce their own set of values, the members of this category content themselves with imitating the behaviour of the bourgeoisie. What they want is to obtain the symbolic and material rewards attached to the bourgeois condition (Bourdieu 1984). In China's case, the source of the established dominant class's position was less culture than wealth and political power. As a result, the middle class has taken charge in the process of setting cultural norms. By definition, there is no Chinese traditional bourgeoisie which could define good tastes and good manner and the middle class claims to take the lead in that matter. The rich are viewed as parvenus and the peasants as uncivilized (Rocca 2016: Ch.4). In terms of material rewards, the middle class blames the dominant class for using 'tricks' (social capital, money, cultural capital) instead of 'moral means' (education, personal efforts, talent). In that struggle for social norms, laws and regulations are viewed as efficient tools for guaranteeing 'fair competition' by middle-class people because they can hoard opportunity.

A final way of identifying the middle class is through their politics, which is supposed to lead to change. Composed of ordinary and middle-rank cadres, professionals, and petite bourgeoisie, this middle class is not a class in Marxist terms but a collection of individuals which rarely express their view as a collective. That does not mean they are passive and do not defend their interests and rights but they do it from a particularistic point of view, typically using their own personal connections and experience.

Expressing views on social networks is a form of action. But in Marxist terms participating in social movements is a much more mature form of political engagement involving class consciousness. It remains though far from certain that this new middle class will lead to action in any specific, coherent direction. The CCP sees the middle class as being able to cushion the changes and shocks of reform. The Party sees the middle class as an aspiration for those at the bottom of society who take seriously the discourse about opportunities to move up the social ladder (Guan Renting 2003; Liao and Tan 2005). The middle class themselves certainly criticizes the Party and sometimes launches protest movements but they do not aim at overthrowing the regime. On the contrary, as they favour negotiation and legality, they contribute to reinforce the legal system and ease social conflicts. Some researchers and activists expect more and in particular the emergence of large-scale social movements (Rocca 2016: Ch.4; Rocca 2013; Franceschini 2014). Some 'specific intellectuals' (Foucault 1980) have strived to give more impact to protests in order to change the power balance and possibly to compel the Party to respect freedom of expression and organizations but they do not seriously envisage the establishment of an election-based political system and certainly not the launch of a revolution. One aspect of the globalization process is the globalization of criticism of democracy which contributes to strengthen the fear about the potential danger of an election-based system in China (Frenkiel 2014).

Middle-class social movements in China have remained linked to local disputes, and their participants were mainly interested in obtaining immediate and material benefits. Social protest does not go beyond 'not in my backyard' attitudes. NGOs or associations were set up and leaders emerged but, until now, the local administration never lost control of the middle class. This results as much from the characteristics of middle-class protest, as from the ability of the CCP. As Bourdieu indicated in another context:

> The fear of losing all they have won, by trying to get all they have been promised (particularly through education and qualifications), does not fully explain the form taken by petit bourgeois bargaining strategies. The ordinary means of the workers' struggle, strikes or demonstrations, are for them a last resort, which they will consider only when driven to extremities by excessive injustice ('If need be, we'll take to the streets'). They prefer symbolic weapons . . . and that particular form of collective action which is achieved through the 'association', a strictly serial grouping of individuals assembled solely by the same 'cause'.
>
> (Bourdieu 1984: 456–457)

These essentially conservative attitudes do not mean that the middle class has not and will not change politics in China. It certainly has contributed to reshaping the power balance but within a framework designed by the CCP. The Party has refused to accept the institutionalization of fundamental relationships among the Party, the state, and citizens but it has created and is developing new modes of managing these relationships within the existing institutions and structures. The objective of leaders is to be able to anticipate conflicts by allowing unsatisfied individuals and social groups to bargain and to a certain extent to be incorporated in decision-making.

The process is obvious regarding the homeowners' movements where some activists became experts in conflict management with and for local governments. On the one hand, the neighbourhood has become a place of self-governance where inhabitants – typically retired people – are in charge of making rules within the residence. On the other hand, self-governance requires a wider supervision. It is the case with the 'grid governance' scheme implemented in middle-class neighbourhoods. In each grid (a few hundred inhabitants), a team was established including 'resident volunteers from each building, staff members of the residents' committee, representatives from residents' social activity groups, representatives from the homeowner association, and building managers, who represent the property management company' (Tang 2020: 40). In addition to organizing social activities, these teams are responsible for ensuring the residents do not get involved in home-owning-related disputes which 'might lead to larger scale social unrest'. The objective is not to suppress but to prevent disputes from occurring by mediating conflicts and finding solutions.

The same phenomenon concerns the use of online participation. In the whole country, local authorities have opened channels in order to enable citizens to express their grievances. 'They must deal with citizens' online complaints. Chinese local governments differentiate their responses according to the publicity surrounding an issue and the cost of resolving it. 'Local governments feel the pressure of responsiveness when their malfeasance or governance failures are exposed. Furthermore, unresolved grievances cause citizens to link their complaints to the political system or the central government' (Cai and Zhou 2019: 350).

And so it is too with NGOs.

> The Xi Jinping administration gave a further boost to sub-contracting services to selected groups by rolling out the policy across China, whilst simultaneously curbing foreign funding through the new restrictive Foreign NGO law and strictly requiring registered social organizations to form a party cell'. This welfarist incorporation agenda advanced further under the new Xi leadership that was keen on improving welfare services both to satisfy a more demanding middle class and allay social unrest in a context of global recession.
>
> (Howell 2019: 78)

The dream of the CCP seems to be to manage a classless society, to control a mass middle class with no political but only social problems: income, consumption, property rights, jobs, saving, education, and pollution. The issue of course is that every social problem can become a political problem. The middle class calls not only for reproduction of their status and transmission of it to their offspring but also for a constant increase in living standards and improvement of living conditions. From this perspective, there is no dilemma between revolution and stability, between liberal and conservative. As the power balance has changed between the CCP and society, middle-class politics has no substance in itself and can shift according to the situation.

Notes

1 Two students encountered in Tsinghua were children of second-generation migrant workers. One grandparent had gone to Beijing and another to a middle-sized city in Hebei in the 1980s. Their parents worked in a small factory before setting up their own workshop. Finally, one son was put in a boarding school and the other entrusted to an aunt living in Beijing. Both had brilliant results in the university entrance exam.
2 Interviews as part of research program on the Xi Jinping generation (Rocca interviews 2018–2019).

7
THE DOMINANT CLASS AFTER 1978

Elite persistence and the ironies of social change

David S. G. Goodman

Political stability and the development of market socialism since 1978 have resulted in new elite configurations and the emergence of a dominant class not solely rooted in the revolutionary history of the CCP. While there is widespread agreement among commentators that political power, economic wealth, and social status have all come to contribute to dominant class formation in the changing political economy, there are different views about the relative importance of each and the consequences overall for leadership and authority. Regardless of the precise interpretation subsequently adopted the dominant class of 2021 necessarily did not emerge in full with the changes of the late 1970s. The former revolutionary generation of the leadership had to pass, or be passed from the scene and be replaced: a process begun in earnest in September 1985 at the special National CCP Conference, and then essentially completed at the 13th Congress of the CCP in October/November 1987. The move from state to market socialism also required adjustments in the dominant discourses about the political economy not least to provide legitimacy to the role of entrepreneurs, even as they had already contributed to the economic growth already under way. This was a process not really completed until 2002 when businesspeople were formally able to become CCP members.

Interpretations of the changes in the composition of the dominant class have been varied. The debate has been dominated by commentators beginning to consider the consequences of the introduction of market forces on the operation of the political economy. There had been a general recognition with respect to earlier times and other countries that under state socialism wealth, political power, and to some extent social status are determined by redistribution: state and Party leaders and officials make decisions about the distribution of wealth and power in the absence of a functioning economic market or competitive polity (Szelényi 1978). The key issue is then (after 1978) what happens when market forces are introduced into a once state socialist political economy. Victor Nee has played a major role

DOI: 10.4324/9781003255017-8

in trying to understand these consequences. In 1989, he postulated that with the introduction of market forces there would be a 'transfer of power favouring direct producers over redistributors' (Nee 1989: 666). Subsequently, Nee both on his own and with a variety of collaborators then undertook a number of studies that demonstrated that rural stratification had moved to market determination (Nee 1996); that cadres have incentives to move into the private sector because of market transition (Nee and Lian 1994); and that cadres had indeed moved out of State-Owned Enterprise management and into private enterprises (Nee and Su 1998).

This and later research led Nee to two conclusions. One was that 'The spread of markets erodes commitment to the party and paves the way for regime change' (Nee and Lian 1994: 285). Of course, this then led to questions about the speed of the change that might consequently be envisaged. Nee made it clear that his 'Market transition theory is not a theory of radical change; instead, it turns on the cumulative causation of decentralized market processes in promoting discontinuous change at the margins of the pre-existing stratification order' (Nee and Cao 2002: 36). He nonetheless predicted that at some point there would be a tipping point, and in 2012 he signalled its arrival through a study (with Sonja Opper) of enterprise development in East China. At that time, they argued 'The market has replaced redistributed power; political capital does not lead to economic success' (Nee and Opper 2012: 55).

The second and equally important conclusion to result from Nee's research was that path dependence would often impede the market transition. Change would not simply come slowly but would also necessarily be made manifest in different parts of the country at different times, and even in different ways. In particular, he highlighted that urban areas would change more slowly than rural districts. Each situation would be highly localized, determined by the different kinds of markets that existed in different localities, and dependent to a high degree on which sector was dominant in any particular location. Clearly, conditions were not the same in areas on the coast, which were more exposed to the market reforms and the rest of the world's economic involvement, and those inland, which were more sheltered from the impact of globalization. Even on the East Coast – which was most integrated into the external economy – there could be and were clear differences, as, for example, between Zhejiang Province, where the emerging economy was characterized by the private sector, with individual owner-operators; and Jiangsu Province where collective sector enterprises predominated in the new sectors of the economy (Nee 1991, 1992; Nee and Cao 1999).

In contrast, other commentators have seen little evidence of declining political influence and its replacement by the power of the market. Instead, they emphasize even more than Nee the significance of path dependence in economic management and development, and the continued institutional and associational power of the Party-state. In this, such commentators echo the universal notion in China of the importance and continued influence of anyone and any operation which is *tizhinei* [体制内]: literally 'inside the system', within or part of the Party-state.

The key question for these commentators is the extent to which the political elite have found their room for action determined by economic development and reactions to the market, on the one hand, and the extent to which entrepreneurs depend on their relationship with the Party-state, on the other. One strong argument is that politically based privilege is embedded in the economy (Bian and Logan 1996: 741). From this perspective, class background, CCP membership, and political position remain crucial to the local level distribution of wealth and power (Xie and Hannum 1996; Walder 2002, 2003; Bian and Zhang 2004; Gustafsson and Ding 2010). Szelenyi has identified contemporary China's political economy as a form of state socialism, largely because of the continuing domination of the Party-state (Szelényi 2008). This was a view also found in Bruce Dickson's description of China as Crony Capitalism: 'a system of interaction between economic and political elites that is based on patrimonial ties and in which success in business is due more to personal contacts in the official bureaucracy than to entrepreneurial skill or merit' (Dickson 2008).

It would seem clear that in the determination of the new post-1978 elite it is impossible to ignore the significance of both market forces and political factors, as well as of social capital (Walder et al. 2000; Zang 2001, 2004). Such observations, and particularly the role of historically determined social capital, necessarily move the examination from just discussion of the elite towards a wider consideration of the development of the dominant class. While Nee has regarded the introduction of market forces into a socialist system as necessarily leading to a transition in favour of the latter and a wider pluralism, Szelenyi and Kostello have suggested otherwise. Drawing on research into reforming East European state socialism (before and after 1989), they argued that it had been 'the technocratic fraction of the former *nomenklatura*' (the leadership positions that require state and party approval, and their occupants) and the children of former cadres who 'would become the new system's political and economic elite, not the current private entrepreneurs' (Szelényi and Kostello 1998).

Some intergenerational transfer of privilege was present even under state socialism, despite the dominant discourse of revolutionary social change. In the post-1978 period, that possibility has expanded quite considerably, including the influence of both the pre-1978 revolutionary generation and the pre-1949 local elite. The transfer of post-1949 political privilege into economic wealth clearly attends enterprise development alongside the large-scale co-optation of entrepreneurs into the realm of the Party-state. The intergenerational transfer of influence and privilege has been made even more visible, particularly in the development of economic activities. This is readily apparent in the later adult behaviour of the children of cadres in the Party-state who have gone on to become businesspeople. Research has also demonstrated the ways in which a significant proportion of the pre-1949 local elite morphed into the post-1978 elite. Most dramatically, an examination of the extremely wealthy from the last two decades suggests that in large measure the roots of their social capital are to be found in the local elite from before the establishment of the PRC, when in addition a substantial proportion had also joined the CCP.

The political elite

The obvious place to start any consideration of the dominant class in a post-state socialist transition is *tizhinei*: the Party-state. The Central Committee of the CCP represents the most senior level of the PRC's political elite. Overall though there are about half a million leading cadres at the country or division level or above. This includes about 900 in the offices of the central CCP and government; 2,500 ministers, provincial leaders, and senior managers of State-Owned Enterprises (SOE) (also appointed as leading officials of the Party-state). Lower down the politico-administrative hierarchy are some 39,000 leading cadres at district and department levels, with some 460,000 more down to and including the county level (Burns 2006; Walder 2006b). The passage of time, as well as the changed development strategy of 1978, has meant significant changes not only in the career background of the political elite, their qualifications, and social characteristics, but also in the ways their appointments have been managed.

In 1978, the political elite could largely have been characterized in exactly the same terms as that which came to power in 1949, reflecting the earlier experience of the CCP's revolution, its geographic and social origins. On the whole, the political elite were generalists – former guerrilla soldiers and political activists whose political loyalty to the CCP was assured but who had little professional or technical training, including only accidentally in state administration (Zang 2004: 43). There were essentially two reasons for the similarities in elite profile between 1949 and 1978. The first was that when the political elite came to power in 1949 they were still relatively young, and as a consequence aged in office. Even Mao's Cultural Revolution and the attack on leading cadres in the late 1960s did little to change this characteristic – for the most part 'those in authority taking the capitalist road' were replaced by others from the same generation. After Mao's death in 1976, many of those senior leaders who had been removed during the late 1960s began to be rehabilitated in large numbers. Their political reputations were restored; many were re-appointed to similar positions as those they had held before. This was the second reason for a similar profile to the political elite over a 30-year span. In many cases, they were not just individuals of the same generalist profile; they were exactly the same individuals.

The subsequent long-term change in the composition of the political elite was both inevitable and necessary. Necessary because the new development strategy adopted in 1978 had a need for greater specialization and a higher level of knowledge, skills, and qualifications in the political elite if its aims were to be achieved; and inevitable because with the passage of time the political leadership was ageing. As Deng Xiaoping remarked in August 1980, aged leading cadres were likely to be weak, ill, and quite simply not capable of doing their jobs properly

(Deng Xiaoping 1980). First, though the coalition whose support had led to the changes of December 1978 in the CCP leadership had to be satisfied with their individual positions as well as China's political future. There had to be a political agreement on 'the mistakes' of the recent past, which would include the rehabilitation of almost all those who had been the victims of the Cultural Revolution, not least to restore their long-term pension rights and (somewhat paradoxically) to organize their retirement.

Reinterpretation of the past was a process that had already started after the death of Mao Zedong in September 1976 but gathered pace after the 3rd Plenum of the 11th Central Committee of December 1978. There was the development of a new discourse to replace the idea of 'cultural revolution' that focused on the concept of 'socialist democracy' – essentially the importance of the Party as opposed to the leader (Schram 1983). This discourse focused on four main criticisms of past practices. The first was the over-concentration of power both in the hands of individuals and of the CCP. In theory, the CCP made policy and directed the state administration to implement them. In practice, there was an in-built tendency for officials in the state administration not to act on their own because they knew that CCP officials would be breathing down their necks, either to catch them out when slips were made or to intrude and run things themselves. The CCP's involvement in the state administration was even more counter-productive. It tended to step in to do others' jobs and rapidly became over-stretched and inefficient in the execution of both its own tasks and those of others. These problems were not assisted by the lack of clear lines of authority between different institutions and individuals. Particularly before 1979, multiple office-holding in different parts of the CCP and state administration had been commonplace. This was connected to the second criticism of past practices – the abuse of office. Under attack here were the worst excesses of what was then described as the 'bureaucratic work style': the lifelong tenure of officials, increasing corruption and abuse of privileged position, and the authoritarian attitudes of many leaders. The last two criticisms of past practices were relatively self-explanatory: for the best part of the previous 20 years, the legal system and democratic processes had been disregarded as 'bourgeois' and harmful to the cause of socialism (Goodman 1985: 218).

The rehabilitation of leading cadres as well as the establishment of new legitimacies culminated at the 11th Central Committee's 6th Plenum in June 1981 where the senior leadership of the CCP was restructured and the Party adopted the 'Resolution on certain questions in the history of our party since the founding of the People's Republic of China'. This essentially criticized Mao Zedong during 1962–1976 as favouring his views on change at the expense of the principle of collective leadership within the CCP, and held him responsible for 'leftist' errors in those years. It also formally restored to the leadership a number of senior CCP figures who had been victims of both the Cultural Revolution and Mao's opposition earlier. Among these were not only Deng Xiaoping (appointed to head the CCP's Military Commission) but also Hu Yaobang (now becoming Chairman of the CCP's Central Committee of the CCP), Zhao Ziyang (already Premier of the

State Council and now a Vice Chairman of the CCP Central Committee), and Xi Zhongxun (out of favour since 1962 though now added to the CCP Secretariat). The spirit of the times was definitely, to quote Deng Xiaoping in 1980 'Under the united leadership of the CCP, we quickly overcame the grave difficulties of 1959, 1960 and 1961. It is worth recalling that' (Goodman 1981).

The longer term changes to rejuvenate and re-skill the leadership, and to re-engineer the leadership processes started in earnest in 1982 and lasted throughout the 1980s. Immediately there was a need to recruit younger and technically more competent individuals to ensure that cadres were 'younger, better educated, more specialised, and politically correct' – or the 'Four Modernisations of Cadres' as the new campaign was described. Starting in 1982, compulsory retirement at age 60 was introduced and new age limits were set for appointments: county leaders could not be older than 45, division leaders no older than 50. Leading cadres were now expected to be college graduates with some additional technical knowledge and expertise (Goodman 1985: 230).

The CCP's control of appointments to the political elite changed dramatically with the shifts in strategic development that started in 1978. The system of control of appointments leadership positions in the PRC is usually referred to in terms of the 'table of ranks'. This system is derived from earlier operation in the Soviet Union where each position in the Party-state hierarchy is assigned a rank, and each individual is graded similarly by rank, through regular periods of study at a Party School (Pieke 2009). An individual can only be appointed to a position for which they have the qualified rank. Each CCP committee at each level has a list of positions for which it is responsible. The list has two sections: those positions that can be filled by the CCP committee in question directly; and those that must obtain an additional approval from the CCP's Organization Department.

Before the early 1980s, the CCP process of appointments to leadership positions was highly centralized with appointment to a position at a given level a matter of report to the Organization Department of the CCP Committee two levels above the decision being taken. One of the important reforms in the early 1980s was to replace this injunction so that report was only to one superior level of CCP committee Organization Department. Another, equally important was a large reduction in the number of positions being supervised in this way by the Organization Department of the Central Committee, the senior Organization Department in the system (Burns 1994). At the start of the reform era, some 13,500 were under review by the Central Organization Department. This was reduced to about 4,000 positions including those in the Central Party and government, the 2,500 elite positions at ministerial and provincial-level, and an unspecified number of appointments to the leadership of SOEs (Burns 2003; Brodsgaard 2006).

The call to renew the cadre force and the changed procedures for appointment led almost immediately to dramatic changes in the membership of the political elite, sanctioned by the 12th Congress of the CCP in September 1982. From March 1983 to August 1985, there was a turnover in the leadership of the CCP and the state administration greater than that which had occurred during the Cultural

Revolution, though this time the aims were both to remove those individuals who had come to positions of political authority at that time and to retire their victims, in order to provide younger, more educated, and more technically skilled leading cadres. The impact of these rapid turnovers in personnel can be seen at the provincial level where there were sweeping leadership changes during March and April 1983, and again later between May and July 1985 (Mills 1985). In February 1983, the average age of secretaries of CCP Provincial Committees had been approximately 63 years, and some 53% of all provincial leaders had been first appointed to positions of leadership before the Cultural Revolution. By the middle of 1983, the average age of provincial CCP secretaries was approximately 57 years, and the proportion of pre-Cultural Revolution provincial leaders still in office fell to 27%. By August 1985, the average age of secretaries of CCP Provincial Committees had fallen to approximately 50 years, and the proportion of pre-Cultural Revolution cadres still in leadership positions at provincial level had fallen to 1.5%. In addition and overall, the average educational level of the leadership had started to rise dramatically. Though some members of the earlier Revolutionary Generation had received formal higher education, on the whole, this was necessarily a limited proportion. By 1985, some 52% of secretaries of CCP Provincial committees were graduates from institutes of higher education (Goodman 1986: 126).

These dramatic changes foreshadowed the unusual calling of a CCP National Conference in September 1985. On the previous occasion when there had been a Party Conference of this kind (as opposed to a CCP National Congress) in 1955, it had followed a major conflict in the leadership between Mao Zedong and the leadership of Northeast China (Teiwes 1990). As in 1955, the September 1985 Party Conference also concentrated on personnel changes. The Party Conference was preceded immediately by the 4th Plenum of the CCP's 12th Central Committee, and followed immediately by its 5th Plenum. At the former plenary session, 10 of 24 of the CCP's Political Bureau resigned, as did 64 full and alternate members of the CCP Central Committee, all previously elected at the 12th CCP National Congress in 1982. The 5th Plenum appointed six new full members of the CCP Political Bureau and added 91 new members to the CCP Central Committee and three people to the CCP Secretariat. There were apparently three motivations in these changes: to rejuvenate the leadership, to remove the influences of the Cultural Revolution, and to ensure the political commitment of individual leaders to the reform programme. Rejuvenation and rectification of the leadership were real enough but need to be kept in perspective. The 10 members of the CCP Political Bureau who retired certainly had an average age of over 80. Nonetheless, four of the members of the CCP Political Bureau who remained were still older than 80 years old, and the six new replacements still averaged well over 60 years old (Goodman 1986: 124).

The more complete passing of the Revolutionary Generation though had to wait until the 13th CCP National Congress at the end of October and the beginning of November 1987. The delay was the result of differences of opinion among the leadership about the speed and direction of reform, and also, less surprisingly, the speed of change in the leadership. At one point, one of the CCP's senior leaders, Peng Zhen (the first major victim of the Cultural Revolution in 1966 when Mayor of Beijing) gave an interview in which he said:

> It would never do for the Political Bureau to be made up of young people. Not that I do not respect young comrades. It is just that for complicated work there is a need for a certain amount of experience. If people are too young, I am afraid it will not do. It would be better to have a combination of the rather elderly, the old, the middle-aged, and the young.
> *(Peng Zhen 1987)*

In the event though the 13th CCP Congress delivered both an agreement on the political recipe for change and a new leadership in terms of generational change. At the Congress, Zhao Ziyang explicated the formulae associated with the idea of China being in 'the primary stage of socialism' which significantly highlighted the continued need to combat the possibilities of 'bourgeois liberalisation'. The new leadership represented a significant shift into a technocratic, modernizing elite. Most of the new CCP Central Committee were college graduates (67%), young (average age 55), and with wide administrative and professional experience. The change is emphasized at the level of the CCP Political Bureau. Almost none of the new CCP Political Bureau (16%, compared to a third of the CCP Political Bureau on the eve of the 1987 Congress) had participated in the Long March, and less than half (42%) had actually been involved in CCP activities before 1949. Several of the new Political Bureau members had not even joined the CCP before the late 1950s. Just under half (48%) of the new Political Bureau were university or college educated and one-third could readily be described as technocrats – higher education graduates in technology and professional studies with appropriate career experience before joining the cadre force – compared to less than one-tenth of the previous CCP Political Bureau (Goodman 1988).

Since the late 1980s, recruitment to the CCP has been considerably more open than in the past, through education, the workplace, and the professions, with those destined for leadership identified at an early stage. Indeed, it is estimated that about a quarter of all CCP members go on to become leading cadres at some level. The political elite has come to be characterized by its high levels of educational qualification and its representativeness of the wider society more generally, especially in terms of geographical distribution around China (Kou and Zang 2013). The one obvious exception to the greater representativeness of the political elite is in terms of its gender balance. During the Cultural Revolution, about one-fifth of the members of the CCP Central Committee had been women, but there are now even fewer than there had been in the past, with no more than a small handful in the political elite and at any level of the leadership (Zheng and Fook 2003; Victor Shih et al. 2010).

The education levels of the political elite have become particularly impressive. By 2012, by way of example, 74% of members of the Standing Committees of CCP

Committees at the provincial-level were holders of master's degrees and 22.8% were doctoral graduates (Li Cheng 2012: 604). Andrew Walder's observations on the role of education in leading to appointment as a leading cadre are instructive:

> A party member with a college education was 26 times more likely to become a cadre than a non-Party member with less than a high school education, and over four times more likely than a party member with only a high school education.

As he points out too, even in rural China the role of education in determining the appointment of cadres is crucial: each year of schooling increases the likelihood that an individual will become a cadre by one-third, and someone with six years of schooling is six times more likely to become a cadre than someone without (Walder 2006b).

Education may have become a necessary condition for entry to the political elite, but there was always a significant sector of the elite recruited through education even before 1978. Even before 1978, there had been previously two segmented paths to elite status: one determined by ideological conformity and political appropriateness leading to political appointment; and another generated by educational qualifications and leading to a professional position (Walder et al. 2000; Andreas 2009). One of the consequences of the elite dualism of the Mao era is its persistence, albeit in a modified form. There is a difference in political elite appointments between CCP and government positions, supported by two different career paths. Everyone is required to have educational credentials and political capacity. At the same time, human capital is emphasized when government leadership appointments are made and political loyalty for appointments to the CCP hierarchy. In appointments to leadership in the CCP, party seniority is more important. Professional and administration experience count more for appointment to a government position. University education is a particular determinant of advance to a leading position in government (to such an extent that professionals and intellectuals may be co-opted), whereas particularistic ties seem more important for appointments to the CCP hierarchy (Zang 2004).

Enterprises, entrepreneurs, and the economic elite

China's economic elite head a wide and complex range of different kinds of economic enterprises. The introduction of market forces into a state socialist economic system since the early 1980s and the various different waves of economic restructuring that have taken place subsequently has led to a sometimes bewildering array of enterprises in terms of ownership and control (Naughton 2016). The result is an economic elite composed of state-owned and other enterprise managers, businesspeople, private entrepreneurs, and leading political cadres, particularly at the most local of levels. Two defining characteristics of the development of the economy under reform have shaped both enterprise development and the newly emergent economic elite. The first is that structural development has resulted from marketization not for the most part from privatization – the sale or transfer in other ways of state assets – as occurred in other reforming state socialist systems (Naughton 1995; Walder 2006a). The second is that though direct state management of enterprises as branch agencies of the ministries of central government in a planned economy has mostly disappeared, the Party-state's role in the economy remains central to its operation. The Party-state's influence is dominant and way beyond the control of state-owned enterprises [SOE] (Pearson 2015: 44).

There are very few clues to the wealth, status, and political linkages of economic elites from the categorization of enterprises (and indeed of economic sectors). One reason for uncertainty is that such descriptions in the PRC are no clear guide to their systems of ownership and control, or indeed their operation. The state sector includes SOEs and other public-sector enterprises, including public service units, and central and local government enterprises. In 2017 there were 110 large-scale and strategically important SOEs at the national level (under the State Asset Supervision and Administration Commission) with a further 110,000 or so at other levels of the politico-administrative hierarchy, and more than 300,000 collective sector enterprises (Naughton 2017). In 2019, there were estimated to be about 38 million small- and medium-sized enterprises, expected to grow to 43 million in 2020. The private sector is estimated to contribute more than 60% of GDP, with some 340 million employees or 44% of the working population. The foreign-invested sector is estimated to contribute about 10% of GDP with about 26 million employees or just over 3% of the workforce. Those figures are very approximate but the numbers for the state sector are even more elastic. As a proportion of GDP, the state sector is estimated to provide somewhere between 21 and 39%, with somewhere between 114 million and 205 million employees or 14 to 26%of the workforce (Zhang Chunlin 2019).

A key reason for these uncertainties is that the public sector, the private sector, and the foreign-invested sector are almost inherently interrelated and hybrid companies dominate in terms of the economy's ownership systems (Dickson 2008: 60; Naughton 2010). In 2013, the 110 national SOEs had 38,423 subsidiary companies. One-quarter of all private enterprises are subordinate companies of SOEs; foreign-invested companies often have SOE shareholders; and the huge local government section of the public sector often has private, local government, and foreign equity coming together in a variety of different ways. Shareholding is widespread across all the economic sectors, and SOEs even have private shareholders (Garnaut et al. 2006; Naughton 2017).

Enterprise development has generally passed through several stages since 1978 (Dickson 2008: 32–65; Goodman 2008: 27–30; Zhang, H. 2012; Naughton 2016). Town and village enterprises (TVEs) were first developed as part of the opening up of rural China during the early reform era. In 1984, small-scale individual businesses started to be developed in urban China, though ambiguity remained about their status. That ambiguity worsened for a couple of years after the Tian'anmen Incident of mid-1989, as the CCP appeared resistant to the idea of private enterprise and the role of foreign investment in China. This all only started to change in 1992, when Deng Xiaoping encouraged the development of private enterprises, those with more than eight employees. In the mid-1990s, large numbers of TVEs were restructured, becoming private enterprises, shareholding collectives, or corporate entities of other kinds; and in 1995 the decision was taken to restructure SOEs. The growing systemic confidence that came with the expansion of the private sector and the restructuring of public-sector enterprises also led to more open and unrestricted opportunities for foreign investment, first in joint ventures and then in wholly owned companies.

TVEs came about during the 1980s as villages and households were permitted to operate in the market. They developed fastest and in greater numbers in the suburban and peri-urban areas of cities, in the coastal regions, rapidly becoming a major adjunct to the state sector. In many such urban cases too, the development of rural industry rapidly ensured that villages ceased agricultural activities altogether. Though all were designated as collective sector enterprises – enterprises owned technically by the people who live in a given area or work in the enterprise – there were in practice different kinds of TVEs (Alpermann 2006; Zhang, J. 2007). One model was indeed that of a TVE collectively owned and developed by local government. This is often referred to as the Sunan Model, named after Southern Jiangsu, the area of the Lower Yangtze River Delta, where it originated, centred on the cities of Suzhou, Wuxi, and Chagzhou (Oi 1995; Walder 1995; Whiting 2001). The second variety of TVE was actually a private enterprise. Private entrepreneurs in the last 30 years have always had more difficulties obtaining access to loans, labour, and land than state and collective sector enterprises. In the 1980s and early 1990s, this was particularly acute for both ideological and political reasons, and so many private entrepreneurs became what have been known as 'red hat' entrepreneurs: collective sector managers in name but private entrepreneurs in practice. Private enterprise TVEs are also sometimes spoken of as the Wenzhou Model, after the town in Zhejiang Province, where the practice was both prevalent and particularly successful (Parris 1993; Whiting 2001). Official estimates in 1996 calculated that about half of all TVEs were 'collectives' of this second kind (Lau 1999: 64). The third variety was that of TVEs that were essentially cooperative ventures between villages in Guangdong, Fujian, and to a lesser extent Zhejiang Provinces, on the one hand, and Chinese investors from Hong Kong and Taiwan, on the other, often though not exclusively by any means returning to their ancestral homes (Chan et al. 2009; Saich and Hu 2012: 73).

The varied development of TVEs generated a wide variety of entrepreneurs and managers with different social backgrounds and experiences, ranging from those who had been at the centre of local communities before 1979, sometimes with substantial education and training, to those who been denied access to power and status by the earlier regime's discrimination against class enemies. Many of the individual business owners who started operations in the 1980s were those who had been previously dispossessed: those with bad class labels during the Mao era and those who had been urban youth rusticated to the countryside during the Cultural Revolution and deprived of education and training, but now allowed back into the cities (Gold 1989; Davis 1992). These businesses were technically permitted in order to provide the goods and services that the state and collective sectors were not able to supply, although their legal and political status remained somewhat unclear (Parris 1999: 268). This uncertainty worsened after the Tian'anmen Incident of June 1989, when businesspeople were criticized for their alleged role in supporting the demonstrations, and the CCP banned entrepreneurs from joining the Party (Dickson 2008: 36).

After 1992, there was substantial growth in small- and medium-sized private enterprises. Many of those who became private entrepreneurs in the 1990s came out of the Party-state. Subsequently, it has become more usual for graduates to move into business both working for others and working for themselves. Backgrounds and educational levels have changed dramatically. Before 1992, 37% of entrepreneurs were former peasants or factory workers; by 1996, only 7% came from these backgrounds. In the 1980s, only 40% of entrepreneurs had more than a junior high school education; by 2002, 88% had at least graduated from high school (Nee and Opper 2012: 36). With the restructuring of TVEs and SOEs that started in the mid-1990s, these characteristics of private entrepreneurs were intensified. A survey of private entrepreneurs in five coastal provinces during 2006–2007 found that 51% had formerly worked in the state economic sector and 19% had previously been Party or government cadres (Chen, J. and Dickson 2010: 37).

Changes in the private sector during the 1990s inevitably brought pressure for change both to TVEs and to the state sector. In both cases, there was a shortage of funds for investment, and competition was increasing. TVEs were transformed by turning most of them into shareholding companies, largely through management buyouts (Sun Laixiang 2005; Naughton 2007: 291–292). One survey found that, by 1999, 86% of TVEs in Jiangsu and Zhejiang had at least partially changed in this way, and 57% had completed the process (Li, H. and Rozelle 2003).

SOE restructuring proceeded differently, not least because enterprises had been both substantially larger and work units with social and political as well as economic functions. One consequence was that SOEs had been weighed down not just by inefficient and outdated equipment, and so in need of re-investment, but also by the burden of retirees who remained on the enterprise payroll and of a workforce privileged by the CCP's ideology. SOE managers had attempted to meet the challenge of reform by setting up subsidiary companies that effectively moved former company assets and staff elsewhere, usually into the collective and private sectors, while retaining a share of the equity in the new enterprises, but these moves necessarily exacerbated the problems they faced (Ding 1999; Lin, Y. and Zhang 1999). The corporate restructuring programme that started in the mid-1990s resulted in bankruptcies as well as the public offerings of shares, employee and management buyouts, development of leasing arrangements, and the establishment of joint ventures with foreign investors (Garnaut et al. 2006; Oi and Han 2011; Zeng and Tsai 2011). A 2004 survey found that some 37% stayed public-sector enterprises, 32% became corporate enterprises, 24% became private enterprises, and 5% had become foreign-invested enterprises (Oi and Han 2011: 23).

The state sector of the economy and SOEs in particular remained an inefficient part of the economy, employing large numbers of people but not contributing proportionately to national economic output or development. Further reform and restructuring of SOEs was a major item on the agenda at the 3rd Plenum of the 18th Central Committee of the CCP in November 2013. There were three major goals for change: greater SOE autonomy ensuring incentives to improve efficiency of operation; greater supervision by the CCP of SOEs to ensure that the development of greater autonomy is not abused; and greater innovation in technology and operations. As Barry Naughton points out, these three goals were largely contradictory and without considerable difficulty mutually exclusive. SOEs might be expected to operate according to market forces but their whole operational culture mitigated against that, not to mention that the largest SOEs all have leaders appointed by the Party-state. These circumstances explain why innovation has been and remains the preserve of private enterprise rather than SOEs, and why SOEs become involved in almost all sectors of the economy rather than focusing on new developments as the 3rd Plenum of 2013 had suggested. As Naughton points out, SOEs have been unable to concentrate in the ways envisaged: 'State firms have stopped investing in breath mints and pleasure boats, but they continue to invest something in virtually every significant economic sector' (Naughton 2017: 286). Unsurprisingly, the private sector contributes not only a higher proportionate share of GDP but also 80% of urban employment and 90% of new jobs.

Elite interdependence and class formation

With the development of the PRC economy, the political elite has not so much lost its monopoly position in society as transformed itself into part of a new dominant class in which the interests of economic and political management intersect now in the new configurations of market socialism. That dominant class has both political and economic elite components but is characterized by both their institutional and their associational interdependence, as the examination of the evolution of post-state socialist economic forms has just in no small measure indicated. A large part of the economic elite comes from or remains employed in the state sector. Even where that is not the case, the successful entrepreneur needs just links not only to the Party-state in order to prosper but also to take a role in the Party-state's networks of formal institutions and associations. For government at all levels, the business of government is now most definitely business and economic development, and cadres at all levels need the skills and experience to deal with that.

By definition and operation, those who run enterprises in the state sector of the economy are fundamentally part of the political as well as the economic elite, even where their appointments to positions of leadership or management need not be formally approved by CCP committees at any level. Almost all are members of the CCP, and their career backgrounds are largely indistinguishable from leading cadres in the Party-state in terms of education and experience. More remarkable perhaps is that the economic elite whose enterprises are not in the state sector, who are private entrepreneurs and owner-operators, share many of the same social and demographic characteristics. A survey of the economic elite in Shanxi Province during the reform era to 2000 found similar levels of education, and that 56% of private entrepreneurs were members of the CCP, even before that possibility was sanctioned by the Party itself. One exception to that common background was that the same survey found that entrepreneurs and managers in private enterprises were more likely than cadres to have had a parent who was or who had been a member of the CCP or who had worked in the Party-state (Goodman 2001).

Given that many of the very earliest reform era private entrepreneurs and owner-operators of businesses had also been those discriminated against during the Cultural Revolution, it is clear that CCP membership was surreptitiously sought and approved. The reasons for this are relatively clear. From the CCP's side, there was always, especially in the early days of reform, some nervousness about the political consequences of private enterprise. Individual household businesses had been accepted as 'non-exploitative' from the beginning. TVEs were understood as collective sector developments, whatever the realities of economic formation, and so less political confronting to local cadres. In the 1980s, private business was accepted as 'a necessary and beneficial supplement to the public economy' and in 1997 it became 'an important component' of the national economy. It was not until 2007 (at the 17th National CCP Congress) that the Party determined to 'unswervingly encourage, support and guide the development of the non-public sector' granting in theory the same status to private enterprises, corporate entities, and those based on shares or other notions of equity as granted to SOEs.

For entrepreneurs in the non-state sectors of the economy, CCP membership provided not only a degree of political surety but also considerable financial benefit. The key problem facing private entrepreneurs and owner-operators has always been access to land, labour, and loans. Private entrepreneurs have repeatedly said (through regular surveys) that they feel a need to be in 'the system' (Dickson 2008: 94–5) and large numbers have reported feeling discriminated against in comparison to the Party-state's relationship to the public sector (Tsai 2007: 84). Access to financing and business opportunities and concerns about tax and industrial and commercial management policy are usually given as the main reasons for their wanting to be involved in the various activities of the Party-state and not just CCP membership (Zhang, H. and Ming 1999: 50).

Quite apart from CCP membership, entrepreneurs were encouraged to participate in the state's representative political institutions. In 2004, for example, more than 9,000 entrepreneurs were delegates to people's congresses at county, provincial, and national levels, and a further 30,000 had been elected to various people's political consultative conferences (Zhang Houyi 2004: 318). As many of the economic elite had in fact emerged from within the Party-state they could hardly be said to have been politicized in this way. Perhaps a better indicator of that process is the near-universal membership by private entrepreneurs in Chambers of Commerce and business associations organized by and through local government (Chen, J. and Dickson 2010: 45). It is certainly clear that those private entrepreneurs who engaged in such activities were successful: studies of private entrepreneurs and their level of political embeddedness have shown that those who joined the CCP and participated in formal institutions in these ways were more likely to obtain bank loans and financing (Zhou Wubiao 2009; Talavera et al. 2010). It remains then no surprise to find that three-quarters of private enterprises have CCP branches; or for that matter that when China's then richest individual, Jack Ma, founder of Alibaba, retired in late 2019 it emerged that he too was a member of the CCP.

The interdependence of economic and political elites is highlighted not only by the large numbers of former local leading cadres who became entrepreneurs, and the recruitment into the CCP and co-optation into the activities of the Party-state of successful entrepreneurs, but also by the recruitment into the political elite of individuals with specialized non-political skills. As might be expected, most of the political elite had worked their way up the administrative hierarchy. On the whole, cadres were better educated than members of the local economic elite; urban-based elites were better educated than rural-based elite groups; and those from the leadership of the state and public-sector enterprises were better educated than entrepreneurs in the private sector. At the same time, a study of cadres in Shanxi Province reveals that substantial proportions of the cadres interviewed in the provincial administration, district offices, and county authorities had not spent the majority of their working lives within the offices of the Party-state. In all cases, these were (former) businesspeople, technocrats, and intellectuals who had been politically suspect (usually on grounds of family background) in the Mao-dominated era of China's politics. Though a few had been permitted to join the CCP even before the reform era, all had chosen to make their careers outside the Party-state. With the advent of reform, they were recruited to government office by a provincial leadership anxious to utilize their skills and expertise (Goodman 2000). This phenomenon is undoubtedly one reason that generally across the country 38% of local cadres are not members of the CCP.

From the mid-1990s on it became clear that the main business of local government was economic development. An early study of Shulu County in Hebei Province detailed the ways in which local government developed an industrial and commercial infrastructure that it did not immediately control or administer (Blecher and Shue 1996). Research a little later based on local governments in ten different provinces described the emergence of 'local state corporatism' in the ways county, township, and village each operate as a corporate entity on its own, and as a system together where county government essentially becomes the corporate headquarters for local economic activity (Oi 1999: 99). Landry's still later research shows how important management of the local economy remains to the subsequent career of local cadres: success in this regard leads to promotion, though interestingly poor performance of the local economy does not necessarily lead to dismissal or demotion (Landry 2008: 261).

The interdependence of economic and political institutions at the national level appears understandably to have taken different forms, more focused on strategy and policymaking. There is some evidence in particular of the development of a kind of lobbying process in which individuals, companies, and governments campaign on behalf of interests and initiatives. Provincial and local governments have long-established liaison offices in the capital, major metropolitan centres, and other cities in a practice that dates from imperial times. These liaison offices not only represent the interests of localities around China but also provided a place where natives can come and stay and find people who speak the same language and eat the same food. In addition, there are newly formed pro-active corporate and industrial interest agencies, notably those representing the state monopolies of banking, oil, electricity, coal, telecommunications, aviation, rail, tobacco, and shipping, whose function is solely to interact with government and the CCP. Important lobby groups have also been formed for state, foreign, and private firms on a sectoral basis, one of the most important of which is for real estate development (Sun Liping 2006). In 2010, the central government issued regulations on the establishment and activities of these various lobby groups and liaison offices (Li Cheng 2012: 614).

The interdependence of economic and political elites leading to the emergence of new dominant class interest is certainly not unobserved in the PRC itself. Yan Ye of the North China Institute of Science and Technology described the situation where 'there is a lot of space and almost a bottomless pit for rent-seeking by those with power' (Yan 2012: 202). Zhou Xiaohong of Nanjing University, equally negatively suggests that

> The upper "capitalist class" and a fraction of the middle class in Chinese society . . . are derived from the former power centre or, at least, have something to do with it. Part of their wealth is acquired through unfair competition or utilization of the loopholes in the state system and policies. More importantly, this group of people, while small in number and proportion, owns a great part of the social wealth.
> *(Zhou Xiaohong 2008: 11)*

And Sun Liping, Professor of Sociology at Tsinghua University has written even more pointedly

> The process of the strengthening of the government's capacity to extract resources . . . concentrated more and more money in the hands of the government. And he who has wealth speaks loudest. . . . Vested interests have now become entrenched, the result being tremendous social unfairness. In dealing with this social unfairness, the government has been utterly helpless.
> *(Sun Liping 2013)*

To some extent, the introduction of compulsory retirement at 60 has led some cadres to look for employment in the private sector at 59 (Li Cheng 2012: 603). A survey of CCP and government officials undertaken in 2005 by the CCP organization department revealed that cadres often approached private entrepreneurs with three aims in mind: to gain economic benefit for themselves and their families; to look for opportunities for themselves to leave a Party or government position and find a job in the business world; and to seek political support from the private sector owing to its increasing political importance (Zheng 2006).

The intergenerational transfer of privilege

While elite interdependence highlights the understanding of the dominant class in the fundamental sense of class as shared economic interest, the intergenerational transfer of privilege provides a more contemporary understanding. Although modernizing societies often promote the myth that education and work can trump social status, wealth, and power in the determination of individual success, in practice social standing is pre-determined for just under three-quarters of the population in most industrialized societies (Clark 2014). The evidence from the PRC differs only in the scale of the intergenerational transfer of class. Research undertaken through Peking University and the PRC National Bureau of Statistics highlights 'an extremely high level of intergenerational persistence . . . (which) implies that intergenerational mobility is much lower in China than in most developed nations' (Gong et al. 2010: 6). This research concludes that a child's socio-economic position is determined by their parents' income, level of education, occupation, and CCP membership. One particular finding is of near certainty that a daughter will follow her father's occupation and social status; another a 74% certainty that a son will do the same (Gong et al. 2010: 16). From this intergenerational perspective, it seems that dominant class formation after 1978 is embedded in both the PRC's political elite and those whose social capital has its origins with the pre-1949 local elite across China.

The links between political power and economic advantage across generations seem almost self-evident. A survey of 1700 central and provincial leaders found that they had 3,100 children then holding official positions at or above bureau level, and that another 900 were the leaders of large and medium-sized SOEs (Li Cheng 2001: 128–129). One internal report by the CCP's organization department recorded that in 2012, of 8,370 senior executives in the major SOEs directly under the State-Owned Assets Supervision and Administration Commission, 6,370 have immediate family members who live overseas or have foreign citizenship (Li Cheng 2012: 617). A publicly available study from 2013 suggests that the children of cadres earn 15%more in their first employment than do the children of other people (*Global Times* 2013). An internal report by the CCP's organization department recorded that 90%of millionaires in 2006 were the children of high-ranking officials (Dickson 2008: 23).

At the local level, there have been a number of studies that suggest the importance of the intergenerational link to fame and fortune. A study of entrepreneurs in Shanxi during the mid-1990s highlighted how many of those who came to the fore as provincial models of entrepreneurship had a father who worked in the Party-state and was usually a leading cadre, where they themselves were originally at least not even CCP members. Hu Jianping's father had been a Korean War veteran and a former leader of the local militia. Hu Jianping himself had become a lorry driver and then a large-scale coke manufacturer, eventually persuaded to become secretary of his home village's CCP branch. Wang Jijun's father had been a cadre in the Eighth Route Army of the War of Resistance to Japan and later became a leading cadre in the provincial public security system. Wang Jijun himself became a policeman and then a lawyer establishing the province's largest practice. Wang Hualun was the President of the Shanxi Rongtong Credit Cooperative. His father had been a pre-Cultural Revolution mayor of both Yangquan and Datong. His elder brother was a cadre of the Provincial Legal Commission; and his younger brother a cadre in the Provincial Planning Commission. Wang Hualun himself served in the PLA during the early 1970s, before moving into management (Goodman 1998: 45–52).

A later study of women entrepreneurs in Mianyang (Sichuan), Qiongshan (Hainan), and Jiaocheng (Shanxi) also highlighted the role of parental influence associated with the Party-state in the evolution of entrepreneurial activism. Where the female entrepreneurs were not themselves CCP members, almost all had a father or mother who was (Chen Minglu 2008: 114). In many of the reported interviews of entrepreneurs, there is a decided hint that the children of cadres and CCP members did not need to either join the CCP or serve in the Party-state in order to access the necessary networks of influence. On a number of occasions when private entrepreneurs were asked about their lack of CCP membership, they often responded along the lines of: why should I join the CCP. I have grown up locally, and my father, mother, or some other relative was the village head (or county party secretary, or some other local position of leadership) (Goodman 2004: 151).

The intense localism that characterizes business elites is also reflected in the attitudes and behaviour of local cadres. A survey of local cadres at county level and below in Shanxi Province found that most were locals, overwhelmingly of the province, with the majority from the same or a neighbouring county where they served. Many fewer of the local political elite had parents who were CCP members or worked in the Party-state than was the case for the local business elites. On the other hand, a three-generation pattern is observable in which the parent, usually the father, is born into a peasant family, becomes a cadre as an adult, and has a child or children who then go on to become businesspeople. To a large extent, the local business elite are the children of the local political elite (Goodman 2000).

The intergenerational transfer of privilege goes far beyond a linear relationship to the PRC's political elite, strong though that may be. There is also the continuation of specific family influence from the pre-1949 local elite, through the establishment and development of the PRC's political elite into the contemporary economic elite. One illustrative piece of research details the development of a local elite family from the early 1930s on. The eldest son of a rich landlord family in North China decided, at the point at which Japanese invasion seemed likely, to give away the family's historic land-holdings in a kind of land redistribution without the formal processes of land reform, and joined the CCP. He then marched into the Taihang Mountains with one of the CCP columns when the Japanese invasion came and joined the War of Resistance, almost inevitably as a leader. This then set him on a career which led to provincial leadership positions after 1949, membership of the CCP Central Committee, persecution in the Cultural Revolution, and rehabilitation afterwards. His children had in one case an almost equally as noteworthy political career, and in the other, a professional career with later political service. His grandchildren then became local businesspeople in the places where they had been born and brought up (Minglu Chen 2012).

Life history research in the mid-1990s indicated the extent to which the pre-1949 local elites contributed to the later PRC leadership. About a quarter of the CCP's leadership in the early days of the PRC came from a local elite background. Even those who had not been members of the CCP before 1949 were able to find leading positions in economic and social management, and sometimes even in state operations. The Cultural Revolution fell disproportionately heavily on those who had been pre-1949 members of the local elite and early members of the CCP, though as already noted they and their families had their social and political positions restored after 1978. At that time those who had been from the pre-1949 local elite and who had not been associated with the earlier Communist Movement were able to resume their social and economic leadership positions and were almost necessarily at the forefront of the rapidly expanding business sector (Walder and Hu 2009).

Later research into wealthy entrepreneurs in Qingdao, Lanzhou, Kunming, Taiyuan, and Nanjing also emphasized the intergenerational transfer of privilege going back to both earlier PRC political elites and the pre-1949 local elite. The conclusions from 469 interviewees were that while there had been changes in the contemporary configurations of wealth and power, there had been less certain change in the social composition of the new elite which remains a product of social capital alongside wealth and political influence. Of those prepared to divulge information about their family's political affiliations before 1949, 80% reported having a close family member in the CCP at that time, which was almost 60% of all those interviewed. Similar proportions were reported when interviewees were questioned about having a family member in a local elite family before 1949: 81%, 53% of all those interviewed. Just under a quarter of those interviewed identified at least one individual member of their immediate family before 1949 who was simultaneously at that time both a member of the CCP and from a local elite family.

Equally interesting perhaps in the context of the intergenerational transfer of status was the interviewees' sense of their privileged place in society and China's history. Almost 10% of those interviewed were prepared to describe themselves as elite or upper class. A quarter came from families that still maintained family history books (many such books were destroyed by people from former elite families during the Cultural Revolution), and many talked (when given the opportunity) of their long family history. There were claims to be descendants of famous emperors, of a family history going back thousands of years, and in the modern era of involvement in many of the key events and with many of the key people of China during the twentieth century, let alone owning large amounts of property before the establishment of the PRC. Far-fetched and fanciful as some of these claims may sound, they nonetheless point to the importance of social status and social capital through family narratives, as well as the stories that people tell themselves in personal motivation (Goodman 2018).

The dominant class

The dominant class of 2021 is to be found in the intersections of politics, wealth, and social capital. It is embedded in the PRC's political system as established in and after 1949; in the economic restructurings of the late 1980s, the mid-1990s, and the late 1990s and early 2000s; and in the pre-1949 political economy. Wealth creation, the exercise of political power, and the acknowledgement of social status all play their role in defining the boundaries of the dominant class. China is though still a political economy in transition, and the precise composition of the dominant class is likely to continue developing even if change may not be a constant factor. Partly as a result its boundaries may be a little unclear at times, most obviously in the identification of the still relatively small Chinese middle classes, who are inevitably sometimes best regarded as a subordinate part of the dominant class not least because of their strong relationship to the system created by the Party-state.

It is the existence and operation of the Party-state that remains the defining feature of China's political economy and its dominant class. There are certainly entrepreneurs who appear to operate to some extent like capitalists in other parts of the world, and there is equally as certainly a community of interest that has developed and been developed between wealth creation and political power. At the same time though, the Party-state retains the ultimate authority in determining not simply the direction of the economy but also the development potential for specific companies and enterprises (Li Chunling 2013: 23).

BIBLIOGRAPHY

Abercrombie, N., and J. Urry (1983) *Capital, Labour, and the Middles Classes*. London: Allen & Unwin.

ACFTU (1999) (All-China Federation of Trade Unions) Policy Research Office *Zhongguo zhigong zhuangkuang diaocha, shijuchuan* [A Survey of the Condition of Chinese Workers and Staff, Statistical Volume]. Beijing: Xiyuan Press.

ACFTU (2006) (All-China Federation of Trade Unions) Research Office *Diwuci Zhongguo zhigong zhuangkuang diaocha, shijuchuan* [Fifth Survey of the Condition of Chinese Workers and Staff, Statistical Volume]. Beijing: Workers Press.

All China Industry and Business Association (2005) *China's Private Economy Yearbook 2002–2004*. Beijing: Zhongguo Zhigong Chubanshe.

Alpermann, Bjorn (2006) '"Wrapped Up in Cotton Wool": The Political Integration of Private Entrepreneurs in Rural China' in *The China Journal*, no. 56, 33–61.

Anagnost, Ann (1997) *A National Past-Times Narrative, Representation, and Power in Modern China*. Durham, NC: Duke University Press.

Anagnost, Ann (2004) 'The Corporeal Politics of Quality (*suzhi*)' in *Public Culture*, no. 16, 189–208.

Anagnost, Ann (2008) 'From "Class" to "Social Strata": Grasping the Social Totality in Reform-Era China' in *Third World Quarterly*, vol. 29, 497–519.

Anderlini, Jamil (2013) 'Chinese National People's Congress Has 83 Billionaires' in *Financial Times*, 7 March.

Anderson, Alistair R., Jin-Hai Li, Richard T. Harrison, and Paul J. A. Robson (2003) 'The Increasing Role of Small Business in the Chinese Economy' in *Journal of Small Business Management*, vol. 41, no. 3, July, 310–316.

Andreas, Joel (2009) *Rise of the Red Engineers: The Cultural Revolution and the Origins of China's New Class*. Palo Alto Ca: Stanford University Press.

Andreas, Joel (2012) 'Industrial Restructuring and Class Transformation in China' in Beatriz Carrillo and David S. G. Goodman (eds) *China's Peasants and Workers: Changing Class Identities*. Cheltenham Edward Elgar, pp. 102–123.

Appleton, Simon, John Knight, Linda Song, and Qingjie Xia (2006) 'Contrasting Paradigms – Segmentation and Competiveness in the Formation of the Chinese Labour Market' in Shi Li and Hiroshi Sato (eds) *Unemployment, Inequality and Poverty in Urban China*. Abingdon: Routledge, pp. 212–235.

Bibliography

Aron, Raymond (1960) 'Social Class, Political Class, Ruling Class' in *European Journal of Sociology*, vol. 1, 260–281.
Atkinson, Will (2009) 'Rethinking the Work – Class Nexus: Theoretical Foundations for Recent Trends' in *Sociology*, vol. 43, no. 5, 898.
Bai, Limin (2006) 'Graduate Unemployment: Dilemmas and Challenges in China's Move to Mass Higher Education' in *The China Quarterly*, no. 185, 128–144.
Becker, Jeffrey, and Manfred Elfstrom (2010) *The Impact of China's Labor Contract Law on Workers*. Washington, DC: International Labor Rights Forum.
Bendix, R., and S. M. Lipset (1967) 'Karl Marx's Theory of Social Class' in R. Bendix and S. M. Lipset (eds) *Class, Status and Power*. 2nd ed. London: Routledge.
Benney, Jonathan (2016) 'Weiwen at the Grassroots: China's Stability Maintenance Apparatus as a Means of Conflict Resolution' in *Journal of Contemporary China*, vol. 25, no. 99, 389–405.
Berger, P. L., and T. Luckmann (1966) *The Social Construction of Reality*. London: Allen Lane.
Bergère, Marie-Claire (1983) 'The Chinese Bourgeoisie, 1911–37' in John K. Fairbank (ed) *Republican China 1912–1949, Part 1*. Cambridge: Cambridge University Press, pp. 721–825.
Bergère, Marie-Claire (1989) *The Golden Age of the Chinese Bourgeoisie 1911-1937*. Cambridge: Cambridge University Press.
Bernstein, Basil (1975) *Class, Codes, and Control*. London: Routledge & Kegan Paul.
Bian, Yanjie (1994) *Work and Inequality in Urban China*. SUNY Series in the Sociology of Work. Albany: State University of New York Press.
Bian, Yanjie (2002) 'Chinese Social Stratification and Social Mobility' in *Annual Review of Sociology*, no. 28, 91–116.
Bian, Yanjie, and J. R. Logan (1996) 'Market Transition and the Persistence of Power: The Changing Stratification System in Urban China' in *American Sociological Review*, vol. 61, 739–758.
Bian, Yanjie, and Zhanxin Zhang (2004) 'Urban Elites and Income Differential in China: 1988–1995' in *Japanese Journal of Political Science*, vol. 5, 51–68.
Bjorklund, E. M. (1986) 'The Danwei: Socio-Spatial Characteristics of Work Units in China's Urban Society' in *Economic Geography*, vol. 62, no. 1, January, 19–29.
Blau, P., and O. D. Duncan (1967) *The American Occupational Structure*. New York: John Wiley.
Blau, Peter Michael, and Otis Dudley Duncan (1978) *The American Occupational Structure*. New York: Free Press.
Blecher, Marc (2002) 'Hegemony and Workers' Politics in China' *China Quarterly*, vol. 170, 283–303.
Blecher, Marc (2004) 'The Working Class and Governance in China' in Jude Howell (ed) *Governance in China*. Lanham, MD: Rowman and Littlefield, pp. 193–206.
Blecher, Marc (2006) 'Hegemony and Workers' Politics in China' in Lowell Dittmer and Guoli Liu (eds) *China's Deep Reform* Lanham, MD: Rowman and Littlefield, pp. 405–427.
Blecher, Marc (2008) 'What – and How – Have Tianjin Workers Been Thinking?' in *Journal of Chinese Political Studies*, vol. XIII, no. 3, October, 249–267.
Blecher, Marc (2021) 'The Political Economy of Working Class Re-formation' in Lowell Dittmer (ed) *China's Political Economy in the Xi Jinping Epoch: Domestic and Global Dimensions*. Hackensack, NJ: World Scientific.
Blecher, Marc (various years) Interviews.
Blecher, Marc, and Vivienne Shue (1996) *Tethered Deer: Government and Economy in a Chinese County*. Palo Alto, CA: Stanford University Press.
Blecher, Marc, and Gordon White (1979) *Micropolitics in Contemporary China: A Technical Unit During and After the Cultural Revolution*. London: Macmillan and White Plains: M. E. Sharpe.

Boehler, Patrick (2013) 'The Chinese Dream in Surveys: A Happy Middle Class' in *South China Morning Post*, 18 December.
Boltanski, Luc (1987) *The Making of a Class. Cadres in French Society*. Cambridge: Cambridge University Press.
Boltanski, Luc and Eve Chiapello (2005) *The New Spirit of Capitalism*. London and New York: Verso.
Bourdieu, Pierre (1984) *Distinction: A Social Critique of the Judgement of Taste*. Cambridge: Cambridge University Press.
Bourdieu, Pierre (1989) *The State of Nobility: Elite Schools in the Field of Power*. Palo Alto, CA: Stanford University Press.
Bourdieu, Pierre (1987) 'What Makes a Social Class?' in *Berkeley Journal of Sociology*, vol. 22, 1–18.
Bourdieu, Pierre, and Jean-Claude Passeron (1990) *Reproduction in Education, Society, and Culture*. London: Sage.
Bo Yibo (1996) *Ruogan zhongda juece yu shijian de huigu* [A Memoir of Major Decisions and Events], vol. 1. Beijing: Zhonggong dangshi chubanshe.
Bramall, Chris (2001) 'The Quality of China's Household Income Surveys' in *The China Quarterly*, no. 167, 689–705.
Braverman, Harry, *Labor and Monopoly Capital: The Degradation of Work in the Twentieth Century*, New York: Monthly Review Press, 1974.
Bray, David (2005) *Social Space and Governance in Urban China: The Danwei System from Origins to Reform*. Stanford, CA: Stanford University Press.
Bray, David (2006) 'Building "Community": New Strategies of Governance in Urban China' in *Economy and Society*, vol. 35, no. 4, 530–549.
Breen, Richard, and Jan O. Jonsson (2005) 'Inequality of Opportunity in Comparative Perspective: Recent Research on Educational Attainment and Social Mobility' in *Annual Review of Sociology*, vol. 31, 223–244.
Brint, S. G., and J. Karabel (1989) *The Diverted Dream: Community College and the Promise of Educational Opportunities in America 1900–1985*. New York: Oxford University Press.
Brodsgaard, Kjeld Erik (2006) '*Bianzhi* and Cadre Management in China: The Case of Yangpu' in Kjeld-Erik Brodsgaard and Yongnian Zheng (eds) *The Chinese Communist Party in Reform*. New York: Routledge.
Brook, Timothy (2005) *Collaboration: Japanese Agents and Local Elites in Wartime China*. Cambridge, MA: Harvard University Press.
Brown, P. (1990) 'The "Third Wave": Education and the Ideology of Parentocracy' in *British Journal of Sociology of Education*, vol. 11, no. 1, 65–85.
Burnham, James (1941) *The Managerial Revolution: What Is Happening in the World*. New York: Norton.
Burns, John P. (1994) 'Strengthening Central CCP Control of Leadership Selection: The 1990 *Nomenklatura*' in *The China Quarterly*, vol. 138, 474–480.
Burns, John P. (2003) 'Downsizing the Chinese State: Government Retrenchment in the 1990s' in *The China Quarterly*, vol. 175, 775–802.
Burns, John P (2006) 'The Chinese Communist Party's Nomenklatura System as a Leadership Selection Mechanism: An Evaluation' in Kjeld Erik Brodsgaard and Yongnian Zheng (eds) *The Chinese Communist Party in Reform*. Abingdon: Routledge.
Burr, V. (1995) *An Introduction to Social Constructionism*. London: Routledge.
Cai Yongshun (2002) 'The Resistance of Chinese Laid-off Workers in the Reform Period' in *The China Quarterly*, no. 170, 327–344.
Cai Yongshun (2005) 'China's Moderate Middle Class: The Case of Homeowners Resistance' in *Asian Survey*, no. 45, 777–799.

Cai Yongshun, and Zhou Titi (2019) 'Online Political Participation in China: Local Government and Differentiated Response' in *The China Quarterly*, no. 238, June, 331–352.
Cao, Yongshun (2001) 'Careers Inside Organizations: A Comparative Study of Promotion Determination in Reforming China' in *Social Force*, vol. 80, 1–29.
Carrillo, Beatriz (2011) *Small Town China: Rural Labour and Social Inclusion*. London: Routledge.
Carroll, Lewis (1975) *Through the Looking Glass*. London: Hart-Davis MacGibbon.
CASS (Chinese Academy of Social Sciences) (2013) *Blue Book of Cities in China*. Beijing: Shehui kexue wenxian chubanshe.
Castel, Robert (2002) *From Manual Workers to Wage Laborers: Transformation of the Social Question*. London: Routledge.
CCP Constitution (2017) Constitution of the Communist Party of China, 5 November 2017.
CEIC Data (n.d.) 'China Migrant Worker: Average Age'. Available at www.ceicdata.com/en/china/migrant-worker/migrant-worker-average-age.
Central Committee of the Chinese Communist Party (1953) 'Zhongguo Gongchandang zhongyang weiyuanhui guanyu nongye shengchan hezuoshe de jueyi' (16 December 1953) [The Resolution of the Central Committee of the Chinese Communist Party on Agricultural Cooperatives], in Guofang daxue dangshi dangjian zhenggong jiaoyanshi (ed) *Zhonggong dangshi jiaoxue cankao ziliao* [Reference Materials for Teaching the History of the CCP] vol. 20. Beijing: Guofang daxue, 1989.
Central Committee of the Chinese Communist Party (1978) 'Communiqué of the Third Plenary Session of the Eleventh Central Committee of the Communist Party of China' (adopted on 22 December 1978). Available at http://cpc.people.com.cn/GB/64162/64168/64563/65371/4441902.html.
Chan, Anita (1995) 'The Emerging Patterns of Industrial Relations in China and the Rise of Two New Labour Movements' in *China Information*, vol. 9, no. 4, 36–59.
Chan, Anita, Richard Madsen, and Jonathan Unger (2009) *Chen Village: Revolution to Globalization*. Berkeley, CA: University of California Press.
Chan, Anita, and Jonathan Unger (2009) 'A Chinese State Enterprise under the Reforms: What Model of Capitalism?' in *The China Journal*, vol. 62, 1–28.
Chan, Chris King-Chi (2012) 'Class or Citizenship? Debating Workplace Conflict in China' in *Journal of Contemporary Asia*, vol. 42, 308–327.
Chan, Chris King-Chi (2013) 'Contesting Class Organization: Migrant Workers' Strikes in China's Pearl River Delta, 1978–2010' in *International Labor and Working-Class History*, vol. 83, 112–136.
Chan, Chris King-Chi, and Pun Ngai (2009) 'The Making of a New Working Class? A Study of Collective Actions of Migrant Workers in South China' in *The China Quarterly*, no. 198, 287–303.
Chan, Hon S., and Jie Gao (2018) 'The Politics of Personnel Redundancy: The Non-leading Cadre System in the Chinese Bureaucracy' in *The China Quarterly*, no. 235, September, 622–643.
Chan, Jenny, and Pun Ngai (2010) 'Suicide as Protest for the New Generation of Chinese Migrant Workers: Foxconn, Global Capital, and the State' in *The Asia-Pacific Journal: Japan Focus*, vol. 37, 23–37.
Chan, Kam Wing, and Will Buckingham (2008) 'Is China Abolishing the *Hukou* System?' in *The China Quarterly*, no. 195, 582–606.
Chan, Kam Wing, and Guanghua Wan (2017) 'The Size Distribution and Growth Pattern of Cities in China, 1982–2010: Analysis and Policy Implications' in *Journal of the Asia and Pacific Economy*, vol. 22, no. 1, 136–155.

Chang, Ching-li (1970) *The Chinese Gentry*. 2nd ed. Seattle: University of Washington Press.

Chen, Calvin (2008) *Some Assembly Required: Work, Community and Politics in China's Rural Enterprises*. Cambridge, MA: Harvard University Asia Center.

Chen, Dan (2017) 'Supervision by Public Opinion or by Government Officials? Media Criticism and Central-Local Government Relations in China' in *Modern China*, vol. 43, no. 6, 620–645.

Chen Duxiu (1921) 'Jiaoyu yu shehui – zai Guangdong jiaoyuhui de yanjiang' [Education and Society – A Lecture at the Guangzhou Association of Education] (20 January 1921), in Qi Xiemei and Shao Zude (eds) *Chen Duxiu jiaoju lunzhu xuan* [Selected Essays on Education by Chen Duxiu]. Beijing: Renmin jiaoyu chubanshe, 1995.

Chen Duxiu (1923) 'Zhongguo nongmin wenti' [China's Peasant Question] (I July 1923), *Chen Duxiu wenzhang xuanbian* [Selected Articles of Chen Duxiu]. Shanghai: Sanlian shudian, 1984.

Chen, Feng (2006) 'Privatization and its en in Chinese Factories' in *The China Quarterly*, no. 185, 42–60.

Chen, J., D. Dai, M. Pu, W. Hou, and Q. Feng (2010) 'The Trend of the Gini Coefficient of China'. BWPI Working Paper. Brooks World Poverty Institute.

Chen, Jerome (1973) 'The Development and Logic of Mao Tse-tung's Thought, 1928–1949' in Chalmers Johnson (ed) *Ideology and Politics in Contemporary China*. Seattle: University of Washington Press.

Chen, Jiaxin, and Dan Wang (2020) 'Class Consciousness of Rural Migrant Children in China' in *The China Quarterly*, 23 November, 1–21.

Chen, Jie (2013) *A Middle Class Without Democracy: Economic Growth and the Prospects for Democratization in China*. New York: Oxford University Press.

Chen, Jie, and Bruce J. Dickson (2008) 'Allies of the State: Democratic Support and Regime Support among China's Private Entrepreneurs' in *The China Quarterly*, vol. 196, 780–804.

Chen, Jie, and Bruce J. Dickson (2010) *Allies of the State: China's Private Entrepreneurs and Democratic Change*. Cambridge, MA: Harvard University Press.

Chen, Jie, and Lu Chunlong (2006) 'Does China's Middle Class Think and Act Democratically? Attitudinal and Behavorial Orientations Towards Self-Government' in *Journal of Chinese Political Science*, vol. 11, no. 2, 1–20.

Chen, Meixuan (2002) *Workers' State(s): Changing Self-Images and Social Relations of Chinese Workers 1970–2002*. Thesis, School of Foreign Studies, Nanjing University.

Chen, Minglu (2008) 'Entrepreneurial Women: Personal Wealth, Local Politics And tradition' in David S. G. Goodman (ed) *The New Richps 10 in China: Future Rulers, Present Lives*. Abingdon: Routledge.

Chen, Minglu (2012) 'Being Elite, 1931–2011: Three Generations of Social Change' in *Journal of Contemporary China*, vol. 21, 741–756.

Chen, Shuhong (2008) 'Zhongchan jieji jiaoyu chuancheng zhong de wenhua zaishengchan wenti' [The Problem of Cultural Reproduction in the Education Inheritance of the Middle Class] in *Shehui zongheng* [Social Review], no. 8–9, 143–147.

Chen, Xi (2011) *Social Protest and Contentious Authoritarianism in China*. Cambridge University Press.

Chen, Yi, and Frank Cowell (2015) 'Mobility in China' in *Review of Income and Wealth*, vol. 63, 203–218.

Chen, Yuanyuan, and Shuaizhang Feng (2013) 'Access to Public Schools and the Education of Migrant Children in China' in *China Economic Review*, vol. 26, 75–88.

Chen, Yun (1989) cited in Li Debin *Zhongguo nongcun jingjie jishi* [A Chronicle of the Rural Economy in New China]. Beijing: Beijing daxue chubanshe.

Cheng, Yingfang (2006) 'Xingdong li yu zhidu xianzhi' [The Strength of Movement and the Institutional Limits: the Middle Class in Metropolis Movements] in *Shehuixue yanjiu* [Social Studies Research], no. 4, 24–32.

China Daily, 26 September 2006. 'Defining "Middle Class"'. Available at http://english.peopledaily.com.cn/200609/26/eng20060926_306436.html

China Labour Bulletin (n.d.) 'China Strike Map'. Available at https://maps.clb.org.hk/?i18n_language=en_US&map=1&startDate=2019-01&endDate=2019-12&eventId=&keyword=&address=&industry=&parentIndustry=&industryName=

Cho, Mun Young (2013) *The Specter of "The People": Urban Poverty in Northeast China*. Ithaca: Cornell University Press.

Chow, Yung-Teh (1966) *Social Mobility in China: Status Careers Among the Gentry in a Chinese Community*. New York: Atherton Press.

Chung, Him, and Jonathan Unger (2013) 'The Guangdong Model of Urbanisation: Collective Village Land and the Making of a New Middle Class' in *China Perspectives*, no. 3, 33–41.

Clark, G. (2014) *The Son Also Rises: Surnames and the History of Social Mobility*. Princeton: Princeton University Press.

Clark, T. et al. (1993) 'The Declining Political Significance of Social Class' in *International Sociology*, vol. 8, no. 3, 279–293.

Clark, T., and S. M. Lipset (1991) 'Are Social Classes Dying?' in *International Sociology*, vol. 6, no. 4, 397–410.

Cleveland, John (2003) 'Does the New Middle Class Lead Today's Social Movements' in *Critical Sociology*, no. 29, 163–188.

Cohen, Philip N., and Feng Wang (2009) 'Market and Gender Pay Equity: Have Chinese Reforms Narrowed the Gap?' in Deborah Davis and Feng Wang (eds) *Creating Wealth and Poverty in Postsocialist China*. Stanford, CA: Stanford University Press, pp. 37–53.

Coleman, James S. (1992) 'Some Points on Choice in Education' in *Sociology of Education*, vol. 65, no. 4, 260–262.

Collins, James (2009) 'Social Reproduction in Classrooms and Schools' in *Annual Review of Anthropology*, vol. 38, 33–48.

Collins, R. (1979) *The Credential Society*. London: Academic Press.

Constitution of the People's Republic of China (1954) passed at the first session of the First National People's Congress, 20 September. Available at www.npc.gov.cn/wxzl/wxzl/2000-12/26/content_4264.htm.

Croll, Elisabeth (2006) *China's New Consumers: Social Development and Domestic Demand*. London and New York: Routledge.

Crompton, Rosemary (1993) *Class and Stratification: An Introduction to Current Debates*. Cambridge: Polity Press.

Crompton, Rosemary (2006) 'Class and Family' in *The Sociological Review*, vol. 54, 658–677.

Crompton, Rosemary, and M. Mann (1986) *Gender and Stratification*. Cambridge: Cambridge University Press.

Crowley, Stephen (1997) *Hot Coal, Cold Steel: Russian and Ukrainian Workers from the End of the Soviet Union to the Post-Communist Transformations*. Ann Arbor: University of Michigan Press.

Dahrendorf, R. (1959) *Class and Class Conflict in Industrial Society*. London: Routledge and Kegan Paul.

Dangdai Zhongguo bianjibu [Editorial Committee of *Modern China*] (1990) *Dangdai Zhongguo de laodongli guanli* [Management of the Labour Force in Contemporary China]. Beijing: Zhongguo shehui kexue chubanshe.

Davis, Deborah S. (1992) 'Job Mobility in Post-Mao cities: Increases on the Margins' in *The China Quarterly*, vol. 132, 1062–1085.

Davis, Deborah S. (2003) 'From Welfare Benefit to Capitalized Asset' in R. Forrest and J. Lee (eds) *Chinese Urban Housing Reform*. London: Routledge, pp. 183–196.

Davis, Deborah S. (2005) 'Urban consumer culture' in *The China Quarterly*, no. 183, 677–694.

Davis, Deborah S., Yanjie Bian, and Shaoguang Wang (2005) 'Material Rewards to Multiple Capitals Under Market-Socialism in China' in *Social Transformations in Chinese Societies*, vol. 1, 31–58.

Davis, Deborah S., and Feng Wang (eds) (2009) *Creating Wealth and Poverty in Postsocialist China*. Stanford, CA: Stanford University Press.

Deng Liqun (1991) 'Have a Correct Understanding of Contradictions in Socialist Society, Grasp Initiative in Handling Contradictions' in *The People's Daily*, 23 October, p. 5, trans. FBIS-CHI, 29 October 1991, pp. 22–29.

Deng Liqun (2001) cited in Willy Wo-Lap Lam, 'China's Struggle for "Democracy"'. available at www.cnn.com/Asia, accessed 1 August 2001.

Deng Xiaoping (1956) 'Report on the Work of the Secretariat' in *Eighth National Congress of the Communist Party of China*. Peking: Foreign Languages Press, vol. 2.

Deng Xiaoping (1980) 'On the Reform of the System of Party and State Leadership' in *Selected Works of Deng Xiaoping*. Beijing: Foreign Languages Press, 1984, p. 302.

Deng Xiaoping (1993) 'Zai Wuchang, Shenzhen, Zhuhai, Shanghai dengdi de tanhua yaodian' [Essential Points from Talks in Wuchang, Shenzhen, Zhuhai, Shanghai and other Places] in *Deng Xiaoping wenxuan* (Selected Works of Deng Xiaoping), vol. 3. Beijing: Renmin chubanshe.

Deng Yanhua, and Yang Guobin (2013) 'Pollution and Protest: Environmental Mobilization in Context' in *The China Quarterly*, no. 214, 321–336.

Deng, Zhong, and Donald J. Treiman (1997) 'The Impact of the Cultural Revolution on Trends in Educational Attainment in the People's Republic of China' in *American Journal of Sociology*, vol. 103, 391–428.

Dickson, Bruce J. (2000) 'Cooptation and Corporatism in China: The Logic of Party Adaptation' in *Political Science Quarterly*, vol. 115, 517–540.

Dickson, Bruce J. (2003) *Red Capitalists in China: The Party, Private Entrepreneurs, and Prospects for Political Change*. New York: Cambridge University Press.

Dickson, Bruce J. (2007) 'Integrating Wealth and Power in China: The Communist Party's Embrace of the Private Sector' in *The China Quarterly*, vol. 192, 827–854.

Dickson, Bruce J. (2008) *Wealth into Power: The Communist Party's Embrace of China's Private Sector*. New York: Cambridge University Press.

Dickson, Bruce J. (2010) *Allies of the State. China's Private Entrepreneurs and Democratic Change*. Cambridge, MA: Harvard University Press.

Ding, N., and Y. Wang (2008) 'Household Income Mobility in China and Its Decomposition' in *China Economic Review*, vol. 19, 373–380.

Ding, X. L. (1999) 'Who Gets What, How? When Chinese State-Owned Enterprises become Shareholding Companies' in *Problems of Post-Communism*, vol. 46, 32–41.

Djilas, Milovan (1957) *The New Class: An Analysis of the Communist System*. New York: Praeger.

Donald, Stephanie H., and Zheng Yi (2008) 'Richer than before – the Cultivation of Middle-Class Taste Education Choices in Urban China' in David S. G. Goodman (ed) *The New Rich in China: Future Rulers, Present Lives*. Abingdon: Routledge, pp. 71–82.

Duan, Ruopeng et al. (2002) *Zhongguo xiandaihua jincheng zhong de jieceng jiegou biandong yanjiu* [The Transformation of China's Stratum Structure in the Process of Modernization]. Beijing: Renmin chubanshe.

Duara, Prasenjit (2003) *Sovereignty and Authenticity: Manchukuo and the East Asian Modern*. Lanham, MD: Rowman and Littlefield.
Eberhard, W. (1975) 'The Upper-Class Family in Traditional China' in C. E. Rosenberg (ed) *The Family in History*. Pittsburgh: University of Pennsylvania Press, pp. 59–94.
Economy, Elizabeth (2004) *The River Runs Black: The Environmental Challenge to China's Future*. Ithaca: Cornell University Press.
Edgell, Stephen (1993) *Class*. London: Routledge.
Engels, Frederick (1895) 'The Peasant Question in France and Germany' in *Selected Works of Marx and Engels*, vol. 3. Moscow: Progress Publishers, 1993.
Engels, Frederick (1934) *Anti-Dühring*. Moscow: Co-operative Publishing Society.
Ergenc, Ceren (2014) 'Political Efficacy through Deliberative Participation in Urban China: A Case Study on Public Hearings' in *Journal of Chinese Political Science*, vol. 19, no. 2, 191–213.
Erikson, Robert, and J. H. Goldthorpe (1988) 'Women at Class Crossroads: A Critical Note' in *Sociology*, vol. 22, 545–553.
Erikson, Robert, and J. H. Goldthorpe (1992) *The Constant Flux: A Study of Class Mobility in Industrial Societies*. New York: Oxford University Press.
Esherick, Joseph (1981) 'Numbers Games: A Note on Land Distribution in Prerevolutionary China' in *Modern China*, vol. 7, 387–411.
Fallada, Hans (1933) *Little Man, What Now?* Chicago: Academy Press.
Fang, Jiyou (2007) 'Zhongchan jieji de yanbian ji shehui gongneng' [Social Function and Evolution of the Middle Classes] in *Guowai shehui kexue* [Social Sciences outside China], no. 3, 54–57.
Featherman, D. L., F. L. Jones, and R. M. Hauser (1975) 'Assumptions of Mobility Research in the United States: The Case of Occupational Status' in *Social Science Research*, vol. 4, 329–360.
Featherman, David L., and Robert Mason Hauser (1978) *Opportunity and Change*. Studies in Population. New York: Academic Press.
Feng, Xiaojun (2019) 'Trapped in Precariousness: Migrant Agency workers in China's State Owned Enterprises' in *the China Quarterly*, no. 238, June, 396–417.
Fischer, Andrew Martin (2014) *The Disempowered Development of Tibet in China: A Study in the Economics of Marginalization*. Lanham, MD: Lexington Books.
Florence, Eric (2008) *Struggling around 'Dagong': Discourses about and by Migrant Workers in the Pearl River Delta*. Ph. D. dissertation, Université de Liège.
Foucault Michel (1980) 'Truth and Power' in C. Gordon (ed) *Power/knowledge: Selected Interviews and other Writings 1972–1977*. New York: Pantheon Books, pp. 109–133.
Fourastié, Jean (1979) *Les trente glorieuses ou la révolution invisible de 1946–1975* [Thirty Glorious Years or the Invisible Revolution, 1946–1975]. Paris: Fayard.
Franceschini, Ivan (2014) 'Labour NGOs in China, A Real Force for Political Change' in *The China Quarterly*, vol. 218, June, 474–492.
Frazier, Mark (2004) 'China's Pension Reform and Its Discontents' in *The China Journal*, no. 51, 97–114.
French, Howard (2007) 'Citizens' Groups Take Root across China' in *New York Times*, 15 February.
Frenkiel, Emilie (2014) *Parler politique en Chine. Les intellectuels chinois pour ou contre la démocratie* [Talking Politics in China: Chinese Intellectuals for and against Democracy]. Paris: Presses universitaires de France.
Friedman, Eli (2017) 'Teachers' Work in China's Migrant Schools' in *Modern China*, vol. 43, no. 6, 559–589.
Galbraith, J. K. (1968) *The New Industrial Revolution*. London: Allen Lane.

Gallagher, Mary (2005) *Contagious Capitalism: Globalization and the Politics of Labor in China*. Princeton: Princeton University Press.

Gallelli, Beatrice (2018) 'Doing Things with Metaphors in Contemporary China: Analysing the Use of Creative Metaphors in the Discourse on the Chinese Dream' in *AnnalidiCa'Foscari. Serie orientale,* vol. 54 – Supplemento – 2018.

Ganzeboom, H. B. G., D. J. Treiman, and W. C. Ultee (1991) 'Comparative Intergenerational Stratification Research: Three Generations and Beyond' in *Annual Review of Sociology,* vol. 17, no. 1, 277–302.

Gao, Qin, and Carl Riskin (2009) 'Market versus Social Benefits: Explaining China's Changing Income Inequality' in *Creating Wealth and Poverty in Postsocialist China,* 20–36.

Gao, Qin, Yang Sui, and Zhai Fuhua (2019) 'Hu-Wen Era 2003–2013' in *The China Quarterly,* no. 237, March, 82–107.

Gardner, John (1969) 'The *Wu-fan* Campaign in Shanghai: A Study in the Consolidation of Urban Control' in A. D. Barnett (ed) *Chinese Communist Politics in Action*. Seattle, WA: University of Washington Press, pp. 477–539.

Garnaut, Ross, Ligang Song, and Yang Yao (2006) 'Impact and Significance of State-owned Enterprise Restructuring in China' in *The China Journal,* no. 55, 35–63.

Gerth, H., and C. W. Mills (eds) (1946) *From Max Weber: Essays in Sociology*. Oxford: Oxford University Press.

Gerth, H. and C.W. Mills (eds.), *From Max Weber: Essays in Sociology*, Oxford: Oxford University Press, 1967.

Gerth, Karl (2003) *China Made: Consumer Culture and the Creation of the Nation*. Cambridge, MA: Harvard University Press.

Gerth, Karl (2010) *As China Goes, So Goes the World: How Chinese Consumers Are Transforming Everything*. New York: Hill & Wang.

Gerth, Karl (2013) 'Compromising with Consumerism in Socialist China: Transnational Flows and Internal Tensions in "Socialist Advertising"' in *Past & Present,* no. 218, Spring, 203–232.

Gerth, Karl (2020) *Unending Capitalism: How Consumerism Negated China's Communist Revolution*. New York: Cambridge University Press.

Giddens, A., *Social Theory and Modern Sociology* (Cambridge: Polity Press, 1987.

Giddens, A., *Studies in Social and Political Theory*, London: Hutchinson of London, 1977.

Giddens, A. (1973) *The Class Structure of the Advanced Societies*. London: Hutchinson and Company.

Giddens, A. (1990) *The Consequences of Modernity*. Stanford, CA: Stanford University Press.

Giddens, A., and David Held (eds) (1982) *Classes, Power, and Conflict*. Berkeley: University of California Press.

Giersch, C. Patterson (2020) *Corporate Conquests: Business, the State, and the Origins of Ethnic Inequality in Southwest China*. Stanford, CA: Stanford University Press.

Gillin, Donald G. (1967) *Warlord Yen Hsi-shan in Shansi Province 1911–1949*. Princeton, NJ: Princeton University Press.

Global Times (2013) 'New Study Shows Children of Officials Earn More in First Professional Job', 7 May.

Gold, Thomas (1989) 'Guerrilla Interviewing among the *Getihu*' in Perry Link, Richard Madsen, and Paul G. Pickowicz (eds) *Unofficial China: Popular Culture and Thought in the People's Republic*. Boulder: Westview Press, pp. 175–192.

Gold, Thomas (1990) 'Urban Private Business and Social Change' in Deborah Davis and Ezra F. Vogel (eds) *Chinese Society on the Eve of Tiananmen*. Cambridge, MA: Harvard University Press, pp. 157–178.

Goldthorpe J.H. and G. Marshall, The Promising future of Class Analysis: A Response Recent Critiques, *Sociology*, 26 (3), 1992, pp. 381-400.

Goldthorpe, J. H. (1980) *Social Mobility and Class Structure in Modern Britain*. Oxford: Clarendon Press.
Goldthorpe, J. H., C. Llewellyn, and C. Payne (1987) *Social Mobility and Class Structure in Modern Britain*. Oxford: Clarendon Press.
Gong, C. H., A. Leigh, and X. Meng (2010) 'Intergenerational Income Mobility in Urban China' IZA DP No. 4811.
Goodburn, Charlotte (2009) 'Learning from Migrant Education: A Case Study of the Schooling of Rural Migrant Children in Beijing' in *International Journal of Educational Development*, vol. 29, no. 5, 495–504.
Goodman, David S. G. (1981) 'The Sixth Plenum of the 11th Central Committee of the CCP: Look Back in Anger?' in *The China Quarterly*, no. 87, 518–527.
Goodman, David S. G. (1985) 'The Chinese Political Order after Mao: Socialist Democracy and the Exercise of State Power' in *Political Studies*, no. 33, 218.
Goodman, David S. G. (1986) 'The National CCP Conference of September 1985 and China's Leadership Changes' in *The China Quarterly*, no. 105, 123–130.
Goodman, David S. G. (1988) 'The 13th Congress of the Chinese Communist Party' in *The Pacific Review*, vol. 1, no. 1, 97–101. doi: 10.1080/09512748808718754
Goodman, David S. G. (1994) *Deng Xiaoping and the Chinese Revolution: A Political Biography*. London: Routledge.
Goodman, David S. G. (1995) 'Collectives and Connectives, Capitalism and Corporatism: Structural Change in China' in *The Journal of Communist Studies and Transition Politics*, no. 11, 12–32.
Goodman, David S. G. (1996) 'The People's Republic of China: The Party-state, Capitalist Revolution and New Entrepreneurs' in R. Robison and David S. G. Goodman (eds) *The New Rich in Asia: Mobile Phones, McDonalds and Middle-Class Revolution*. London: Routledge, pp. 225–242.
Goodman, David S. G. (1998) 'In Search of China's New Middle Classes: The Creation of Wealth and Diversity in Shanxi during the 1990s' in *Asian Studies Review*, vol. 22, no. 1, March, 39–62.
Goodman, David S. G. (1999) 'The New Middle Class' in M. Goldman and R. MacFarquhar (eds) *The Paradox of China's Post-Mao Reforms*. Cambridge, MA: Harvard University Press, pp. 241–261.
Goodman, David S. G. (2000) 'The Localism of Local Leadership: Cadres in Reform Shanxi' in *Journal of Contemporary China*, vol. 9, 159–183.
Goodman, David S. G. (2001) 'The Interdependence of State and Society: The Political Sociology of Local Leadership' in Chien-min Chao and Bruce J. Dickson (eds) *Remaking the Chinese State: Strategies, Society and Security*. London: Routledge, pp. 132–156.
Goodman, David S. G. (2004) 'Localism and Entrepreneurship: History, Identity and Solidarity as Factors of Production' in Barbara Krug (ed) *China's Rational Entrepreneurs: The Development of the New Private Business Sector*. London: Routledge, pp. 139–165.
Goodman, David S. G. (2008) 'Why China Has No New Middle Class: Cadres, Managers and Entrepreneurs' in David S. G. Goodman (ed) *The New Rich in China*. Abingdon: Routledge, pp. 23–37.
Goodman, David S. G. (2013) 'Reinterpreting the Sino – Japanese War: 1939–1940, Peasant Mobilisation, and the Road to the PRC' in *Journal of Contemporary China*, vol. 22, no. 79.
Goodman, David S. G. (2014a) *Class in Contemporary China*. Cambridge: Polity.
Goodman, David S. G. (2014b) 'New Economic Elites: Family Histories and Social Change' in Sujian Guo (ed) *State Society Relations and Governance in China*. Lanham: Lexington Books, pp. 15–38.

Goodman, David S. G. (2014c) 'Middle Class China: Dreams and Aspirations' in *Journal of Chinese Political Science,* vol. 19, no. 1, 49–67.

Goodman, David S. G. (2016) 'Locating China's Middle Classes: Social Intermediaries and the Party-state' in *Journal of Contemporary China,* no. 25, 1–13.

Goodman, David S. G. (2018) 'The Changing Face of China's Local Elite: Elite Advantage and Path Dependence in Business Communities' in *Chinese Political Science Review,* vol. 3, no. 2, 115–128.

Goodman, David S. G., and Xiaowei Zang (2008) 'Introduction the New Rich in China: The Dimensions of Social Change' in David S. G. Goodman (ed) *The New Rich in China: Future Rulers, Present Lives.* Abingdon: Routledge, pp. 1–20.

Gu, Shanjie et al. (1995) *Dangdai Zhongguo shehui liyi qunbti fenxi* [Analysis of Interest Groups in Contemporary China]. Harbin: Heilongjiang jiaoyu chubanshe.

Guan, Renting (2003) 'Zhongjian yu shehui wending' [The Middle Strata and Social Stability] in *Hubeisheng shehuizhuyi xueyuan xuebao* [The Academic Journal of Hubei Province College of Socialism], no. 4, 33–35.

Guo, G. (2005) 'Party Recruitment of College Students in China' in *Journal of Contemporary China,* vol. 14, no. 43, 371–393.

Guo, Xuezhi (2001) 'Dimensions of Guanxi in Chinese Elite Politics' in *The China Journal,* no. 46, July, 69–90.

Guo, Yingjie (2004) *Cultural Nationalism in Contemporary China: The Search for National Identity under Reform.* London: RoutledgeCurzon.

Guo, Yingjie (2008) 'Class, Stratum and Group: The Politics of Description and Prescription' in David S. G. Goodman (ed) *The New Rich in China: Future Rulers, Present Lives.* London: Routledge.

Guo, Yingjie (2009) 'Farewell to Class, Except the Middle Class: The Politics of Class Analysis in Contemporary China' in *The Asia-Pacific Journal,* no. 26, 189–205.

Guo, Yingjie (2013) 'Political Power and Social Inequality' in Sun Wanning and Guo Yingie (eds) *Unequal China.* Abingdon: Routledge, pp. 12–26.

Guo, Yuhua, Shen Yuan, and Chen Peng (2014) *Juzhude zhengzhi* [Politics of Dwelling]. Guilin: Guiyang Shehui kexue chubanshe.

Guojia tongjiju [National Statistics Bureau] (1956) *Zhongguo renkou tongji nianjian* [China Statics Yearbook 1956]. Beijing: Zhongguo shehui kexue chubanshe.

Guojia tongjiju [National Statistics Bureau] (1984) *Zhongguo tongji nian 1984* [China Statistical Yearbook 1984]. Beijing: Zhongguo shehui kexue chubanshe.

Guojia tongjiju [National Statistics Bureau] (1998) *Zhongguo tongji nianjian 1997* [China Statistical Yearbook]. Beijing: Zhongguo tongji chubanshe.

Guojia tongjiju [National Statistics Bureau] (2001) *Zhongguo tongji nianjian 2000* [China Statistical Yearbook 2000]. Beijing: Zhongguo tongji chubanshe.

Guojia tongjiju [National Statistics Bureau] (2020a) 'Zhonghua renmin gongheguo 2019 nian guomin jingji he heshui fazhan tongji gongbao' [A Statistical Report on the Economic and Social Development in the People's Republic of China, 2019], 28 February. Available at www.stats.gov.cn/tjsj/zxfb/202002/t20200228_1728913.html.

Guojia tongjiju [National Statistics Bureau] (2020b) '2019 nian nongmingong jiance diaocha baogao' [Investigation Report on Migrant Workers]. Available at www.stats.gov.cn/tjsj/zxfb/202004/t20200430_1742724.html.

Gustafsson, Bjorn (2016) 'Ethnic Disparities in Economic Well-Being in China' in Xiaowei Zang (ed) *Handbook on Ethnic Minorities in China.* Cheltenham, UK: Edward Elgar, pp. 341–363.

Gustafsson, Bjorn, and Ding Sai (2010) 'New Light on China's Rural Elites' UNU-WIDER WP No. 2010/108.

Halsey, A. H. (ed) (1988) *British Social Trends since 1900*. Basingstoke and London: Macmillan.

Han, Chunping, and Martin King Whyte (2009) 'The Social Contours of Distributive Injustice Feelings in Contemporary China' in Deborah Davis and Feng Wang (eds) *Creating Wealth and Poverty in Postsocialist China*. Palo Alto, CA: Stanford University Press, pp. 193–212.

Han, Han (2003) *Tan geming* [On Revolution]. Available at http://blog.sina.com.cn/twocold.

Han, Han (2008) *Zhe yidai ren* [Politics of Dwelling]. Available at http://blog.sina.com.cn/s/blog_4701280b01008eh7.html.

Han, Heejin (2014) 'Policy Deliberation as a Goal: The Case of Chinese ENGO Activism' in *Journal of Chinese Political Science*, vol. 19, no. 2, 173–190.

Han, Zhang (2015) 'Party Building in Urban Business Districts: Organizational Adaptation of the Chinese Communist Party' in *Journal of Contemporary China*, vol. 24, no. 94, 4 July, 644–664.

Hannum, Emily (1999) 'Political Change and the Urban-Rural Gap in Basic Education in China, 1949–1990' in *Comparative Education Review*, vol. 43, no. 2, 193–211.

Hannum, Emily, and Jennifer Adams (2009) 'Beyond Cost: Rural Perspectives on Barriers to Education' in Deborah Davis and Wang Feng (eds) *Creating Wealth and Poverty in Postsocialist China*. Redwood City: Stanford University Press, pp. 156–171.

Hannum, E., and M. W. Wang (2006) 'Geography and Educational Inequality in China' in *China Economic Review*, vol. 17, 253–265.

Hanser, Amy (2008) *Service Encounters: Class, Gender, and the Market for Social Distinction in Urban China*. Redwood City: Stanford University Press.

Harvey, David (2007) *A Brief History of Neoliberalism*. New York: Oxford University Press.

He, Baogang, and Stig Thogersen (2010) 'Giving the People a Voice? Experiments with Consultative Authoritarian Institutions in China' in *Journal of Contemporary China*, vol. 19, no. 66, 675–692.

He, Jin (2012) 'The Transformation and Power of "Middle Class" Language in Chinese Media Publications' in Li Chunling (ed) *The Rising Middle Class*. Beijing: Social Sciences Academic Press, pp. 64–84.

He, Shenjing, and Fulong Wu (2009) 'China's Emerging Neoliberal Urbanism: Perspectives from Urban Redevelopment' in *Antipode*, no. 41(2), 282–304.

He, Shenjing, Yuting Liu, Webster Chris, and Fulong Wu (2009) 'Property Rights Redistribution, Entitlement Failure and the Impoverishment of Landless Farmers in China' in *Urban Studies*, vol. 9, no. 46, 1925–1949

Heath, A., and N. Britten (1984) 'Women's Jobs Do Make a Difference' in *Sociology*, vol. 18, 475–490.

Heberer, Thomas, and Christian Göbel (2011) *The Politics of Community Building in Urban China*. Chinese Worlds. Abingdon, Oxon and New York: Routledge.

Hindess, B. (1986) 'Actors and Social Relations' in M. Wardell and S. Turner (ed) *Sociological Theory in Transition*, London: Allen and Unwin.

Hindess, B. (1987) *Politics and Class Analysis*, Oxford, UK: Basil Blackwell.

Ho, Ping-Ti (1962) *The Ladder of Success in Imperial China: Aspects of Social Mobility, 1368–1911*. New York: Columbia University Press.

Holton, R. J., and B. Turner (1989) *Max Weber on Economy and Society*. London: Routledge, p. 194.

Howell, Jude (2019) 'NGOs and Civil Society: The Politics of Crafting a Civic Welfare Infrastructure in the Hu-Wen Period' in *The China Quarterly*, no. 237, March, 58–81.

Hsiao, Hsin-Huang Michael (1999) *East Asian Middle Classes in Comparative Perspective*. Taipei: Institute of Ethnology, Academia Sinica.

Hsiao, Hsin-Huang Michael (2010) 'Placing China's Middle Class in the Asia-Pacific Context' in Cheng Li (ed) *China's Emerging Middle Class Beyond Economic Transformation.* Washington, DC: Brookings Institution Press, pp. 245–263.

Hsing, You-tien (2010) *The Great Urban Transformation: Politics of Land and Property in China.* Oxford: Oxford University Press.

Hsu, Carolyn L. (2007) *Creating Market Socialism: How Ordinary People Are Shaping Class and Status in China.* Durham, NC: Duke University Press.

Hu Angang (2014) 'Cong "yiguo liangzhi" dao "yiguo yizhi": Zhongguo huji zhidu zhuangui lujing touxi' [From 'One County Two Systems' to 'One Country One System': An Analysis of the Transformation of China's Household Registration System] *Renmin luntan* [The People's Forum], vol. 24, 60–62.

Hu Jingbei (2019) 'Nongye laodongli zhuanyi de dingliang tezheng' [Quantitative Features of the Transfer of Agricultural Labour Force] *Jingji ziliao yicong* [Economic Materials Review], vol. 2, 1–14.

Hu Jintao (2007) 'Full Text of Hu Jintao's Report at 17th Congress'. Available at http://news.xinhuanet.com/eng- lish/2007–10/24/content_6938749_3.htm.

Hu Jintao (2012) 'Full Text of Hu Jintao's Report at 18th Congress'. Available at www.china.org.cn/china/18th_cpc_congress/2012-11/16/content_27137540_3.htm

Hu, Xiuhong, and David H. Kaplan (2001) 'The Emergence of Affluence in Beijing: Residential Social Stratification in China's Capital City' in *Urban* Geography, no. 22, 54–77.

Huang, Philip C. (1995) 'Rural Class Struggle in the Chinese Revolution' in *Modern China,* vol. 21, 105–143.

Huang, Xianghuai (2003) 'Dangdai zhongguo zhongjian jieceng de zhengzhixue jiedu' [Political Reading of the Middle Strata in Contemporary China] in *Kexue shehuizhuyi* [Scientific Socialism], no. 2, 13–16.

Huang, Yasheng (2008) *Capitalism with Chinese Characteristics: Entrepreneurship and the State.* Cambridge: Cambridge University Press.

Huang, Youqin (2005) 'From Work-unit Compounds to Gated Communities: Housing Inequality and Residential Segregation in Transitional Beijing' in L. J. C. Ma and F. Wu (eds) *Restructuring the Chinese City: Changing Society, Economy and Space.* New York: Routledge, pp. 192–221.

Huang, Youqin, and Yi Chengdong (2015) 'Invisible Migrant Enclaves in Chinese Cities: Underground Living in Beijing, China' in *Urban Studies*, vol. 52, no. 15, 2948–2973.

Hung, Eva P. W., and Stephen W. K. Chiu (2009) 'Voices of Xiagang: Naming, Blaming and Framing,' in Thomas B. Gold et al. (eds) *Laid-off Workers in a Workers' State.* New York: Palgrave Macmillan.

Hurst, William (2009) *The Chinese Worker After Socialism.* Cambridge: Cambridge University Press.

Inglehart, R. (1977) *The Silent Revolution: Changing Values and Political Styles Among Western Publics.* Princeton, NJ: Princeton University Press.

Inglehart, R. (1990) *Culture Shift in Advanced Industrial Society.* Princeton, NJ: Princeton University Press.

Ishida, H., W. Muller, and J. Ridge (1995) 'Class Origin, Class Destination, and Education: A Cross-National Comparison of Ten Industrial Nations' in *American Journal of Sociology,* vol. 101, no. 1, 145–193.

Jaffrelot, Christophe, and Peter van der Veer (eds) (2008) *Patterns of Middle Class Consumption in India and China.* London: Sage Publications.

Jiang, Shunxing, and Li Liangyu (1990) (ed) *Shanxi wang Yan Xishan* [Yan Xishan, King of Shanxi]. Zhengzhou: Henan renmin chubanshe.

Jiang Zemin (2001) 'Zai qingzhu Zhongguo gongchandang chengli bashi zhouniandahu shang de jianghua' [Speech at the Celebration of the Eightieth Anniversary of the Founding of the Chinese Communist Party] in Jiang Zemin *Lun sange daibiao* [On the Three Represents]. Beijing: Zhongyang wenxian chubanshe.

Jiang Zemin (2002) 'Full Text of Jiang Zemin's Report at 16th Congress'. Available at www.china.org.cn/english/features/49007.

Jiaotong daxue yanjiusuo [Communications University Research Institute] (1954) *Jiefang qian yangmai jinkou qingkuang* [The Import of Foreign Wheat before Liberation]. Shanghai: Jiaotong daxue chubanshe.

Jingji Ziliao Bianji Weiyuanhui [The Committee for the Compilation of Economic Data] (1957) *Ba sheng nongcun jingji dianxing diaocha* [A Survey of Typical Types of Rural Economy in Eight Provinces]. Beijing: Caizheng jingji chubanshe.

Johnson, Thomas (2013) 'The Health Factor in Anti-Waste Incinerator Campaigns in Beijing and Guangzhou' in *The China Quarterly*, no. 214, 356–375.

Jones, David M. (1995) 'Democratization and the Myth of the Liberalizing Middle Class' in Daniel Bell et al. (eds) *Towards Illiberal Democracy in Pacific Asia*. Basingstoke: Palgrave Macmillan, pp. 78–106.

Jorgensen, M., and L. Phillips (2002) *Discourse Analysis as Theory and Method*. London: Sage Publications.

Keane, Michael (2006) 'From Made in China to Created in China' in *International Journal of Cultural Studies*, vol. 9, no. 3, 285–296.

Kernen Antoine, and Jean-Louis Rocca (2000) 'The Social Responses to Unemployment and the 'NewUrban Poor. Case Study in Shenyang City and Liaoning Province' in *China Perspectives*, no. 27, 35–51.

Khan, Azizur Rahman, and Carl Riskin (2001) *Inequality and Poverty in China in the Age of Globalization*. New York: Oxford University Press.

Kim, Jæsok (2013) *Chinese Labor in a Korean Factory*. Stanford, CA: Stanford University Press.

Kim, Jæsok (2015) 'From "Country Bumpkins" to "Tough Workers": The Pursuit of Masculinity among Male Factory Workers in China' in *Anthropological Quarterly*, vol. 88, no. 1, 133–161.

Kipnis, Andrew (2006) 'Suzhi: A Keyword Approach' in *The China Quarterly*, no. 186, 295–313.

Klein, Jacob A. (2013) 'Everyday Approaches to Food Safety in Kunming' in *The China Quarterly*, no. 214, 376–393.

Knight, J., S. Li, and H. Wan (2017) 'The Increasing Inequality of Wealth in China, 2002–2013' in *University of Western Ontario Centre for Human Capital and Productivity Working Paper 2017–15*.

Konrad, George, and Ivan Szelenyi (1979) *The Intellectuals on the Road to Class Power*. New York: Harcourt Brace Jovanovich.

Koo, Hagen (1991) 'Middle Classes, Democratization, and Class Formation: The Case of South Korea' in *Theory and Society*, no. 4, 485–509.

Korzec, M., and M. K. Whyte (1981) 'The Chinese Wage System' in *The China Quarterly*, vol. 86, 248–273.

Kou, Chien-Wen, and Xiaowei Zang (2013) *Choosing China's Leaders*. Abingdon: Routledge.

Kraus, Richard Curt (1981) *Class Conflict in Chinese Socialism*. New York: Columbia University Press.

Kwong, Julia (2004) 'Educating Migrant Children: Negotiations between the State and Civil Society' in *The China Quarterly*, vol. 180, 1073–1088.

Lake, Robert W. (1986) *Resolving Locational Conflicts*. New Brunswick, NJ: The Center of Urban Policy Research Rutgers University.

Lake, Robert W. (1993) 'Rethinking NIMBY' in *Journal of the American Planning Association*, vol. 59, no. 1, 87–93.
Lam, Willy Wo-Lap (2001) 'China's Struggle for "Democracy"'. Available at www.cnn.com/Asia, accessed 1 August 2001.
Lan, Pei-Chia (2014) 'Segmented Incorporation: The Second Generation of Rural Migrants in Urban China' in *The China Quarterly*, vol. 216, 1–23.
Landry, Pierre F. (2008) *Decentralized Authoritarianism in China: The Communist Party's Control of Local Elites in the Post-Mao Era*. Cambridge: Cambridge University Press.
Lareau, Annette (2003) *Unequal Childhoods: Class, Race and Family Life*. Berkeley: University of California Press.
Lau, W. K. (1999) 'The 15th Congress of the Chinese Communist Party: Milestone in China's Privatization' in *Capital and Class*, vol. 68, 50–87.
Lee, Ching Kwan (2007) *Against the Law: Labor Protests in China's Rustbelt and Sunbelt*. Berkeley: University of California Press.
Lee, Ching Kwan (2009) 'From Inequality to Inequity: Popular Conceptions of Social (in)Justice in Beijing' in Deborah Davis and Feng Wang (eds) *Creating Wealth and Poverty in Postsocialist China*. Palo Alto, CA: Stanford University Press, pp. 213–231.
Lee, Ching Kwan (2010) 'Pathways of Labour Activism' in Elizabeth J. Perry and Mark Selden (eds) *Chinese Society: Change, Conflict and Resistance*. New York: Routledge, pp. 57–79.
Lejeune, Dominique (2015) *La France des trente glorieuses: 1945–1974* [France's Thirty Glorious Years]. Paris: Armand Colin.
Lenin (Vladimir Ilyich Ulyanov) (1917) 'Imperialism, the Highest Stage of Capitalism'. Available at www.marxists.org/archive/lenin/works/1916/imp-hsc/ch09.htm.
Lenski, Gerhard E. (1966) *Power and Privilege: A Theory of Social Stratification*. New York: McGraw-Hill.
Le Roux, Brigitte, Henry Rouanet, Mike Savage, and Alan Warde (2008) 'Class and Cultural Dvision in the UK' in *Sociology*, vol. 42, 1049–1071.
Leung, Parry, and Alvin Y. So (2012) 'The Making and Re-making of the Working Class in South China' in Beatriz Carrillo and David S. G. Goodman (eds) *China's Peasants and Workers: Changing Class Identities*. Cheltenham: Edward Elgar, pp. 62–78.
LeVine, Steve (2017) 'The Big Layoff in China' in *Axios*, 22 November. Available at www.axios.com/the-big-layoff-in-china-1513307124-6bf18f3d-834d-430e-9a32-a42403f794ba.html.
Li, Bobai, and Andrew G. Walder (2001) 'Career Advancement as Party Patronage' in *American Journal of Sociology*, vol. 106, 1371–1408.
Li Cheng (2001) *China's Leaders: The New Generation*. Lanham: Rowman and Littlefield.
Li Cheng (ed) (2010a) *China's Emerging Middle Class Beyond Economic Transformation*. Washington, DC: Brookings Institution Press.
Li Cheng (2010b) 'Chinese Scholarship on the Middle Class: From Social Stratification to Political Potential' in Cheng Li (ed) *China's Emerging Middle Class*. Washington, DC: Brookings Institution Press, pp. 55–83.
Li, Cheng (2010c) 'Introduction: The Rise of the Middle Class in the Middle Kingdom' in Cheng Li (ed) *China's Emerging Middle Class Beyond Economic Transformation*. Washington, DC: Brookings Institution Press, pp. 3–31.
Li Cheng (2012) 'The End of the CCP's Resilient Authoritarianism? A Tripartite Assessment of Shifting Power in China' in *The China Quarterly*, 211, 595–623.
Li Chunling, 'Guodu shiqi de chengzhen shehui jieji jiegou' [The Class Structure in Towns and Cities during China's Transition], *Shehuixue yanjiu* [Sociological Research], 2002, pp. 85–92.

Li Chunling (2003) 'Multiple Measurement Needed for Identifying Chinese Middle Class' in *People's Forum (Renmin Luntan)*, no. 3, 71–72.

Li Chunling (2005) *Duanlie yu suipian: dangdai Zhongguo shehui jieceng fenhua shili fenxi* [Cleavage and Fragmentation: An Empirical Analysis of Social Stratification in Contemporary China]. Beijing: Shehui kexue chubanshe.

Li Chunling (2010a) 'Characterizing China's Middle Class: Heterogeneous Composition and Multiple Identities' in Cheng Li (ed) *China's Emerging Middle Class*. Washington, DC: Brookings Institution Press, pp. 135–156.

Li Chunling (2010b) 'Gaodeng jiaoyu kuozhang yu jiaoyu jihui bupingdeng' [The Expansion of Higher Education and the Inequality of Education Opportunity] in *Shehuixue yanjiu* [Sociology Research], no. 3, 82–113.

Li Chunling (ed) (2012) *The Rising Middle Class*. Beijing: Social Sciences Academic Press.

Li Chunling (2013) 'Sociopolitical Attitude of the Middle Class and the Implications for Political Transition' in Minglu Chen and David S. G. Goodman (eds) *Middle Class China: Identity and Behaviour*. Cheltenham: Edward Elgar, pp. 12–33.

Li Chunling (2016a) 'Zhongdeng shouru quti yu zhongjian jieceng he gainian dingyi-shehuixue and jingjixue quxiang de bijiao' [Conceptual Definition of Middle-income Group and Middle Class – a Comparison of Sociology and Economics Orientations] in *Guojia xingzheng xueyuan xuebao* [The Academic Journal of the State Administrative College], no. 6, January, 53–58.

Li Chunling (2016b) 'Zhongguo zhongchan jieji de buanquangan he jiaolüxintai' [The Feeling of Insecurity and Anxiety among the Chinese Middle Class] in *Wenhua Zongheng* [Cultural Considerations], no. 4, 32–39.

Li Chunling (2017) 'Xin shehui jieceng de guimo he goucheng tezheng-jiyu tizhi neiwai xinzhongchan de bijiao' [The Scope and Structural Characteristics of New Social Strata – Comparisons between within and outside the New Middle Classes] in *Zhongyang shehui zhuyi xueyuan xuebao* [The Academic Journal of the Central College of Socialism], no. 4, August, 63–69.

Li Dezheng (2002) 'Lun zhongguo zhongchan jieceng de shehui xiandaihua gongneng' [On the Social Modernizing Function of the Chinese Middle Strata] in *Nanjing shehui kexue* [Nanjing Social Science], no. 10, 44–48.

Li Hongbin, and Scott Rozelle (2003) 'Privatizing Rural China: Insider Privatization, Innovative Contracts and the Performance of Township Enterprises' in *The China Quarterly*, vol. 176, 981–1005.

Li Hongyan (2017) 'Zhongguo zhongchan jieji: zizai yihuo ziwei?' [The Chinese Middle Class: In itself or for itself?] in *Nanjing shehui kexue* [Nanjing Social Science], no. 2, 66–73.

Li Jian, and Xiaohan Niu (2003) 'The New Middle Class(es) in Peking: A Case Study' in *China Perspectives*, no. 45, 4–20.

Li Keqiang (2014) 'Li Keqing: Xinxing chengzhenhua guizai "xin" xiehao "ren"' [Li Keqiang: 'New Urbanization' Is New and Focuses on 'People']. Available at *Zhongguo zhengfu wang*, www.gov.cn/guowuyuan/2014-09/19/content_2753267.htm.

Li Lulu (2003) *Zai shengchan de yanxu. Zhidu zhuanxing yu zhongguo chengshi shehui fenceng jiegou* [Reproduction Continues. Systemic Transition and the Structures of Social Stratification in Chinese Cities]. Beijing: Zhongguo renmin daxue chubanshe.

Li Lulu, and Kong Guoshu (2017) 'Zhongchan jieji de "yuanwenti" [Stratified Society and Middle Class Anxiety] in *Kaifang shidai* [The Open Era], no. 3, 90–100.

Li Peilin (1995) *Zhongguo xin shiqi jieji jieceng baogao* Social Stratification during China's Market Transition in China]. Shenyang: Liaoning renmin chubanshe.

Li Peilin (2004) 'Zhongguo jingji shehui fazhande wenti he qushi' [Issues and Trends in China's Economic and Social Development] in Xin Ru, Lu Xueyi and Li Peilin (eds)

2004 nian: Zhongguo shehui xingshi fence yu yuce [*2004: Analysis and Forecast of Chinese Society*] Beijing: Social Science Documentary Press. Cited in David S. G. Goodman, *Class in Contemporary China*. Cambridge, UK: Polity, 2014, p. 13.

Li Peilin (2017) 'Zenme jieding zhongdeng shouru qunti' [How to Define the Middle Income Group] in *Beijing ribao* [Beijing Daily], 17 July.

Li Peilin (2018) 'China's Class Structure: Changes, Problems, and Policy Suggestions – A Study of Class Development since 1978' in *International Critical Thought*, vol. 8, no. 4, 574–595.

Li Peilin, and Zhang Yi (2008) *Zhongguo zhongchan jieji de guimo. Rentong he shehui taidu* [The Scope, Identity, and Social Attitudes of the Middle Class in China] in *Shehui* [Society], no. 2, 1–19.

Li Qiang (2002) *Zhuanxing shiqi de Zhongguo shehui fenceng jiegou* [Patterns of Social Stratification during China's Transition]. Harbin: Heilongjiang jiaoyu chubanshe.

Li Qiang (2010) *Social Stratification in Contemporary China: Measurement and Analysis*. Bejing Shifan Daxue Chubanshe.

Li Qiang (2016) 'Zhongguo li ganlanxing shehui haiyou duoyuan' [How Far Is China from an Olive-Shaped Society] in *Shehuixue* [Social Studies], no. 11, 4–12.

Li Qiang (2019) *Social Stratification in Contemporary China*. Hong Kong: Life Bookstore Publishing Co. Ltd.

Li Qiang, and Xu Ling (2017) 'Zenyang jieding zhongdeng shouru qunti?' [How to Define the Middle Income Group] in *Beijing shehui kexue* [Beijing Social Science], no. 7, 4–10.

Li Qiang, and Wang Wu (2017) 'Woguo zhongchan jieceng de guimo, jiegouwenti yufazhan duice' [The Scale, Structural Problems and Development Countermeasures of the Middle Class in China] in *Shehui* [Society], vol. 37, no. 3, 163–179.

Li, S., and H. Wan (2015) 'Evolution of Wealth Inequality in China' in *China Economic Journal*, vol. 8, no. 3, 264–287

Li Shenming et al. (2002) *Dangdai woguo de shehui jieji jieceng jiegou* [Class and Stratum Structure of Contemporary China]. Beijing: Shehui kexue wenxian chubanshe.

Li, Shi, Sicular Terry, and Tarp Finn (2018) 'Inequality in China Development, Transition, and Policy' in *UNU-WIDER Working Paper 2018/174*.

Liang, C., H. Zhang, and Z. Q. Li (2013) *Silent Revolution: Research on Social Origins of College Students from Peking University and Soochow University (1949–2002)*. Beijing: SDX Joint Publishing Company.

Liao, Zhongshuang, and Tan Ya (2005) 'Dangqian kuoda zhongchan jieceng shi lishide biran xuanze' [At Present Expanding the Middle Strata Is a Historical and Inevitable Choice] in *Chongqing youdian xueyuan shehui kexuebao* [Chongqing Electrical College Social Sciences Journal], no. 3, 362–365.

Lin Yifu, Cai Fang and Li 'Dui ganchao zhanlue de fansi' [A Reflection on China's Catching-Up and Overtaking Strategy], *Zhanlue yu guanli* [Management and Strategy], 1994 (6), 1–12.

Lin, Jing, and Xiaoyan Sun (2010) 'Higher Education Expansion and China's Middle Class' in Cheng Li (ed) *China's Emerging Middle Class*. Washington, DC: Brookings Institution, pp. 217–242.

Lin, Juren, Yueyang Zhang, and Wei Xiang (2015) 'Changes in Social Stratification and Citizens' Attitude in the Past Decade – Analysis of CGSS Data' in *Issues of Socialism in Contemporary World*, no. 3.

Lin, Nan, and Yanjie Bian (1991) 'Getting Ahead in Urban China' in *American Journal of Sociology*, vol. 97, 657–588.

Lin, Yi (2011) 'Turning Rurality into Modernity: *Suzhi* Education in a Suburban Public School of Migrant Children in Xiamen' in *The China Quarterly*, vol. 206, June, 313–330.

Lin, Yimin, and Zhanxin Zhang (1999) 'Backyard Profit Centers: The Private Assets of Public Agencies' in Jean Oi and Andrew Walder (eds) *Property Rights and Economic Reform in China*. Palo Alto, CA: Stanford University Press, pp. 203–225.

Lin, Yuming (2003) 'Kuoda zhongjian jieceng shi jianshe quanmian xiaokang shehui de zhongyao jichu' [Expanding Middle Strata Is the Basic Ground for the Construction of a Society of Small Prosperity] in *Zhejiang tongji* [Zhejiang Statistics], no. 6, 16–18.

Lipset, S. M., and R. Bendix (1959) *Social Mobility in Industrial Society*. Berkeley: University of California Press.

Lipset, S. M., and H. L. Zetterberg (1956) 'A Theory of Social Mobility' in *Trans. Third World Cong. Sociol.* vol. 2, 155–177.

Liu Chuanjiang (2000) 'Zhongguo liangshi liutong de zhidu anpai jiqi bianqian' [Arrangements for and the Evolution of China's Systems of Grain Circulation] *Jingji pinglun* [Economic Criticism], vol. 2, 48–58.

Liu Elaine, and Shu Zhang (2013) 'A Meta-analysis of the Estimates of Returns to Schooling in China', *China Academy of Social Sciences*. Available at https://ideas.repec.org/p/hou/wpaper/201309855. html, accessed 12 November 2015.

Liu Jing (2015) 'Understanding Inequality in Public School Admission in Urban China: Analysis of Public Discourses on Zexiao' in *Asian Education and Development Studies*, vol. 4, no. 4, 434–447.

Liu Jing (2018) *Inequality in Public School Admission in Urban China*. Singapore: Springer Nature Singapore

Liu Jingming (2006) 'Gaodeng jiaoyu kuozhang yu ruxue jihui chabie 1978–2003' [The Expansion of Higher Education and Inequalities in Access to University 1978–2003] in *Shehui* [Society], no. 3, 158–179.

Liu, L., W. Wagner, and B. Sonnenberg (2014) 'Independent Freshman Admission and Educational Inequality in the Access to Elite Higher Education' in *Chinese Sociological Review*, vol. 46, no. 4, 41–67.

Liu, Tai-lok, and Liu Shuo (2015) 'The Moral Order of a Middle Class Community' in Li Chunling (ed) *The Rising Middle Classes in China*. Hong Kong: Paths International Ltd.

Liu, Tai-lok, and Liu Shuo (2019) 'The Anxious Middle Class of Urban China: Its Emergence and Formation' in Julie Ren, Bart Wissink, and Ray Forrest (eds) *The City in China: New Perspectives on Contemporary Urbanism*. Bristol: Bristol University Press, pp. 207–230.

Liu Xiaobo (2011) *La philosophie du porc et autres essais* [The Philosophy of Pork and other Essays]. Paris: Gallimard.

Liu, Xin (2010) 'Fahui zhongchan jieceng zai chengshi shehui jianshe zhong de zuoyong' [Developing the Function of the Middle Strata in the Construction of Urban Society] in *Tansuo yu zhengming* [Exploration and Debate], no. 1, 45–58.

Liu, Ye (2016) *Higher Education, Meritocracy and Inequality in China*. Singapore: Springer Science+Business Media Singapore.

Liu, Yi (2018) 'Changes in Assets Held by the Middle Class during Social Transition: An Analysis Based on Surveys of Urban Residents in the Pearl River Delta from 1986 to 2004' in William Hurst (ed) *Residency, Class, and Community in the Contemporary Chinese City*. Leiden, Boston: Brill, pp. 26–38.

Liu, Yuting, SHenjing He, Fulong Wu, and Chris Webster (2010) 'Urban Villages under China's Rapid Urbanization: Unregulated Assets and Transitional Neighbourhoods' in *Habitat International*, vol. 34, 135–144.

Liu, Zhiqiang (2007) 'The External Returns to Education: Evidence form Chinese cities' in *Journal of Urban Economics*, no. 61, 542–564.

Lockwood, D. (1989) *The Blackcoated Worker*. 2nd ed. London: Allen & Unwin.

Logan, John R., and Yanjie Bian (1993) 'Inequality in Access to Community Resources in a Chinese City' in *Social Force*, vol. 72, 555–576.

Logan, John R., Yanjie Bian, and Fuqin Bian (1999) 'Housing Inequality in Urban China in the 1990s' in *International Journal of Urban and Regional Research*, vol. 23, 7–25.

Lora-Wainwright, Anna (2013) 'Dying for Development: Pollution, Illness and the Limits of Citizens' Agency in China' in *The China Quarterly*, no. 214, 243–254.

Loyalka, Michelle Dammon (2012) *Eating Bitterness: Scenes from the Front Lines of China's Great Urban Migration*. Berkeley: University of California Press.

Lu, Feng (1989) 'Tonggou tongxian zhengce yu shichang de jianli' [The Policy of Unitary Purchase and Sales and the Establishment of the Market] *Jiaoxue yu yanjiu* [Teaching and Research], vol. 3, 53–57.

Lu, Hanlong (2010) 'The Chinese Middle Class and *Xiaokang* Society' in Cheng Li (ed) *China's Emerging Middle Class*. Washington, DC: Brookings Institution, pp. 104–131.

Lu, Pierre Xiao (2008) *Elite China: Luxury Consumer Behaviour in China*. New York: Wiley.

Lü, Xiaobo, and Elizabeth J. Perry (eds) (1997) *Danwei: The Changing Chinese Workplace in Historical and Comparative Perspectives*. Armonk, NY: M. E. Sharpe.

Lu, Xueyi (2003) 'An Analysis of the Socialist Class Structure with Two Classes and One Strata' in *Qiushi*, no. 11, 4–6.

Lu, Xueyi (2004) *Dangdai Zhongguo Shehui Liudong* [Social Mobility in Contemporary China]. Beijing: Shehui kexue wenxian chubanshe.

Lu, Xueyi (2006) 'Xietiao ge shehui jieceng de guanxi, goujian hexie shehui' (Harmonize the Relations between All Social Strata and Build a Harmonious Society), *Kexue juece yuekan* [Scientific Policy Monthly], vol. 9, 21–23.

Lu, Xueyi (ed) (2012) *Social Structure of Contemporary China*. Singapore: World Scientific Publishing.

Lu, Xueyi et al. (2002) *Dangdai Zhongguo shehui jieceng yanjiu baobao* [Social Stratification in Contemporary China]. Beijing: Zhongguo shehui kexue chubanshe.

Lu, Xueyi et al. (2005) *Social Mobility in Contemporary China*, trans. by Xiaowen Bao and edited by Harold Bashor. Montreal: America Quantum Media.

Lu, Xueyi et al. (2010) *Dangdai Zhongguo shehui jiegou* [Social Structure of Contemporary China]. Beijing: Zhongguo shehui kexue wenxian chubanshe.

Lu, Yiyi (2009) *Non-Governmental Organizations in China*. Abingdon, UK: Routledge.

Man, Joyce Yanyun (2010) 'China's Housing Reform and Emerging Middle Class' in Cheng Li (ed) *China's Emerging Middle Class*. Washington, DC: Brookings Institution, pp. 179–192.

Mao Tse-tung (Mao Zedong), 'Analysis of the Classes in Chinese Society' (1926), *Selected Works of Mao Tse-tung*, vol. 1, Peking: People's Publishing House, 1960.

Mao Tse-tung (Mao Zedong) (1939) 'The Chinese Revolution and the Chinese Communist Party' (December 1939), *Selected Works of Mao Tse-tung*, vol. 2. Peking: Foreign Language Press.

Mao Tse-tung (Mao Zedong) (1940) 'On New Democracy (January 1940), *Selected Works of Mao Tse-tung*, vol. 2. Peking: Foreign Language Press.

Mao Tse-tung (Mao Zedong) (1949) 'On the People's Democratic Dictatorship' (30 June 1949), *Selected Works of Mao Tse-tung*. Beijing: Foreign Language Press, 1961.

Mao Tse-tung (Mao Zedong) (1953) 'Refute Right Deviationaist Views That Depart from the General Line' (15 June 1953), *Selected Works of Mao Tsetung*, vol. 5. Peking: Foreign Language Press, 1977.

Mao Tse-tung (Mao Zedong) (1955) 'The Debate on the Co-Operatives Transformation of Agriculture and the Current Class Struggle' (11 October 1955), *Selected Works of Mao Tsetung*, vol. 5. Peking: Foreign Language Press, 1977.

Mao Tse-tung (Mao Zedong) (1956a) 'On Ten Major Relationships' in *Selected Works of Mao Tse-tung*, vol. 5. Beijing: Foreign Languages Press, 1977, pp. 267–288.
Mao Tse-tung (Mao Zedong) (1956b) 'Tong Minjian he gongshanglian fuzeren de tanhua' (7 December 1956) [A Conversation with Leaders of the China Democratic National Construction Association and from Industry and Commerce], *Mao Zedong wenxuan* (7) [Collected Works of Mao Zedong, vol. 7]. Beijing: Renmin chubanshe, 1999.
Mao Tse-tung (Mao Zedong) (1965) *Selected Works of Mao Tse-tung*, vol. 1. Peking: Foreign Language Press.
Mao Zedong (1943) 'Zuzhi qilai' (29 December 1943) [Peasants Must Organize Themselves], *Mao Zedong xuanji* (3) [Selected Works of Mao Zedong, vol. 3]. Beijing: Renmin chubanshe, 1991.
Mao Zedong (1950a) 'Wei zhengqu guojia caizheng jingji zhuangkuang de jiben haozhuan er douzheng' (6 June 1950) [Struggle for the Basic Improvement of the Country's Financial Situation], *Mao Zedong xuanji* (5) [Selected Works of Mao Zedong, vol. 5]. Beijing: Renmin chubanshe, 1977.
Mao Zedong (1950b) 'Buyao simian chuji' [Don't Launch Attacks on Every Front] (6 June 1950), *Jianguo yilai Mao Zedong wengao* (1) [Mao Zedong Manuscripts since the Founding of the People's Republic of China, vol. 1]. Beijing: Zhongyan wenxian chubanshe, 1987.
Mao Zedong (1951) 'Ban gongren jieji yeshi lingdao jieji de tifa bixu gaizheng' (15 and 23 December 1951) [The Mistake of Treating the Semi-Proletarian Class as Part of the Leading Class Must Be Corrected], *Mao Zedong wenji* (6) [Collected Works of Mao Zedong, vol. 6]. Beijing: Renmin chubanshe, 1999.
Mao Zedong (1955) 'Guanyu nongye hezuohua wenti' [On the Collectivization of Agriculture], *Mao Zedong xuanji* (6) [Selected Works of Mao Zedong], vol. 6. Beijing: Renmin chubanshe, 1999.
Marx, Karl (1844) *Economic and Philosophical Manuscripts of 1844* in Robert Tucker (ed) *The Marx Engels Reader*. New York: Norton, 1978, pp. 66–125.
Marx, Karl (1847) *Poverty of Philosophy* [1995]. New York: Prometheus Books.
Marx, Karl (1852) *The Eighteenth Brumaire of Louis Napoleon*. Beijing: Foreign Language Press, 1978.
Marx, Karl, and Friedrich Engels (1848) 'Manifesto of the Communist Party' in *Selected Works of Marx and Engels*, vol. 1. Moscow: Progress Publishers, 1969.
Merle, Pierre (2009) *La democratisation de l'enseignement* [Democratisation and Education]. Paris: La decouverte.
McKinsey (2019) Johnny Ho, Felix Poh, Jia Zhou, Daniel Zipser *China Consumer Report 2020*.
Michelson, Ethan, and Sida Liu (2010) 'What Do Chinese Lawyers Want? Political Values and Legal Practice' in Cheng Li (ed) *China's Emerging Middle Class*. Washington, DC: Brookings Institution, pp. 310–333.
Mills, C. Wright (1951) *White Collar: The American Middle Classes*. New York: Oxford University Press.
Mills, C. Wright (1956) *The Power Elite*. New York: Oxford University Press.
Mills, William de B. (1985) 'Leadership Changes in China's Provinces' in *Problems of Communism*, vol. 34, no. 2.
Ministry of Civil Affairs (2018) *China Civil Affairs Statistics Yearbook 2017*. Ministry of Civil Affairs.
Ministry of Education (2011) *Education Statistics Yearbook of China*. Beijing: People's Education Press.
Ministry of Education of the People's Republic of China (2017) '2016 Statistical Bulletin of National Education Development', no. 10, July. Available at www.moe.gov.cn/jybsjzl/sjzlfztjgb/201707/t20170710309042.html.

Bibliography

Ministry of Housing and Urban-Rural Development (2016) *Urban Construction Statistics Yearbook*. Beijing: China Statistics Press.

Mo, Rong (2001) 'Jiuye xinshiji mianjiande yaozhan yu jueze' [Looking for Work: The Challenge and Choices for the New Century] in Li Peilin, Huang Ping, and Lu Jianhua (eds) *2001 nian: Zhongguo shehui xingshi fence yu yuce* [2001: Analysis and Forecast of China's Social Situation]. Beijing: Social Science Anthology Press; cited in Dorothy Solinger, 'Chinese Urban Jobs and the WTO' in *China Journal*, vol. 49, January 2003, 70.

MoE (Ministry of Education) (2001) 'The 211 Project' in Ministry of Education. Available at www.moe.gov.cn/publicfiles/business/htmlfiles/moe/moe_1985/200804/9084.html.

MoE (Ministry of Education) (2015) 'Ministry of Education, Republic of China. Statistics' in Ministry of Education. Available at http://english.moe.gov.tw/ct.asp? xItem=14508&CtNode=11431&mp=11.

Mu, Fu-sheng (1962) *The Wilting of the Hundred Flowers*. New York: Praeger.

N.a. (2000) '10 chengshi qiye xiagang zhigong he lituixiu. Renyuan jiben zhuangjiakuangde youxiang diaocha' [A Sample Investigation of the Situation of 10 Cities' Laid-off Enterprise Employees and Retirees] *Zongguo laodong* [China Labor], vol. 12, 51–53.

N.a. (2009) '20 Million Laid-off Migrant Workers May Send China's Unemployment Rate to 10%' in *China Stakes*, 6 February. Available at www.chinastakes.com/2009/2/20-million-laid-off-migrant-workers-may-send-chinas-unemployment-rate-to-10.html.

N.a. (2013) 'Between the Lines: Listening to Female Factory Workers in China' N.p., *Business for Social Responsibility*, March.

Nan Liangjin, and Xue Jinjun (2002) '1949–1999 nian Zhongguo renkou he laodongli tuisuan' [A Calculation of China's Population and Labour Force between 1949 and 1999], *Zhongguo renkou kexue* [China's Population Science], vol. 3, pp. 1–16.

Nathan, Andrew J. (2003) 'Authoritarian Resilience' in *Journal of Democracy*, vol. 14, 6–17.

National Bureau of Statistics of China (various years) *China Statistical Yearbook*. Beijing: China Statistics Press.

National Health Commission of PRC (2018) *Report on China's Migrant Population Development 2018*. Beijing: China Population Publishing House.

National People's Congress of the People's Republic of China (NPC) (1958) *Zhonghua renmin gongheguo hukou dengji tiaoli* [Regulations on Household Registration of the People's Republic of China], 9 January.

Naughton, Barry (1995) *Growing Out of the Plan: Chinese Economic Reform, 1978–1993*. Cambridge: Cambridge University Press.

Naughton, Barry (1997) 'Danwei: The Economic Foundations of a Unique Institution' in Xiaobo Lü and Elizabeth J. Perry (eds) *Danwei: The Changing Chinese Workplace in Historical and Comparative Perspectives*. Armonk, NY: M. E. Sharpe.

Naughton, Barry (2007) *The Chinese Economy: Transitions and Growth*. Cambridge: Cambridge University Press.

Naughton, Barry (2010) 'China's Distinctive System: Can It Be a Model for others?' in *Journal of Contemporary China*, vol. 19, 437–460.

Naughton, Barry (2015) 'The Transformation of the State Sector: SASAC, the Market Economy, and the New National Champions' in Barry Naughton and Kellee S. Tsai (eds) *State Capitalism, Institutional Adaptation, and the Chinese Miracle*. New York: Ebooks Corporation, pp. 21–71.

Naughton, Barry (2016) 'A Dynamic China Model: The Co-Evolution of Economics and Politics in China' in *Journal of Contemporary China* September doi: 10.1080/10670564. 2016.1206278.

Naughton, Barry (2017) 'The Current Wave of State Enterprise Reform in China: A Preliminary Appraisal' in *Asian Economic Policy Review*, vol. 12, 282–298. doi: 10.1111/aepr.12185

NBS (National Bureau of Statistics) (2011) *Series Reports on China's Economic and Social Development Achievements during the 11th Five-Year Planning Period (2006–2010): No. 9*. National Bureau of Statistics. Available at www.stats.gov.cn/tjfx/ztfx/ sywcj/t20110307_402708357.htm.

NBS (National Bureau of Statistics) (2018) *China Statistical Yearbook*. Beijing: China Statistics Press.

Nee, Victor (1989) 'A Theory of Market Transition: From Redistribution to Markets in State Socialism' in *American Sociological Review*, vol. 54, 663–681.

Nee, Victor (1991) 'Social Inequalities in Reforming State Socialism: Between Redistribution and Markets in China' in *American Sociological Review*, vol. 56, 267–282.

Nee, Victor (1992) 'Organizational Dynamics of Market Transition: Hybrid Forms, Property Rights, and Mixed Economy in China' in *Administrative Science Quarterly*, vol. 37, 1–27.

Nee, Victor (1996) 'The Emergence of a Market Society: Changing Mechanisms of Stratification in China' in *American Journal of Sociology*, no. 101, 908–949.

Nee, Victor, and P. Lian (1994) 'Sleeping with the Enemy: A Dynamic Model of Declining Political Commitment in State Socialism' in *Theory and Society*, no. 23, 253–296.

Nee, Victor, and R. Matthews (1996) 'Market Transition and Societal Transformation in Reforming State Socialism' in *Annual Review of Sociology*, no. 22, 401–435.

Nee, Victor, and Sonja Opper (2012) *Capitalism from Below: Markets and Institutional Change in China*. Cambridge, MA: Harvard University Press.

Nee, Victor, and S. Su (1998) 'Institutional Foundations of Robust Economic Performance: Public Sector Industrial Growth in China' in J. Henderson (ed) *Industrial Transformation in Eastern Europe in the Light of East Asian Experience*. New York: St Martin's Press, pp. 167–187.

Nee, Victor, and Cao Yang (1999) 'Path Dependent Societal Transformation: Stratification in Hybrid Mixed Economy' in *Theory and Society*, no. 28, 799–834.

Nee, Victor, and Cao Yang (2002) 'Postsocialist Inequality: The Causes of Continuity and Discontinuity' in *The Future of Market Transition*, no. 19, 3–39.

Ngok, Kinglun (2008) 'The Changes in Chinese Labor Policy and Labor Legislation in the Context of Market Transition' in *International Labor and Working-Class History*, vol. 73, Spring, 45–64.

Non, Arkaraprasertkul (2018) 'Gentrification and Its Contentment: An Anthropological Perspective on Housing, Heritage and Urban Social Change in Shanghai' in *Urban Studies*, vol. 55, no. 7, 1561–1578.

Oi, Jean C. (1995) 'The Role of the Local State in China's Transitional Economy' in *The China Quarterly*, vol. 144, 1132–1149.

Oi, Jean C. (1999) *Rural China Takes Off: Institutional Foundations of Economic Reform*. Berkeley, CA: University of California Press.

Oi, Jean C., and Han Chaohua (2011) 'China's Corporate Restructuring: A Multi-step Process' in Jean Oi (ed) *Going Private in China: The Politics of Corporate Restructuring and System Reform*. Palo Alto, CA: Stanford University Press, pp. 20–37.

Ong, Lynette H. (2014) 'State-Led Urbanization in China: Skyscrapers, Land Revenue and "Concentrated Villages"' in *The China Quarterly*, vol. 217, 162–179.

Orlik, T. (2011) 'Unrest On Rise as Economy Booms' in *Wall Street Journal*, 26 September. Available at http://online.wsj.com/article/SB10001424053111903703604576587070600504108.html.

Orr, Gordon (2014) 'Preparing for China's Middle Class Challenge' *McKinsey Quarterly*, March. Available at www.mckinseychina.com/preparing-for-chinas-middle-class-challenge-part-1/

Pahl, R. E. (1989) 'Is the Emperor Naked? Some Questions on the Adequacy of Sociological Theory in Urban and Regional Research' in *International Journal of Urban and Regional Research*, vol. 13, no. 4, 711–720.

Pakulski, Jan (2005) 'Foundations of a Post-class Analysis' in Erik Olin Wright (ed) *Approaches to Class Analysis*. New York: Cambridge University Press, pp. 152–179.

Pakulski, J., and M. Waters (1996) *The Death of Class*. London: Sage.

Pan, Jennifer, and Yiqing Xu (2018) 'China's Ideological Spectrum' in *The Journal of Politics* vol. 80, no. 1, 254–273.

Pang Song, and Lin Yunhui (1993) *Libang xingguo – 1945–1956 de Mao Zedong* [Establishing the PRC and Making It Thrive – Mao Zedong between 1945 and 1956]. Beijing: Zhongguo qingnian chubanshe.

Parish, W. L., and E. Michelson (1996) 'Politics and Markets: Dual Transformations' in *American Journal of Sociology*, vol. 101, 1042–1059.

Parkin, Frank, *Class Inequality and Political Disorder*, London: Paladin, 1972.

Parkin, Frank (1979) *Marxism and Class Theory: A Bourgeois Critique*. New York: Columbia University Press.

Parris, Kristen (1993) 'Local Initiative and National reform: The Wenzhou Model of Development' in *The China Quarterly*, vol. 134, 242–263.

Parris, Kristen (1999) 'The Rise of Private Business Interests' in Merle Goldman and Roderick Macfarquhar (eds) *The Paradox of China's Post-Mao Reforms*. Boston, MA: Harvard University Press, pp. 262–282.

Pearson, Margaret M. (1994) 'The Janus Face of Business Associations in China: Socialist Corporatism in Foreign Enterprises' in *Australian Journal of Chinese Affairs*, vol. 31, 25–46.

Pearson, Margaret M. (2015) 'State-Owned Business and Party-State Regulation in China's Modern Political Economy' in Barry Naughton and Kellee S. Tsai (eds) *State Capitalism, Institutional Adaptation, and the Chinese Miracle*. New York: Ebooks Corporation, pp. 27–44.

Peng Zhen (1987) 'Peng Zhen Responds to Questions' in *Dagong bao*, 9 April.

Pepper, Suzanne (1996) *Radicalism and Education Reform in 20th-century China. The Search for an Ideal Development Model*. Cambridge: Cambridge University Press.

Pieke, Frank N. (2009) *The Good Communist: Elite Training and State Building in Today's China*. Cambridge: Cambridge University Press.

Polanyi, Karl (1944) *The Great Transformation*. Boston: Beacon Press.

Pollert, Anne (1996) 'Gender and Class Revisited; or, the Poverty of "Patriarchy"' in *Sociology*, vol. 30, 639–659.

Poulantzas, Nicholas (1979) *Class in Contemporary Capitalism*. London: New Left Books.

Pow, Choon-Piew (2009) *Gated Communities in China: Class, Privilege and the Moral Politics of the Good Life*. Abingdon: Routledge.

PRC Constitution (2018) *Constitution of the People's Republic of China*, 11 March.

Pun Ngai (2005) *Made in China: Women Factory Workers in a Global Workplace*. Durham: Duke University Press.

Pun Ngai, and Lu Huilin (2010) 'Unfinished Proletarianization: Self, Anger, and Class Action among the Second Generation of Peasant-Workers in Present-day China', unpublished paper.

Pun Ngai, and Chris Smith (2007) 'Putting Transnational Labour Process in Its Place: The Dormitory Labour Regime in Post-socialist China' in *Work, Employment and Society*, vol. 21, no. 1, 27–45.

Qi Xingfa (2010) 'Zhongguo zhongchan jieceng de zhengzhi dongxiang yanjiu' [Research on Political Tendencies of the Chinese Middle Strata] in *Lilun yu gaige* [Theory and Reform], no. 4, 147–150.

Qian Junxi (2015) 'No Right to the Street: Motorcycle Taxis, Discourse Production and the Regulation of Unruly Mobility' in *Urban Studies*, vol. 52, no. 15, 2922–2947.

Qin Gao, Sui Yang and Fuhua, Zhai (2019) 'Social Policy and Income Inequality during the Hu – Wen Era: A Progressive Legacy?' in *The China Quarterly*, no. 237, March, 82–107.

Qin, Guangqiang (2020) 'Liberal or Conservative? The Differentiated Political Values of the Middle Class in Contemporary China' in *The China Quarterly*, 1–22.

Qiu, Jack Linchuan (2009) *Working-Class Network Society Communication Technology and the Information Have-Less in Urban China*. Cambridge, MA and London, England: The MIT Press.

Qiu, Jack Linchuan, and Hongzhe Wang (2012) 'Working-Class Cultural Spaces: Comparing the Old and the New' in Beatriz Carrillo and David S. G. Goodman (eds) *China's Peasants and Workers: Changing Class Identities*. Cheltenhan: Edward Elgar, pp. 124–146.

Ravallion, M. and S. Chen (2007) 'China's (Uneven) Progress against Poverty' in *Journal of Development Economics*, vol. 82, 1–42.

Read, Benjamin L. (2007) 'Inadvertent Political Reform via Private Associations: Assessing Homeowners' Groups in New Neighborhoods' in Elizabeth J. Perry and Merle Goldman (eds) *Grassroots Political Reform in Contemporary China*. Cambridge, MA and London, England: Harvard University Press.

Reid, I. (1981) *Social Class Differences in Britain*. London: McIntyre.

Rocca (2005–2018) Interviews.

Rocca (2018–2019) Interviews.

Rocca (2019) Interviews.

Rocca, Jean-Louis (2000) 'The Rise of Unemployment in Urban China and the Contradictions of Unemployment Policies' in *China Perspectives*, no. 30, 42–55.

Rocca, Jean-Louis (2001) 'The Banalisation of the State in China', paper prepared for the *Annual meeting of the Association for Asian Studies* Chicago, 11–14 March.

Rocca, Jean-Louis (2003) 'Old Working Class, New Working Class' in Fisac Badell and Leila Fernandez-Stembridge (eds) *China Today: Economic Reforms, Social Cohesion and Collective Identities*. London: Routledge, pp. 77–104.

Rocca, Jean-Louis (2006a) 'Through the Social Jungle' in Dorothy Solinger (ed) *Narratives of the Chinese Economic Reforms: Individual Pathways from Plan to Market*. New York: Mellen Press, pp. 87–96.

Rocca, Jean-Louis (2006b) *La condition chinoise: capitalisme, mise au travail et résistances dans la Chine des réformes* [The Chinese Condition: Capitalism put to work and resisted in Reform China]. Paris: Karthala Editions.

Rocca, Jean-Louis (2008) 'Power of Knowledge: The Imaginary Formation of the Chinese Middle Class Stratum in an Era of Growth and Stability' in Christophe Jaffrelot and Peter van der Veer (eds) *Patterns of Middle Class Consumption in India and China*. Los Angeles, London, New Delhi and Singapore: Sage, pp. 127–139.

Rocca, Jean-Louis (2009) 'Old Working Class Resistance in Capitalist China: A Ritualised Social Management (1995–2006)' in Khun Eng Kuah-Pearce and Gilles Guiheux (eds) *Social Movements in China and Hong Kong. The Expansion of Social Space*. Amsterdam: ICAS/Amsterdam University Press, pp. 117–134.

Rocca, Jean-Louis (2013) 'Homeowners' Movements: Narratives of the Political Behaviour of the Middle Class' in Chen Minglu and David Goodman (eds) *Middle Class China: Identity and Behaviour*. Cheltenham: Edward Elgar Publishing, pp. 110–134.

Rocca, Jean-Louis (2017) *The Making of the Chinese Middle Class. Small Comfort and Great Expectations*. Basingstoke: Palgrave Macmillan.

Rocca, Jean-Louis (2017) 'Governing from the Middle? Understanding the Making of China's Middle Classes' in Vivienne Shue and Patricia Thorton (eds) *To Govern China: Evolving Practices of Power*. Cambridge: Cambridge University Press, pp. 231–255.

Rocca, Jean-Louis (2018) 'Le récit de vie d'une génération: la trajectoire de Chinois nés avec la Chine socialiste' [Life Narrative of a Generation: Trajectory of Chinese Born with Socialist China] in *Les Etudes du CERI* [CERI Studies] no. 238, décembre.

Ross, Kristin (1996) *Fast Cars, Clean Bodies: Decolonization and the Reordering of French Culture*. Cambridge: The MIT Press.

Saich, Tony, and Biliang Hu (2012) *Chinese Village, Global Market: New Collectives and Rural Development*. New York: Palgrave Macmillan.

Samara, Tony Roshan (2015) 'Politics and the Social in World-Class Cities: Building a Shanghai Model' in *Urban Studies*, vol. 52, no. 15, 2906–2921.

Savage, Mike (1995) 'Class Analysis and Social Research' in Butler Tim and Mike Savage (eds) *Social Change and the Middle Classes*. London: UCL Press, pp. 15–25.

Savage, Mike (2000) *Class Analysis and Social Transformation*. Buckingham: Open University Press.

Schram, Stuart R. (1983) *Mao Zedong: A Preliminary Reassessment*. Hong Kong: Chinese University Press.

Selden, Mark (1988) *The Political Economy of Chinese Socialism*. New York: M E Sharpe.

Selden, M., and P. Eggleston (eds) (1979) *People's Republic of China: A Documentary History of Revolutionary Change*. New York: Monthly Review Press.

Shambaugh, David (2008) *China's Communist Party: Atrophy and Adaptation*. Berkeley: University of California Press.

Shavit, Y., R. Arum, and A. Gamoran (2007) *Stratification in Higher Education: A Comparative Study*. Palo Alto, CA: Stanford University Press.

Shavit, Y., and Hans-Peter Blossfeld (1993) *Persistent Inequality: Changing Educational Attainment in Thirteen Countries*. Boulder, CO: Westview Press.

Shavit, Y., and V. Kraus (1990) 'Educational Transitions in Israel: A Test of the Industrialization and Credentialism Hypotheses' in *Sociology of Education,* vol. 63, no. 2, 133–141.

Shen, Liren (2004) 'Peiyu zhongdeng shouru jieceng de yiyi, mubiao he lujing' [Fostering the Trajectory, Aims and Significations of Middle Incomers] in *Nanjing shenji xueyuan xuebao* [Academic Journal of Nanjing Audit College], no. 1, 16–18 and 69.

Shieh, Leslie, and John Friedmann (2008) 'Restructuring Urban Governance' in *City,* vol. 12, no. 2, 183–195.

Shih, Victor, Wei Shan, and Mingxing Liu (2010) 'The Central Committee Past and Present' in Allen Carlson, Mary E. Gallagher, Kenneth Lieberthal, and Melanie Manion (eds) *Contemporary Chinese Politics*. Cambridge: Cambridge University Press, pp. 51–68

Sigley, Gary G. (2004) 'Liberal Despotism: Population Planning, Subjectivity, and Government in Contemporary China' in *Alternatives*, no. 5, 557–575.

Sigley, Gary G. (2009) 'Suzhi, the Body, and the Fortunes of Technoscientific Reasoning in Contemporary China' *Positions: East Asia Cultures Critique*, no. 3, 537–566.

Silverstein, Michael J, Abheek Singhi, Carol Liao, and David Michael (2012) *The $10 Trillion Prize: Captivating the Newly Affluent in China and India*. Boston, MA: Harvard Business Review Press.

So, Alvin Y. (2003) 'The Making of the Cadre-Capitalist Class in China' in Joseph Cheng (ed) *China's Challenges in the Twenty-First Century*. Hong Kong: City University of Hong Kong Press.

So, Alvin Y. (2013) *Class and Class Conflict in Post-Socialist China*. Singapore: World Scientific Publishing.
Solinger, Dorothy (ed) (1984) *Three Visions of Chinese Socialism*. Boulder: Westview Press.
Solinger, Dorothy (1999) *Contesting Citizenship in Urban China: Peasant Migrants, the State, and the Logic of the Market*. Berkeley: University of California Press.
Solinger, Dorothy (2002) 'Labour Market Reform and the Plight of the Laid-off Proletariat' in *The China Quarterly*, vol. 170, 304–326.
Solinger, Dorothy (2004) 'The New Crowd of the Dispossessed: The Shift of the Urban Proletariat from Master to Mendicant' in Peter Gries and Stanley Rosen (eds) *State and Society in 21st-Century China: Crisis, Contention, and Legitimation*. New York and London: RoutledgeCurzon.
Solinger, Dorothy (2012) 'The New Urban Underclass and its Consciousness: Is it a Class?' in *Journal of Contemporary China*, no. 21, 1011–1029.
Solinger, Dorothy (ed) (2018) *Polarized Cities: Portraits of Rich and Poor in Urban China*. Boulder: Rowman and Littlefield.
Song, Geng, and Tracy K. Lee (2010) 'Consumption, Class Formation and Sexuality: Reading Men's Lifestyle Magazines in China' in *The China Journal*, no. 64, 159–177.
Song, Jing, Huimin Du, and Si-ming Li (2020) 'Who Is the Winner? Differentiation within and between Relocated Communities in Urbanizing Northwestern China' in *Journal of Rural Studies*, no. 77, 159–168.
Song, Xi, and Yu Xie (2014) 'Market Transition Theory Revisited: Changing Regimes of Housing Inequality in China, 1988–2002' in *Sociological Science*, vol. 1, 277–291.
Stark, David, 'Class Struggle and the Labour Process, *Theory and Society*, 9 (1), 1980, pp. 89-130.
State Council (2016) *Notice on Implementing Financial Policies on Supporting the Citizenisation Process of Transforming Agricultural Population (Guowuyuan Guanyu Shishi Zhichi Nongye Zhuanyi Renkou Shiminhua Ruogan Caizheng Zhengce de Tongzhi)*. No. 44.
State Statistical Bureau (1986) *Statistical Yearbook of China*. Oxford: Oxford University Press.
State Statistical Bureau (2001) *Statistical Yearbook of China 2001*. Beijing: China Statistics Press.
State Statistical Bureau (2020) *Statistical Yearbook of China 2019*. Beijing: China Statistics Press.
Sun Laixiang (2005) 'Ownership Reform in China's Township and Village Enterprises' in Stephen Green and Guy S. Liu (eds) *Exit the Dragon? Privatization and State Control in China*. Oxford: Blackwell, pp. 90–110.
Sun Liping (2006) 'Duanlie: ershi shiji jiushiniandai yilai Zhongguo shehui jieguo' [Fracture: China's Social Structure since the 1990s] in Y. Li, L. Sun, and Y. Shen (eds) *Dangdai Zhongguo shehui fenceng: lilun yu shizheng* [Social Stratification in Contemporary China: Theory and Evidence]. Beijing: Shehui kexue wenxian chubanshe, pp. 1–35.
Sun Liping (2013) 'Quanli kuibai de di san jieduan' ['The Third Stage in the Failure of Power'], 11 March.
Sun, W., J. Lu, and C. Bai (2007) 'An Analysis of Income Mobility in Rural China' in *Jingji Yanjiu*, vol. 42, no. 8, 43–57.
Sun Wanning (2014) *Subaltern China: Rural Migrants, Media, and Cultural Practices*. Blue Ridge Summit: The Rowman & Littlefield Publishing Group.
Sun, Yanfei, and Zhao Dingxin (2008) 'Explaining Dynamics and Outcomes of Environmental Campaigns in China: Multi-actor State and Diverse Civil Society' in Kevin O'Brien (ed) *Popular Protest in China*. Cambridge, MA: Harvard University Press.
Szelényi, Ivan (1978) 'Social Inequalities in State Socialist Redistributive Economies' in *International Journal of Comparative Sociology*, vol. 19, 63–87.

Szelenyi, Ivan (1983) *Urban Inequalities under State Socialism*. Oxford: Oxford University Press.
Szelényi, Ivan (2008) 'A Theory of Transitions' in *Modern China*, vol. 34, 165–175.
Szelényi, Ivan, and Eric Kostello (1998) 'Outline of an Institutional Theory of Inequality: The Case of Socialist and Postcommunist Eastern Europe' in Mary C Brinton and Victor Nee (eds) *The New Institutionalism in Sociology*. Palo Alto, CA: Stanford University Press, pp. 305–326.
Talavera, Oleksandr, Lin Xiong, and Xiong Xiong (2010) 'Social Capital and Access to Bank Financing: The Case of Chinese Entrepreneurs' Anglia Applied and Financial Economics Working Paper Series 019. Norwich: School of Economics, University of East Anglia.
Tang, Beibei (2013) 'Urban Housing Status Groups: Consumption, Lifestyles, and Identity' in Chen Minglu and David S. G. Goodman (eds) *Middle Class China: Identity and Behaviour*. Cheltenham: Edward Elgar, pp. 54–74.
Tang, Beibei (2015) '"Not Rural but Not Urban": Community Governance in China's Urban Villages' in *The China Quarterly*, vol. 223, September, 724–744.
Tang, Beibei (2018) *China's Housing Middle Class: Changing Urban Life in Gated Communities*. Abingdon: Routledge.
Tang, Beibei (2020) 'Grid Governance in China's Urban Middle-class Neighbourhoods' in *The China Quarterly*, no. 241, March, 43–61.
Tang, Beibei (2021) 'Wujiang in Transition' in Beibei Tang and Paul Cheung (eds) *Suzhou in Transition*. Routledge, pp. 214–232.
Tang, Beibei, and Jonathan Unger (2013) 'The Socio-economic Status, Co-optation and Political Conservatism of the Educational Middle Class: A Case Study of University Teachers' in Minglu Chen and David S. G. Goodman (eds) *Middle Class China: Identity and Behaviour*. Cheltenham: Edward Elgar, pp. 90–109.
Tang, Min, Dwayne Woods, and Zhao Jujun (2009) 'The Attitudes of the Chinese Middle Class Towards Democracy' in *Journal of Chinese Political* Science, no. 14, 81–95.
Tang, Wenfang (2005) *Public Opinion and Political Chang in China*. Palo Alto, CA: Stanford University Press.
Tang, Wenfang (2016) *Populist Authoritarianism: Chinese Political Culture and Regime Sustainability*. Singapore: Oxford University Press.
Teets, Jessica (2012) 'Reforming Service Delivery in China: The Emergence of Social Innovation Model' in *Journal of Chinese Political Science*, vol. 17, no. 1, 15–32.
Teiwes, Frederick C. (1984) *Leadership, Legitimacy, and Conflict in China*. New York: M E Sharpe.
Teiwes, Frederick C. (1990) *Politics at Mao's Court: Gao Gang and Party Factionalism in the Early 1950s*. New York, M E Sharpe.
Thibaud, Andre (2016) 'Indispensable but Sidelined: The Chinese Working Class'. Beijing: Daxue Consulting, 20 October. Available at https://daxueconsulting.com/chinese-working-class/.
Thireau, Isabelle, and Hua Linshan (2003) 'The Moral Universe of Aggrieved Chinese Workers: Workers' Appeals to Arbitration Committees and Letters and Visits Offices' in *China Journal*, vol. 50, 83–103.
Thompson, E.P., *The Making of the English Working Class*, Harmondsworth: Penguin, 1968.
Thornton, Patricia M. (2012) 'The New Life of the Party: Party-Building and Social Engineering in Greater Shanghai' in *The China Journal*, no. 68, 58–78.
Ticktin, Hillel (1981) 'Is Market-Socialism Possible or Necessary' in *Critique*, vol. 14, 13–39.
Tilly, Charles (1998) *Durable Inequality*. Berkeley and Los Angeles: University of California Press.
Tilly, Charles (2001) 'Relational Origins of Inequality', *Anthropological Theory*, vol. 1, no. 3, 355–372.

Tomba, Luigi (2004) 'Creating an Urban Middle Class: Social Engineering in Beijing' in *The China Journal*, no. 51, 1–26.

Tomba, Luigi (2005) 'Residential Space and Collective Interest Formation in Beijing's Housing Disputes' in *The China Quarterly*, vol. 184, 934–951.

Tomba, Luigi (2009) 'Of Quality, Harmony and Community. Civilization and the Middle Class in Urban China' in *Positions: East Asia Cultures Critique*, no. 3, 592–616.

Tomba, Luigi (2010) 'The Housing Effect: The Making of China's Social Distinctions' in Cheng Li (ed) *China's Emerging Middle Class: Beyond Economic Transformation*. Brookings Institution Press, pp. 193–216.

Tomba, Luigi (2012) 'Awakening the God of Earth: Land, Place and Class in Urbanizing Guangdong' in Beatriz Carrillo and David S. G. Goodman (eds) *China's Peasants and Workers: Changing Class Identities*. Cheltenham: Edward Elgar, pp. 40–61.

Tomba, Luigi (2014) *The Government Next Door: Neighborhood Politics in Urban China*. New York: Cornell University Press.

Tsai, Kellee S. (2007) *Capitalism without Democracy: The Private Sector in Contemporary China*. Ithaca, NY: Cornell University Press.

Tsang, Eileen Yuk-Ha (2014) *The New Middle Class in China: Consumption, Politics and the Market Economy*. Singapore: Palgrave Macmillan.

Unger, Jonathan (ed) (2008) *Associations and the Chinese State: Contested Spaces*. Armonk: M.E. Sharpe.

Van de Werfhorst, H. G., and R. Andersen (2005) 'Social Backgrounds, Credential Inflation and Educational Strategies' in *Acta Sociologica*, vol. 48, no. 4, 321–340.

Van de Werfhorst, H. G., and Jonathan J. B. Mijs (2010) 'Achievement Inequality and the Institutional Structure of Educational Systems: A Comparative Perspective' in *The Annual Review of Sociology*, vol. 36, 407–728.

Walder, Andrew G. (1986) *Communist Neo-Traditionalism: Work and Authority in Chinese Industry*. Berkeley: University of California Press.

Walder, Andrew G. (1995) 'Local Governments as Industrial Firms: An Organizational Analysis of China's Transitional Economy' in *American Journal of Sociology*, vol. 101, 1060–1073.

Walder, Andrew G. (1996) 'Markets and Inequality in Transitional Economies: Toward Testable Theories' in *American Journal of Sociology*, vol. 101, 1060–1073.

Walder, Andrew G. (2002) 'Markets and Income Inequality in Rural China: Political Advantage in an Expanding Economy' in *American Sociological Review*, vol. 67, 231–253.

Walder, Andrew G. (2003) 'Elite Opportunity in Transitional Economies' in *American Sociological Review*, vol. 68, 899–917.

Walder, Andrew G. (2006a) 'China's Private Sector: A Global Perspective' in A. S. Tsui, Y. J. Bian, and L. Cheng (eds) *China's Domestic Private Firms: Multidisciplinary Perspectives on Management and Performance*. New York: M.E. Sharpe, pp. 311–326.

Walder, Andrew G. (2006b) 'The Party Elite and China's Trajectory of Change' in Kjeld-Erik Brodsgaard and Yongnian Zheng (eds) *The Chinese Communist Party in Reform*. New York: Routledge.

Walder, Andrew J., Li Bobai, and Donald J. Treiman (2000) 'Politics and Life Chances in a Socialist Regime: Dual Career Paths into the Urban Chinese Elite, 1949–1996' in *American Sociological Review*, vol. 65, 191–209.

Walder, Andrew, and Xiaoxia Gong (1993) 'Workers in the Tiananmen Protests' in *The Australian Journal of Chinese Affairs*, no. 29, 1–29.

Walder, Andrew G., and Songhua Hu (2009) 'Revolution, Reform, and Status Inheritance: Urban China, 1949–1996' in *American Journal of Sociology*, vol. 114, 1395–427.

Walker, Richard, and Daniel Buck (2007) 'The Chinese Road, Cities in the Transition to Capitalism' in *New Left Review,* vol. 46, July/August.

Wang, Chunguang (2012) 'Urban – Rural Structure' in Lu Xueyi (ed) *Social Structure of Contemporary China.* Singapore: World Scientific Publishing, pp. 265–300.

Wang, Feng (2008) *Boundaries and Categories: Rising Inequality in Post-Socialist Urban China.* Stanford, CA: Stanford University Press.

Wang Fenghuang (2013) News.ifeng.com/mainland/detail_2013_08/19/28774327_0.shtml.

Wang, Haiguang (2011) 'Chengxiang eryuan hukou huji zhidu de xingcheng' [The Creation of the Twin Rural – Urban Household Registration System] in *Yanhuang chunqiu,* vol. 12, 6–14.

Wang, Jianying, and Deborah Davis (2010) 'China's New Upper Middle Classes: The Importance of Occupational Disaggregation' in Cheng Li (ed) *China's Emerging Middle Class.* Washington, DC: Brookings Institution, pp. 157–176.

Wang, Kuiming, and Han Zhiming (2020) 'Bie nao da': zhongchanjieceng de celûe xuanze' [Don't Make Trouble: The Middle Class's Strategic Choice] in *Gonggong guanli xuebao* [Public Management Journal], vol. 17, no. 2, April, 84–94.

Wang, Limin, and Jeni Klugman (2020) 'How Women Have Fared in the Labour Market with China's Rise as a Global Economic Power' in *Asia & the Pacific Policy Studies,* vol. 7, no. 1, 43–64. Available at https://onlinelibrary.wiley.com/doi/full/10.1002/app5.293.

Wang, Lu (2008) 'The Marginality of Migrant Children in the Urban Chinese Educational System' in *British Journal of Sociology of Education,* vol. 29, no. 6, 691–703.

Wang, Mengqi (2017) 'Governing the Housing Market in Post-reform China' in Urmi Sengupta and Annapurna Shaw (eds) *Trends and Issues in Housing in Asia: Coming of an Age.* Delhi: Routledge India, pp. 232–250.

Wang, Mengqi (2018) 'Rigid Demand': Economic Imagination and Practice in China's Urban Housing Market' in *Urban Studies,* vol. 55, no. 7, May, 1579–1594.

Wang, Xin (2020) 'Capital, Habitus, and Education in Contemporary China: Understanding Motivations of Middle-class Families in Pursuing Studying Abroad in the United States' *Educational Philosophy and Theory,* no. 52, 1314–1328.

Wank, David (1999) *Commodifying Business, Trust and Politics in a Chinese City.* Cambridge: Cambridge University Press.

Watson, W., and E. Barth (1964) 'Questionable Assumptions in the Theory of Social Stratification' in *Pacific Sociological Review,* vol. 7, 10–16.

Weber, Max (1924) *Essays in Sociology* [1946 translated and edited by H. H. Gerth and C. Wright Mills]. New York: Oxford University Press.

Weber, Max (1978) *Economy and Society: An Outline of Interpretive Sociology.* Berkeley: University of California Press.

Wei, Liqun (2014) 'Actively Carrying Forward Social Management Innovation ('Jiji Tuijin Shehui Zhili Tizhi Chuangxin')' in *Guangming Daily,* 20 June.

Weininger, Elliot B. (2005) 'Foundations of Pierre Bourdieu's Class Analysis' in Erik Olin Wright (ed) *Approaches to Class Analysis.* New York: Cambridge University Press, pp. 82–118.

Wen, Tiejun (2013) '"Nongcun Chengzhenhua Shi Quchengzhenhua" (Rural Urbanization Is De-Urbanization)' in *Xinhuanet,* 23 December. Available at http://news.xinhuanet.com/fortune/ 2013–12/23/c_125899079.htm.

Whiting, Susan H. (2001) *Power and Wealth in Rural China: The Political Economy of Institutional Change.* New York: Cambridge University Press.

Whyte, Martin King (2010) *Myth of the Social Volcano: Perceptions of Inequality and Distributive Injustice in Contemporary China.* Palo Alto, CA: Stanford University Press.

Whyte, Martin King, and William L. Parish (1984) *Urban Life in Contemporary China.* Chicago: University of Chicago Press.

Willis, Paul E. (1981) *Learning to Labor: How Working Class Kids Get Working Class Jobs*. New York: Columbia University Press.
Wong, May (ed) (2008) *Voices from Below: China's Accession to WTO and Chinese Workers*. Hong Kong: Asia Monitor Resource Centre.
Wong, R. Bin (2009) 'Social Stratification: The Legacy of the Late Imperial Past' in Deborah S. Davis and Wang Feng (eds) *Creating Wealth and Poverty in Postsocialist China*. Palo Alto, CA: Stanford University Press, pp. 236–263.
World Bank (2009) 'Poverty Reduction and Economic Management Department, East Asia and Pacific Region' in *From Poor Areas to Poor People: China's Evolving Poverty Reduction Agenda – An Assessment of Poverty and Inequality in China*. Beijing: The World Bank.
World Bank (2012) 'World Bank and Development Research Center of the State Council PRC' in *China 2030: Building a Modern Harmonious and Creative Society*. Washington, DC: International Bank for Reconstruction and Development.
Woronov, T. E. (2011) 'Learning to Serve: Urban Youth, Vocational Schools and New Class Formations in China' in *The China Journal*, no. 66, 77–99.
Wright, Erik Olin (1984) 'A General Framework for the Analysis of Class Structure' in *Politics and Society*, vol. 13.
Wright, Erik Olin (ed) (1989) *The Debate on Classes*. London: Verso.
Wright, Erik Olin (1997) *Class Counts: Comparative Studies in Class Analysis*. New York: Cambridge University Press.
Wright, Erik Olin (ed) (2005) *Approaches to Class Analysis*. New York: Cambridge University Press.
Wright, Teresa (2010) *Accepting Authoritarianism: State-Society Relations in China's Reform Era*. Palo Alto, CA: Stanford University Press.
Wu, Fulong (2010) 'Gated and Packaged Suburban: Packaging and Branding Chinese Suburban Residential Development' in *Cities*, vol. 27, no. 5, 385–396.
Wu, Fulong (2015) *Planning for Growth: Urban and Regional Planning*. London: Routledge.
Wu, Fulong, Zhang Fangzhu, and Chris Webster (2014) *Rural Migrants in Urban China: Enclaves and Transient Urbanism*. London: Routledge.
Wu Jiao (2007) '50% of People Will Be Middle Class by 2020' in *China Daily*, 2 July.
Wu Li (2001) '1949–1978 nianZhongguo "jiandaocha" chae bianzheng' [The Value of China's "Price Scissors" between 1949 and 1978] in *Zhongguo jingjishi yanjiu* [Research on China's Economic History], vol. 4, 3–12.
Wu, Li (2007) '1949–2006 nian chengxiang guanxi de lishi fenxi' [A Historical Analysis of the Evolution of Urban-Rural Relations between 1949 and 2006], *Zhongguo jingjishi yanjiu*, vol. 1, 23–30.
Wu, X., and J. M. Perloff (2005) 'China's Income Distribution, 1985–2001' in *Review of Economics and Statistics*, vol. 87, 763–775.
Wu, Xiaogang (2002) 'Work Units and Income Inequality: The Effect of Market Transition in Urban China' in *Social Forces*, vol. 80, 1069–1099.
Wu, Xiaogang (2017) 'Higher Education, Elite Formation and Social Stratification in Contemporary China: Preliminary Findings from the Beijing College Students Panel Survey' in *Chinese Journal of Sociology*, vol. 3, no. 1, 3–31.
Wu, Xiaogang, and Donald J. Treiman (2004) 'The Household Registration System and Social Stratification in China 1955–1996' in *Demography*, vol. 41, no. 2, 363–384.
Wu, Xiaogang, and Donald J. Treiman (2007) 'Inequality and Equality under Chinese Socialism: The Hukou System and Intergenerational Occupational Mobility' in *American Journal of Sociology*, vol. 113, no. 2, 415–445.
Wu, Xiaogang, and Y. Xie (2003) 'Does Market Pay Off? Earnings Returns to Education in Urban China' in *American Sociological Review*, vol. 68, 425–442.

Wu, Yan, and Wen Wang (2012) 'Does Participatory Budgeting Improve the Legitimacy of the Local Government? A Comparative Case Study of Two Cities in China' in *The Australian Journal of Public Administration*, vol. 71, 122–135.

Xi Jingping (2013) 'Address to the First Session of the 12th National People's Congress' 17 March 2013, in *Xi Jinping: The Governance of China* 2014, Apple Books, p. 110.

Xie, Ying, and Lin Fen (2016) 'Kangzhengxing zhengzhizhong de qunti chayi yu ziyuan jieyong zhongchan kangzheng nongmin kangzheng de gean' [Comparison of Cases of Middle Class Protests and Farmers Protests] in *Shehui pinglun* [Social Comment], vol. 4, no. 1, 34–48.

Xie, Yu, and Emily Hannum (1996) 'Regional Variation in Earnings Inequality in Reform Era Urban China' in *American Journal of Sociology*, vol. 101, 950–992.

Xie, Yu, and Xiaogang Wu (2008) 'Danwei Profitability and Earnings Inequality in Urban China' in *The China Quarterly*, vol. 195, 558–581.

Xie, Yu, Xiaobo Zhang, Jianxin Li, Xuejun Yu, and Qiang Ren (2014) *China Family Panel Studies 2014*. Beijing: Beijing University Press.

Xinhua (2005) *Xinhua* 'Middle Class to Reach 40% of Workforce', 1 February.

Xinhua (2018) 'Report of the CCP Organization Department'. Available at https://baijia hao.baidu.com/s?id=1604678109117460026&wfr=spider&for=pc

Xinhua (2020) 'The CCP Member Record Reaching 91.914 Million' in *Xinhua News*, 30 June. Available at https://xhpfmapi.zhongguowangshi.com/vh512/share/9212201?channel=qq.

Xinhua (2021) *Xinhua*, 2 February. Available at https://baijiahao.baidu.com/s?id=1690540182346000006&wfr=spider&for=pc.

Xiong, Yihan (2015) 'The Broken Ladder: Why Education Provides No Upward Mobility for Migrant Children in China' in *The China Quarterly*, vol. 221, 161–184.

Xiong Yihan (2019) 'Zhongguo zhongchan jieceng de zhengzhi qingxiang jiqi dui yuqing de yingxiang' [The Political Tendency of China's Middle Class and Its Influence on Public Opinion] in *Xiantan daxue xuebao* [Journal of Xiantan University], vol. 43, no. 5, September, 158–161.

Xiong, Yihan (2020) 'Jingxi fencengshehui yu zhongchan jielüzheng' [Stratified Society and Middle Class Anxiety] in *Wenhua Zongheng* [Cultural Review], no. 5, 112–120.

Xu Dixin (ed) (1988) *Dangdai Zhongguo renkou* [Population in Contemporary China]. Beijing: Zhongguo shehui kexue chubanshe.

Xu Haoran (2017) *Renmin guojia: Bijiao shiye xia de Zhongguo zhengzhi* [A People's State: A Comparative Perspective on Chinese Politics]. Beijing: Xinhua chubanshe.

Xu Jingyong (2001) 'Dui woguo shengyu laodongli zhuanyi wenti de lilun sikao' [A Reflection on the Transfer of the Surplus Rural Labour Force in China] in *Zhuzhou Gongxueyuan xuebao* [Journal of Zhuzhou Engineering College], vol. 15, no. 6, 5–9.

Xu Yong, and Xu Zengyang (1999) 'Zhongguo nongcun he nongmin wenti yanjiu de bainian huigu' [20th Century Studies of the Chinese Rural and Peasants Issues in Retrospect] in *Journal of Central China Normal University* (Humanities and Social Sciences), vol. 38, no. 6, 1–10.

Xue, Yong (2009) *Choufu* [The Hatred of the Rich]. Nanjing: Jiangsu wenyi chubanshe.

Yan, Ye (2012) 'Population Structure' in Lu Xueyi (ed) *Social Structure of Contemporary China*. Singapore: World Scientific Publishing, pp. 65–98.

Yan, Zhimin (2002) *Zhongguo xian jieduan jieji jieceng yanjiu* [Research on Class and Strata in Contemporary China]. Beijing: Zhonggong zhongyang dangxiao chubanshe.

Yang, Guobin (2013) 'Contesting Food Safety in Chinese Media: Between Hegemony and Counter Hegemony' in *The China Quarterly*, no. 214, 337–355.

Yang, Jisheng (2000) *Zhongguo shehui ge jieceng fenxi baogao* [Analysis of the Social Strata in China]. Wulumuqi: Xinjiang renmin chubanshe.

Yang, Yunyan (2003) 'Zhongguo renkou de qianyi guimo cesuan yu qiangdu fenxi' [Migration in China: Scale Estimate and Intensity Analysis] in *Zhongguo shehui kexue* [China's Social Science], vol. 6, 97–107.

Yang, Zan, and Jie Chen (2014) *Housing Affordability and Housing Policy in Urban China*. Berlin: Springer.

Yeh, Emily T. (2013) *Taming Tibet: Landscape Transformation and the Gift of Chinese Development*. Ithaca, NY: Cornell University Press.

Yu, Jianping (2003) 'Shixian quanmian jianshe xiaokang shehui de mubiao yu zhongjian jieceng de jueqi' [The Sharp Rise of Middle Strata and the Aim of Comprehensively Achieving Small Prosperity Society] in *Xuexi luntan* [Study Forum], no. 11, 42–43.

Yu, Min, and Christopher B. Crowley (2020) 'The Discursive Politics of Education Policy in China: Educating Migrant Children' in *The China Quarterly*, no. 241, March, 87–111.

Yuan, Zhang, Guanghua Wan, and Niny Khor (2012) 'The Rise of the Middle Class in Rural China' in *China Agricultural Economic Review*, vol. 4, no.1, 36–51.

Zang, Xiaowei (2001) 'Educational Credentials, Elite Dualism, and Elite Stratification in China' in *Sociological Perspectives*, vol. 44, 189–205.

Zang, Xiaowei (2004) *Elite Dualism and Leadership Selection in China*. London: Routledge.

Zeng, Jin, and Kellee S. Tsai (2011) 'The Local Politics of Restructuring State-owned Enterprises in China' in Jean Oi (ed) *Going Private in China: The Politics of Corporate Restructuring and System Reform*. Palo Alto, CA: Stanford University Press, pp. 40–69.

Zhan Shaohua (2011) 'What Determines Migrant Workers' Life Chances in Contemporary China? Hukou, Social Exclusion and the Market' in *Modern China*, vol. 37, no. 3, 243–285.

Zhang, Chunlin (2019) *How Much Do State-Owned Enterprises Contribute to China's GDP and Employment?* World Bank Report, 15 July.

Zhang Houyi (1994) 'Siren qiyezhu jieceng zai woguo, shehui jiegou zhong de diwei' [The Position of Private Entrepreneurs in China's Social Structure] *Zhongguo shehui kexue* [China's Social Science], vol. 6, 59–71.

Zhang Houyi (2004) 'Jinru xinshiqide Zhongguo saying qiyezhu jiceng' [Private Entrepreneurs in China Enter a New Era] in *2004 nian: Zhongguo shehui xingshi fenxi yu yuce* [Blue Book of China's Society 2004: Analysis and Forecast of China's Social Development]. Beijing: Shehui kexue wenxian.

Zhang Houyi (2012) 'Zhongguo siying qiyezhu jieceng 20 nian' [Twenty Years Development of China's Entrepreneurs in Private Sector] in *2012 Shehui lanpishu* [2012 Blue Book of China's Society]. Beijing: Shehui kexue wenxian chubanshe, pp. 273–283.

Zhang Houyi, and Ming Zhili (eds) (1999) *Zhongguo siying qiye fazhan baogao 1978–1998* [Report on the Development of Private Enterprises in China 1978–1998]. Beijing: Shehui kexue wenxuan chubanshe.

Zhang, Jianjun (2007) 'Marketization, Class Structure, and Democracy in China: Contrasting Regional Experiences' in *Democratization*, vol. 14, 159–184.

Zhang, Jun (2019) *Driving toward Modernity: Cars and the Lives of the Middle Class in Contemporary China*. Ithaca, NY: Cornell University Press.

Zhang, Li (2010) *In Search of Paradise: Middle-Class Living in a Chinese Metropolis*. Ithaca, NY: Cornell University Press.

Zhang, Li, and Meng Li (2018) 'Acquired but Unvested Welfare Rights: Migration and Entitlement Barriers in Reform-Era China' in *The China Quarterly*, no. 235, September, 644–668.

Zhang Naiqi (1954) 'Wunian lai de liangshi shengchan gongzuo qingkuang – zai quanguo renmin daibian dahui shand de fayan' [Grain Production in the Last Five Years – Speech at the National People's Congress] September 1954, cited in Yang Jisheng 'Dayuejing zhong de liangshi wenti' [The Grain Problem during the Great Leap Forward] in *Ershiyi shiji* [Twenty-first Century], vol. 12, 2008, 38–51.

Zhang Wanli (1990) 'Jinqi woguo shehui jieji, jieceng yanjiu zongshu' [A Survey of Recent Research on Classes and Strata] in *Zhongguo shehui kexue* [China's Social Science], vol. 5, 173–181.

Zhang Xing (2003) 'Zhongguo zhongchan jieceng texing ji fazhan tiaojian jianxi' [Characteristics of Middle Strata and the Conditions of Development] in *Lishui shifan zhuanke xuexiao xuebao* [Journal of Lishui Teachers Specialist School], no. 6, 14–16.

Zhang Zhongfa (2008) '1949 dao 2007: Zhongguo nongcun gaige yu fazhan 58 nian' [From 1949 to 2007: 58 Years of Reform and Development in Rural China] in *China Report*, no. 2, 39–43.

Zhang, Zhuoni, and Wu Xiaogang (2016) 'The Growth of Chinese Professionals: A New Middle Class in the Making' in Guo Yingjie (ed) *Handbook of Class and Stratification in China*. Cheltenham: Edward Elgar, pp. 292–313.

Zhao, Jing (2015) 'Expert Says Land-Losing Farmers in China Reaching 112 Million' in *Cnstock*, 21 November. Available at www.cnstock.com/v_news/sns_bwkx/201511/3629886.htm.

Zhao, Minghua, and Theo Nichols (1996) 'Management Control of Labour in State-Owned Enterprises: Cases from the Textile Industry' in *China Journal*, vol. 36, 1–2.

Zhao, Yao (2001) 'Xiagang nuzhigong: chu "zaijiuye fuwu zhongxin" qingkuangde diaocha' [Laid-off Women Staff and Workers: An Investigation of the Situation of Leaving the 'Reemployment Service Center'] in *Zhongguo gongren* [China;s Workers], vol. 3.

Zhao, Yaohui, Albert Park, and Song Xiaoqing (2005) 'Economic Returns to Schooling in Urban China, 1988 to 2001' in *Journal of Comparative Economics*, vol. 33, no. 4, 730–752.

Zheng, Yongnian (2006) 'The Party, Class, and Democracy in China' in Kjeld-Erik Brodsgaard and Yongnian Zheng (eds) *The Chinese Communist Party in Reform*. New York: Routledge, pp. 231–260.

Zheng, Yongnian, and Lye Liang Fook (2003) 'Elite Politics and the Fourth Generation of Chinese Leadership' in *Journal of Chinese Political Science* 8, 65–86.

Zhonghua Renmin Gongheguo Liangshibu Bangongting (1959) [The General Office of Food of the People's Republic of China] (ed) *Nongcun liangshi tonggou tongxiao wenjian huibian* (1956–1957) [A Collection of Documents Regarding Unitary Purchase and Sales] internal publication.

Zhou, Feizhou (2009) 'Creating Wealth: Land Seizure, Local Government, and Farmers' in Deborah Davis and Feng Wang (eds) *Creating Wealth and Poverty in Postsocialist China*. Palo Alto, Ca: Stanford University Press, pp. 112–125.

Zhou Luogeng et al. (2002) *Shichang jingji yu dangdai Zhongguo shehui jiegou* [Market Economy and the Social Structure of Contemporary China]. Shanghai: Sanlian shudian.

Zhou Shaojie, and Hu Angang (2020) *Surpassing the Middle-Income Trap*. Basingstoke: Palgrave Macmillan.

Zhou Wubiao (2009) 'Bank Financing in China's Private Sector: The Payoffs of Political Capital' in *World Development*, vol. 37, 787–799.

Zhou, Xiang, and Yu Xie (2019) 'Market Transition, Industrialization, and Social Mobility Trends in Postrevolution China' in *American Journal of Sociology*, vol. 124, no. 6, 1810–1847.

Zhou Xiaohong (2002) 'Zhongguo zhongchan jieji: heyi keneng yu heyi kewei' [Research on Political Tendencies of the Chinese Middle Class] in *Jiangsu Shehui Kexue* [Jiangsu Social Science], no. 6, 7–21.

Zhou Xiaohong (2005) 'Zailun zhongchan jieji: llun, lishi yu leixingxue' [More on the Middle Class: Theory, History and Typology'] in *Shehui* [Society], vol. 3.

Zhou Xiaohong (2008) 'Chinese Middle Class: Reality or Illusion?' in Christophe Jaffrelot and Peter van der Veer (eds) *Patterns of Middle Class Consumption*. London: Sage, pp. 110–126.

Zhou Xiaohong, and Qin Chen (2010) 'Globalization, Social Transformation, and the Construction of China's Middle Class' in Cheng Li (ed) *China's Emerging Middle Class*. Washington, DC: Brookings Institution, pp. 84–103.

Zhou, Xueguang (2000) 'Economic Transformation and Income Inequality in Urban China: Evidence from Panel Data' in *American Journal of Sociology*, vol. 105, 1135–1174.

Zhou, Xueguang (2004) *The State and Life Chances in Urban China*. Cambridge: Cambridge University Press.

Zhou, Xueguang (2009) 'Rethinking Corporatist Bases of Stratification in Rural China' in Deborah Davis and Feng Wang (eds) *Creating Wealth and Poverty in Postsocialist China*. Palo Alto, CA: Stanford University Press, pp. 97–111.

Zhou, Xueguang, Phyllis Moen, and N. B. Tuma (1998) 'Educational Stratification in Urban China: 1949–94' in *Sociology of Education*, vol. 71, 199–222.

Zhou Zhaojun (2009) 'Zhongchan jieceng jueqi: wending Zhongguo shehui chongsuo 'Zhongguo xingge''' [The Rise of the Middle Stratum: Stabilizing Chinese Society and Recasting 'Chinese Character') *Zhongguo xinwen wang* [China News Network], 29 July. Available at www.chinanews.com/home/, accessed 28 December 2010.

Zhu Bin (2017) 'Dangdai zhongguo de zhongchan jieji yanjiu' [Research on the Middle Class in Contemporary China] in *Shehuixue pinglun* [Sociological Commentary], vol. 5, no. 1, January, 9–21.

Zhu Guanglei et al. (2007) *Dangdai Zhongguo shehui ge jieceng fenxi* [Analysis of the Social Strata in Contemporary China]. Tianjin: Tianjin remin chubanshe.

INDEX

Note: Page numbers in *italics* indicate a figure and page numbers in **bold** indicate a table on the corresponding page.

ACFTU see All-China Federation of Trade Unions
Agrarian Revolution 84
All-China Federation of Trade Unions (ACFTU) 107–109
ambiguous class identity 75–77
antagonistic conflicts 5

behaviour 64–65; and CCP-led discourses 70–73; consumption and lifestyles 65–70; perception, class identity, and political participation 73–80; and political leadership 80
Blecher, Marc vii, 23
bourgeoisie 2, 31–35, 84–88, 102, 130–131, 155–156; see also petty bourgeoisie

capitalist urbanization 23, 81–82, 89; objects of 94–100
CCP see Communist Party of China
Chen Duxiu 84
Chen Yonggui 96
Chen Yun 16, 91
China General Social Survey (CGSS) 47, 74, 77
China Household Incomes Project (CHIP) 52
Chinese Academy of Social Sciences (CASS) 20, 36–38, *38*, 147–148

Chinese People's Political Consultative Conference (CPPCC) 78
Chinese Revolution 22–23, 81–89
citizenization 70–72
civilizing 144–145
class 1–3, 25–26, 40–42, 43–44, 64–65; and the CCP 21–24, 70–73; consumption and lifestyles 65–70; economic structure, class consciousness, and class action 26–30; and education inequality 57–62; hegemony of the structure model 35–40; and life chances 54–56; and opportunities 56–57; perception, class identity, and political participation 73–80; and political leadership 80; and social change 11–21; and stratification 3–11, 50–54, 62–63; transformation of class structure 44–50; utility of 30–35; see also specific class categories
class action 26–30
class conflict 1–2, 7, 11–18
class consciousness 26–30, 75–77
classes in themselves 35–40
class formation 170–174
class identity 73–80
classification 13–15
class inequality 50–54
classless society 125–128; the middle class and politics 138–147; the middle class in

wider context 153–157; the new middle class and the petty bourgeoisie 137–138; and the origin of the new middle classes 128–129; and reproduction of the middle class 131–136; return to reality 147–153; and social stratification 129–131
class levelling 13–15
class mobility: and education inequality 57–62; and life chances 54–56; and opportunities 56–57
class structure 41–43; transformation of 44–50
class struggle 15–18, 30, 32
Communist Party of China (CCP) 1; CCP-led discourses 70–73; and class 21–24; class and social change 11–21; class and stratification 3–11; and the dominant class 158–177; and the middle class 125–157; and the peasantry 81–103; the performance of class 64–80; social consciousness and social existence 25–42; and social mobility 43–63; utility of class to 30–35; and working-class decline 104–123
consciousness 25–29, 37, 40–41; divorced from existence 30–35
consumption 65–70; socio-economic modernization through 143–144
Cultural Revolution 17–19, 85–86, 92–93, 161–165, 175–176

Deng Liqun 32
Deng Xiaoping 15, 17–19, 161–163, 168
discourses 70–73
distributional location 5
dominant class 158–161, 177; elite interdependence and class formation 170–174; enterprises, entrepreneurs, and the economic elite 166–170; the intergenerational transfer of privilege 174–177; the political elite 161–166

economic decline 104–107
economic elite 166–170; see also elite
economic growth: and the decline of the working class 104–119; and the ideational 111–119; and the politics of working-class decline 119–122; and the social 107–111; and structural reform 122–123
economic structure 26–30
education expenses 68–70
education inequality 57–62

elite 158–161, 177; enterprises, entrepreneurs, and the economic elite 166–170; interdependence and class formation 170–174; the intergenerational transfer of privilege 174–177; the political elite 161–166
emancipation 5
enterprises 166–170
entrepreneurs 32, 35–38, 45–47, 77–78, 133–134; and the dominant class 177; and the economic elite 166–170; and elite interdependence 171–173; and the intergenerational transfer of privilege 174–176
environmental non-governmental organization (ENGO) 150–151
existence 30–35, 40

GDP see gross domestic product
GMD see Nationalist Party of China, Guomindang (Kuo-min-tang)
Goodman, David S. G. vii, 24, 43–44, 53
Great Leap Forward 16–17, 92
gross domestic product (GDP) 66, 90, 101, 167, 170
Guo, Yingjie vii 22–23
Guomindang see Nationalist Party of China, Guomindang (Kuo-min-tang)

hegemony: market and state 115–116; of the structure model 35–40
historical variation 5
household registration 81–82, 89, 98–100
housing consumption 67–68
housing reform 67–68
Hu Jianping 174–175
Hu Jintao 19, 135
Hu Yaobang 162

ideal class 139–143
ideational decline 111–119
income 27–28, 35–36; and the middle class 125–126, 131–132, 140, 142–144, 148–150; and the peasantry 91–92; and the performance of class 66, 74–75; and social mobility 47–48, 55–59, 62–63
income inequality 22, 51–54, 63, 74
industrialization 81, 83, 87–89, 95–96, 100, 103; auxiliaries to socialist industrialization 89–94
inequality 74–75; see also class inequality; education inequality; income inequality; wealth inequality
interdependence 170–174

intergenerational class mobility 56–57
intergenerational transfer of privilege 174–177
intragenerational class mobility 54–56

Jiang Qing 17
Jiang Zemin 19–20, 31, 60–61, 96, 143–144

landlessness 14, 46–50, 57, 68–69, 71, 76
Land Reform 13–15, 82–86, 90–92, 175
Li Keqiang 98–99
life chances 5, 54–56
lifestyles 64–65; and CCP-led discourses 70–73; consumption and lifestyles 65–70; perception, class identity, and political participation 73–80; and political leadership 80
Lin Biao 17–18
Liu Shaoqi 17

managers 9, 20–21, 35–38, 47–48, 110–114, 168–169
Mao Zedong and Maoism 13–18, 30–36; and the dominant class 161–168; and the peasantry 84–91, 95–96, 100–103; and social mobility 43–45; and working-class decline 107–115, 119–123
market hegemony 115–116
market socialism 3, 18–21
Marx and Marxism 2–10, 21–22, 25–32, 34–41, 86–90, 94–95, 100–103
middle class(es) 125–128; the origin of the new middle classes 128–129; and the petty bourgeoisie 137–138; and politics 138–147; reproduction of 131–136; return to reality 147–153; and social stratification 129–131; in wider context 153–157
migrants see rural migrants
Ministry of Education (MoE) 61–62
mobility 62–63; see also class mobility
modernization 139–144

National Bureau of Statistics (NBS) 68, 142, 174
Nationalist Party of China, Guomindang (Kuo-min-tang, GMD) 84
National People's Congress (NPC) 65, 78, 85, 93–94, 99
new consumers 65–67
new middle classes 128–129, 137–138
'new rich' 65–67
non-governmental organization (NGO) 125, 141, 150, 156–157

opportunity 23–24; and intergenerational class mobility 56–67; and the middle class 130–135; and the peasantry 92–96; and the performance of class 74–75; and working-class decline 121–122; and social mobility 43–44, 51–55, 58, 61–63

peasantry 1–2, 13–14, 18–23, 30–32, 34–35, 81–83; auxiliaries to socialist industrialization 89–94; the future of 100–103; and the middle class 128–132; objects of capitalist urbanization 94–100; and the performance of class 75–76; role and status in the Chinese Revolution 83–89; and social mobility 44–46; and working-class decline 116–117
perception 73–80
performance of class 64–65; and CCP-led discourses 70–73; consumption and lifestyles 65–70; perception, class identity, and political participation 73–80; and political leadership 80
People's Liberation Army (PLA) 17, 175
petty bourgeoisie 137–138, 141
PLA see People's Liberation Army
political elite 161–166; see also elite
politics: and the middle class 138–147; political dilemmas 145–147; political leadership 80; political participation 73–80; of working-class decline 119–122
privilege 174–177
professionals 8–9, 15, 20–21, 35–38; and the dominant class 165–166; and the middle class 128–138, 149–150; and the performance of class 71–72; and social mobility 45–46
professions 58, 144, 165

quality discourse 70–72

reality 147–153
reform 18–21, 125–128; the middle class and politics 138–147; the middle class in wider context 153–157; the new middle class and the petty bourgeoisie 137–138; and the origin of the new middle classes 128–129; and reproduction of the middle class 131–136; return to reality 147–153; and social stratification 129–131
reproduction of the middle class 131–136
Rocca, Jean-Louis vii–viii, 24
ruling class 10, 14, 34, 90
rural migrants 116–119, 149–150
rustbelt atavism 112–115

school education 59–60
self-governance 72–73
social change 13–14, 19, 43–44, 158–161, 177; class, mobility, and stratification 62–63; and the economic 104–107; education inequality and class mobility 57–62; elite interdependence and class formation 170–174; enterprises, entrepreneurs, and the economic elite 166–170; and the ideational 111–119; the intergenerational transfer of privilege 174–177; life chances and intragenerational class mobility 54–56; opportunities and intergenerational class mobility 56–57; the political elite 161–166; and the politics of working-class decline 119–122; and the social 107–111; social stratification and class inequality 50–54; and structural reform 122–123; transformation of class structure 44–50
social consciousness 25–29, 37, 40–41; divorced from existence 30–35
social decline 107–111
social existence 25–26, 40; consciousness divorced from 30–35
socialist distribution 53–54
socialist industrialization 89–94
social mobility 43–44; and education inequality 57–62; intergenerational class mobility 56–57; intragenerational class mobility 54–56; and stratification 50–54, 62–63; transformation of class structure 44–50
social movements 150–153
social stratification 50–54, 129–131
social structure 11–13
social volcano myth 74–75
socio-economic modernization 143–144
sociology 8–11
SOE see state-owned enterprise
stability maintenance 72–73
state hegemony 115–116
state-owned enterprise (SOE) 21, 55, 88, 91–92, 110, 169–170
stratification 2, 14, 20–22, 43–44, 62–63; and class 3–11; and education inequality 57–62; and life chances 54–56; and mobility 54–62, 62–63; social 50–54, 129–131; transformation of class structure 44–50
structural reform 122–123; and the economic 104–107; and the ideational 111–119; and the politics of working-class decline 119–122; and the social 107–111
structure model 27–28; hegemony of 35–40
subjective salient groups 5
subordinate classes 11, 47, 71

Tang, Beibei viii, 22
'two classes and one stratum' 44–46

university education 60–62
University Entrance Examination (UEE) 61–62, 69, 132
urbanization 81–83, 89, 100–103; objects of capitalist urbanization 94–100

wages 54–55, 105–107, 105–106, 115, 119
Wang Hualun 175
Wang Hongwen 17
Wang Jijun 175
wealth 2–3, 56–57, 62–63, 67–68, 173–174, 176–177
wealth inequality 51–53, 62
Weber, Max 3–10, 64–65
workers 15–24, 31–40; and the economic 104–107; and the ideational 111–119; and the middle classes 128–129, 131–138, 144–150; and the peasantry 88–92, 97–103; and the performance of class 71–76; and the politics of working-class decline 119–122; and the social 107–111; and social mobility 45–52, 55–62; and social stratification 129–131
working class 1, 6–7, 21–23, 34–35; and the middle class 136–138; and the performance of class 74–75; and social mobility 44–45; and structural reform 122–123
working-class decline: and the economic 104–107; and the ideational 111–119; the politics of 119–122; and the social 107–111; and structural reform 122–123

Xi Jinping 19, 21, 95, 97, 144, 157
Xi Zhongxun 163

Yao Wenyuan 17

Zhang Chunqiao 17
Zhang Naiqi 93
Zhou Enlai 18

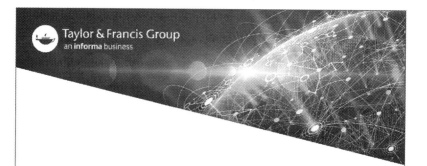

Printed in the United States
by Baker & Taylor Publisher Services